COURT PAINTINGS FROM THE JOSEON DYNASTY

VISUAL KOREAN HERITAGE NO.1

COURT PAINTINGS FROM THE JOSEON DYNASTY

Published in 2016 by Seoul Selection U.S.A., Inc.
4199 Campus Drive, Suite 550, Irvine, CA 92612

Phone: 949-509-6584
Fax: 949-509-6599
Email: publisher@seoulselection.com
Website: www.seoulselection.com

ISBN: 978-1-62412-053-4 53700
Printed in the Republic of Korea

Library of Congress Control Number: 2015957428

VISUAL KOREAN HERITAGE NO.1

COURT PAINTINGS FROM THE JOSEON DYNASTY

WRITTEN BY
PARK JEONG-HYE

Seoul Selection

Contents

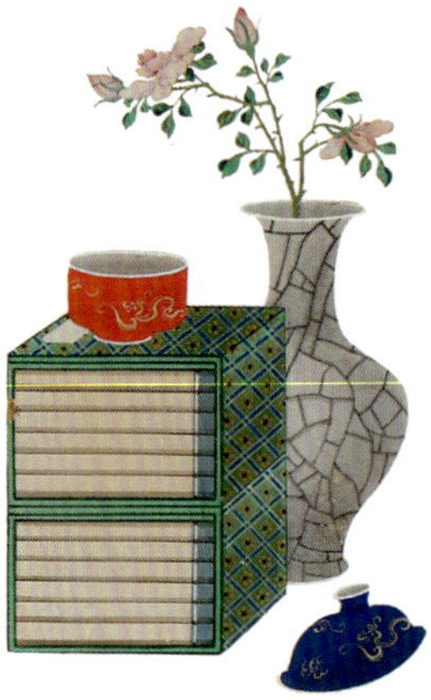

The Beauty of Joseon Court Paintings: Grandeur and Sophistication

The court paintings of the Joseon Dynasty (1392–1910) were artwork created for the appreciation of the king, his family, and high-ranking officials. The type of paintings commissioned for display at court hardly deviated from those pieces created for the common people; in essence, court painters did not adhere to any particular genre of painting for works destined for the court, though pictorial style would vary over time. Unlike pieces created for personal appreciation of the general public, however, court paintings carried far more importance and served a more specific function than those done outside the palace.

One of the major functions of Joseon court paintings was education. Pictures of significant moments of history were used to help the king and prince learn from the past and cultivate a heightened sense of morality and leadership. An example of such "educational painting" was *Golden Chest* (*Geumgwedo*) (p. 153), which depicts the legend of the progenitor of King Munmu (r. 661–681), who unified the three kingdoms of the Korean peninsula into the Unified Silla Kingdom in 668.

Another crucial function of court paintings was both the documentation and conservation of the visual culture of the eras in which they were created. During the Joseon Dynasty, a period whose philosophical foundation rested on Confucian ideals, images played an essential role in the efficient management of the state. For example, a visual record of Confucian rites was used as an official reference for complicated procedures. This was especially prevalent in *banchado*, a commonly produced type of illustration, in which a series of participants are drawn for various state ceremonies, such as weddings, funerals, and the procession to a royal tomb. *Dongga Banchado* (p. 147) is considered one of the best of its kind. Documentary paintings were also used for archival purposes, as seen in books of court rites, also known as *uigwe*. This seminal record serves as a record of important state rites, including not only textual descriptions but also illustrations, hence its importance to the preservation of both the dynasty and royal family's core cultural values for future generations. The illustrations found in *Uigwe for the Sixtieth Anniversary of Lady Hyegyeong's Coming-of-age Ceremony* are considered to be among the most exquisite of the era (p. 125).

The most important genre was portraiture of the king, with royal portraiture signifying the dignity and authority of the king himself. For this reason, the conservation and maintenance of such artwork was directly linked to the continued prosperity of the dynasty. Only a small group—the king, the crown prince, and those who participated in the ceremonies of ancestral worship—was able to appreciate the finished work, which was enshrined as a sacred object. Portrait painters of the Joseon Dynasty aimed not only to accurately represent the painted figure but also to have the subject's personality emanated to the viewer. The epitome of Joseon-era portraits is that of King Taejo (r. 1392–1398), which exudes the solemn charisma of the founder of the dynasty (p. 11).

The majority of the remaining court paintings are so-called documentary paintings, which depict and commemorate the ceremonial scenes of state events. In the absence of modern technology that could capture a pictorial record of a significant occasion, such as a camera, some government officials attempted to memorialize events by commissioning a work that would document the occurrence in detail. Court documentary paintings also served as a means of boasting about one's service to the state and were seen as a gesture of camaraderie among participants. If one of the attendees were to suggest the production of such a painting, a group of other officials would collect money to commission a work that would be kept at the home of each participant for generations as a family treasure; hence, the number of paintings produced equaled the number of commissioners who paid for the production, which occasionally reached more than a hundred. This custom among Joseon government officials is a unique practice that cannot be found in the contemporary societies of China and Japan.

In the production of the commemorative paintings, it was usually the leader of the group who would write an introductory paragraph explaining the reason for the commission, as well as a list of names and titles of the commissioners. Since the paintings were produced for personal collections, images of the king and members of the royal family were not to be included. Instead, their presence was implied through the inclusion of objects used by the royals, such as chairs, mats, and fans.

By the mid-eighteenth century, the production of documentary paintings became widespread enough to attract the attention of the king. It was King Yeongjo (r. 1725–1776) who first recognized the public power of documentary paintings and initiated an official collection within the court. Once the power of documentary paintings became more widely understood—that is, their function as a medium to enhance the authority of the royal family and achievements of the king—the practice of commissioning court documentary paintings blossomed, reaching its heyday during the era of King Jeongjo (r. 1777–1800), grandson of King Yeongjo. One masterpiece from this era is the screen depicting King Jeongjo's visit to Hwaseong (p. 115, p. 121).

Another popular genre of Joseon court paintings was decorative paintings, which adorned both inner and outer spaces of the palace complex. The primary role of decorative paintings was to enhance the dignified and stately ambience of the space by employing various themes and types of imagery relevant to the space and the position of its resident.

Some of the most common motifs used in Joseon court paintings included the sun and moon, pine trees, water, clouds, peaches, and peonies—all symbols of eternity and longevity. Although these motifs and subjects had much in common with those seen elsewhere in contemporary China and Japan, paintings in Joseon developed distinctive themes and composition derived from the needs and aesthetics that were specific to Korean culture. For example, the screen of sun, moon, and five peaks, or *irwol obongdo*, characterized by its simplified composition and use of vivid colors, was an original style that emerged during Joseon Korea. Similarly, *sipjangsaengdo*, or ten symbols of longevity paintings, is a unique Korean painting genre in that it embodies ten symbols selected to highlight the idea of long life.

Some genres experienced changes in form due to the popular use of folding screens in Joseon court. The screens, which were a logical architectural addition to the wooden-framed, multi-windowed traditional Korean houses, became the painting type of choice for both decorative and documentary paintings. The screens were also easier to move than wall-mounted paintings, and could also be used to divide open spaces. For this reason, the narrow, vertical frames of each panel of the screen served as a strong driving force for shaping the unique formal character of the Joseon court paintings.

Due to the extensive amount of time and effort involved in adding color to paintings—a common feature of pieces created for members of court—the paintings of this genre saw little stylistic change over time. Moreover, not much personality of individual artists was revealed in these works.

With few exceptions, the Joseon court paintings were created by court painters who belonged to the Office of Paintings, or Dohwaseo. Due to the fact that the painters would have been summoned to carry out a specific task for the state, they had little opportunity to sign the work. Given that it was considered desirable to continue the artistic traditions from the past, it was customary that the individual painters would refrain from attempting to showcase their own artistic personality. More often than not, the same court painting would be worked on by multiple artists; for documentary paintings, numerous copies would have been produced for multiple commissioners, and for large decorative paintings, a group of painters would be expected to collaborate on the same work. Consequently, court paintings tended to be more conservative in terms of style and conventions.

Overall, the Joseon court paintings were intended to be the pinnacle of contemporary artwork of their time, produced by anonymous court painters to meet the tastes of the commissioners while abiding by past customs.

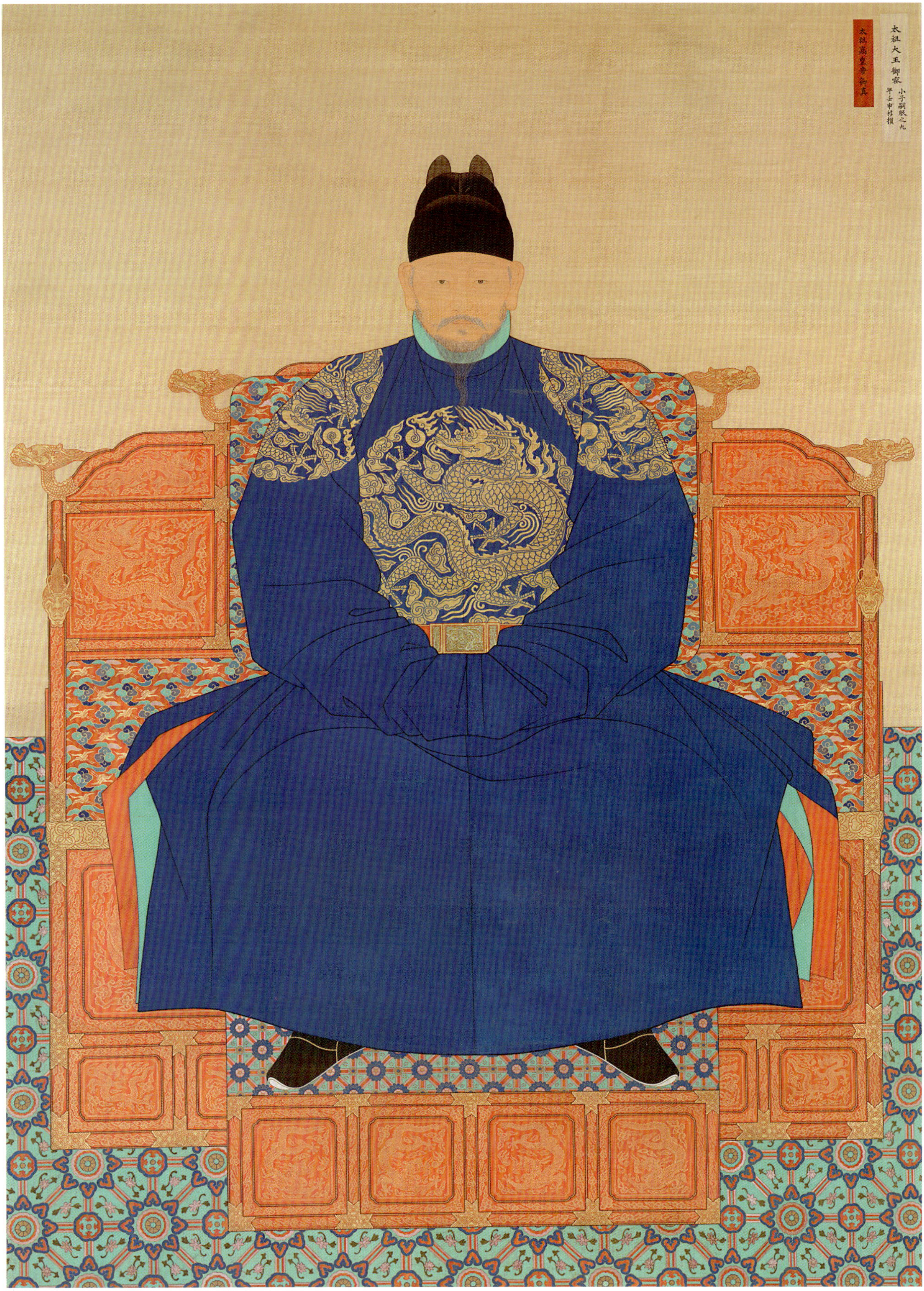
太祖大王御容
小子嗣服之九
太祖高皇帝御真

Portrait of King Taejo *Taejo Eojin*

By **Yi Han-cheol, Jo Jung-muk, Bak Gi-jun, Baek Eun-bae** / 1872 / ink and color on silk / 220 × 151 cm / Royal Portrait Museum

This portrait of King Taejo (r. 1392–1398), the founder of the Joseon Dynasty (1392–1910), was one of the most prized objects within the national sphere. During King Taejo's reign, his portraits were enshrined in the palace and across five provinces as a means of displaying and reinforcing the legitimacy of royal authority. After his death, the original portraits were used as models for a series of reproductions when a previous painting was damaged or when a new shrine was built within the capital.

This particular copy was once preserved at the Gyeonggijeon Shrine in Jeonju, the ancestral hometown of the Yi royal family. It is an 1872 reproduction of a previous version housed at the Yeongheejeon Hall in Seoul, made in 1688, modeled after another that once hung in Gyeonggijeon Shrine, during the reign of King Sukjong (r. 1674–1720). Due to such process of derivation, this copy, though it was produced in the late nineteenth century, retains the stylistic qualities of the original portraiture used in the early Joseon period. For example, King Taejo wears a blue *gollyongpo* (dragon robe) with *ikseongwan* (a black double-crested headpiece); the blue dragon robe had been a dress style adopted by the Joseon kings before they began to follow that of the Ming Dynasty (1368–1644).

The king's dignified posture, focused gaze, and slightly enlarged body all serve to demonstrate his regal majesty, and there is a strong visual contrast among the king's blue robe, the redness of the royal throne, and the elegantly patterned carpet. In accordance with the Joseon adage stating that "a person is no longer the same with another thread of hair," the painting pursues a thorough and truthful rendering of the model's face and expression. Following the technique used in the early Joseon, the background was colored using a method known as *baechae*, in which the color scheme would be applied to both the front and reverse sides of the silk to create a deeper yet subdued look. Overall, this portrait is undoubtedly a prime example of portraiture produced during the Joseon Dynasty.

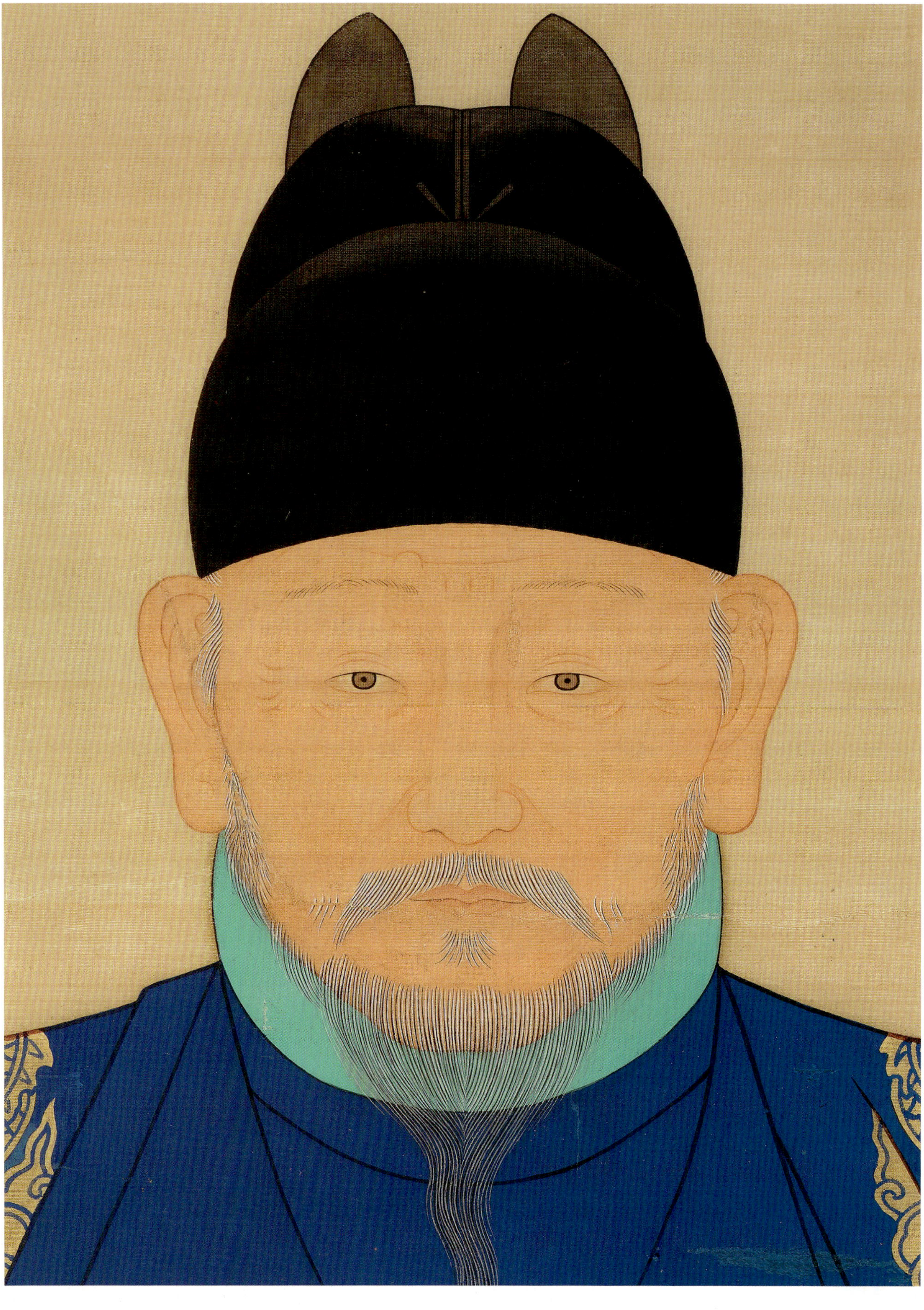

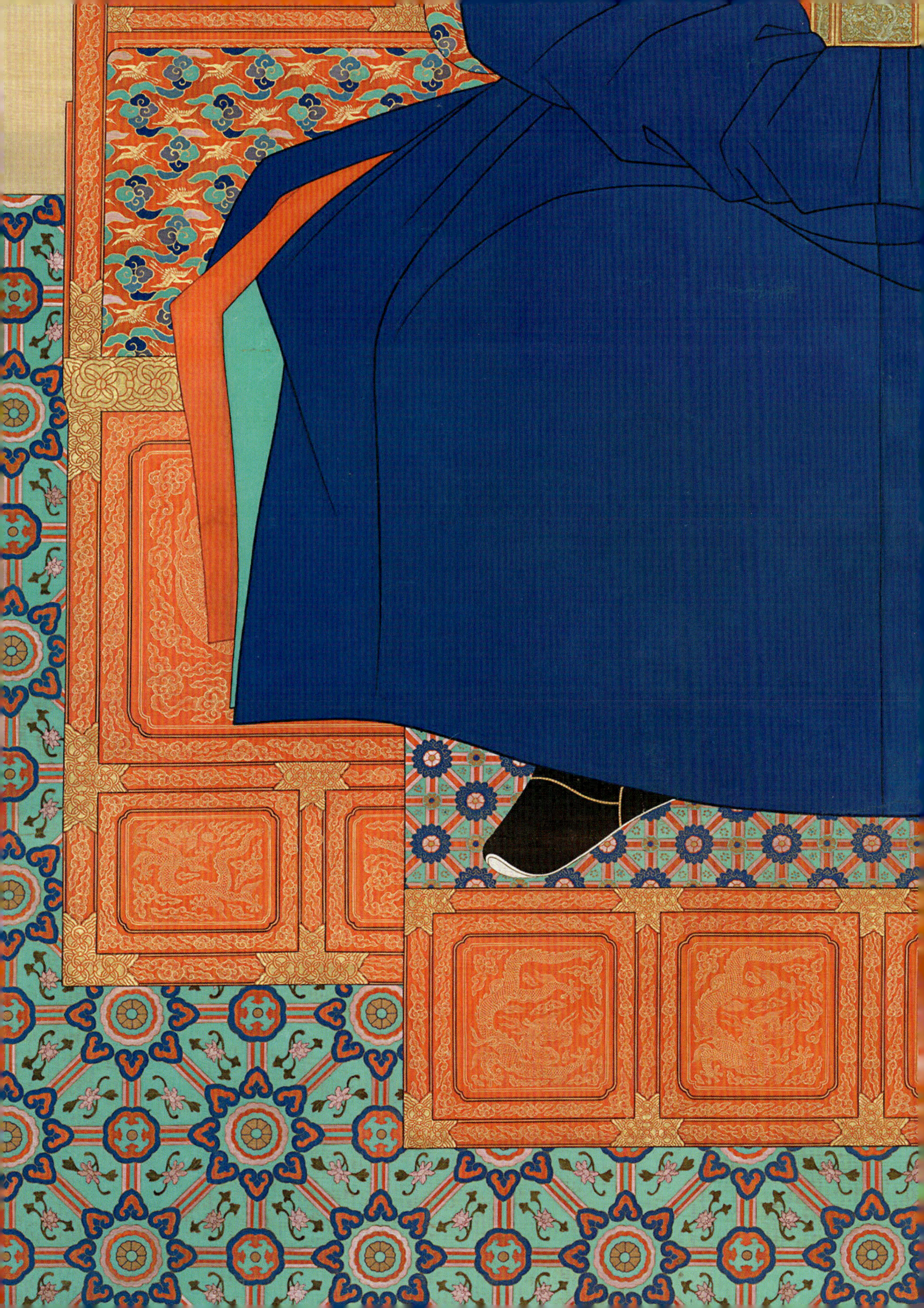

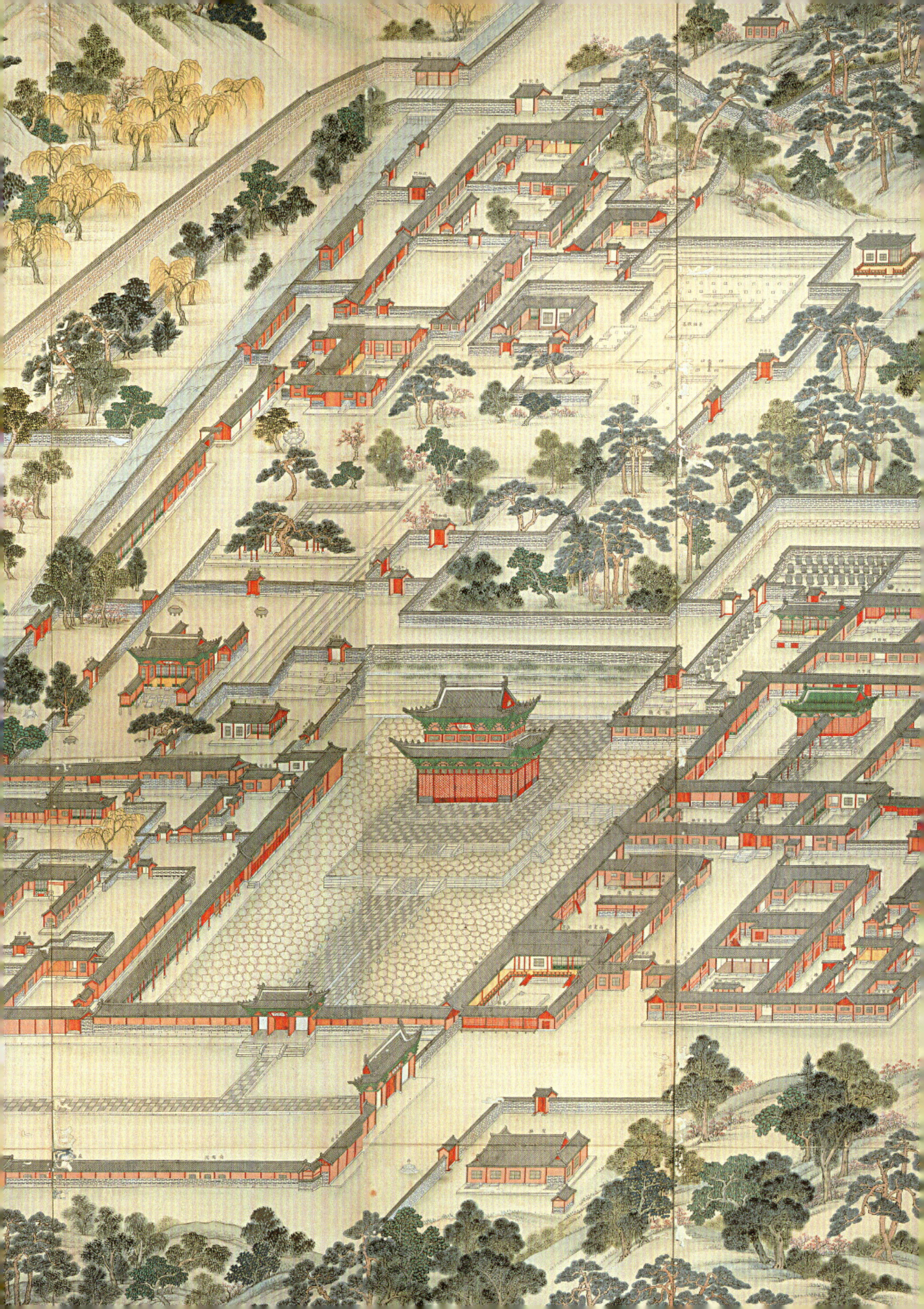

The Eastern Palaces *Donggwoldo*

Ca. 1828 / 16 painting albums / ink and color on silk / 273 × 584 cm / Korea University Museum

The Eastern Palaces (*Donggwoldo*) provides an aerial view of two of the five palaces of Hanyang, the Joseon capital (present-day Seoul). The two palaces in question, Changdeokgung and Changgyeonggung, were nicknamed the "Eastern Palaces," or Donggwol (the term *do* in the work's title simply means "painting"), due to their being situated to the east of Gyeongbokgung, the royal residence that was considered the official palace.

The Eastern Palaces consists of sixteen foldable, accordion-like panels, each of which extends to over 273 centimeters when unfolded from top to bottom. It is only when all sixteen panels are fully expanded and aligned from right to left that the entire, enormous scene of the Eastern Palaces is revealed to full effect. In the complete image, the compositional lines of Changdeokgung and Changgyeonggung are drawn parallel to one another, presented on the left and the right sides of the map, respectively. In the garden of Changdeokgung located in the upper section, a sense of depth is heightened by the use of linear perspective.

The absence of historical records makes it difficult to identify the map's date as well as the motivation for its production. It is likely, however, that Crown Prince Hyomyeong (1809–1830), who served as the proxy of King Sunjo (r. 1800–1834), commissioned the painting around 1828 in an attempt to reinforce his authority.

The architectural rendering in court paintings reached its technical peak during the early nineteenth century. Geometric illustration of the architectural layout became more popular during this era using *jiehua*—a technique of drawing straight lines using rulers.

The significance of *The Eastern Palaces* lies in its detailed recording of the exact layout of palaces as they were during the Joseon Dynasty. The accurate visual details documenting the structure and appearance of numerous edifices, gardens, and various architectural installations as they existed at that time serve as an invaluable graphic record of the Joseon palace complex, some of which is now entirely gone.

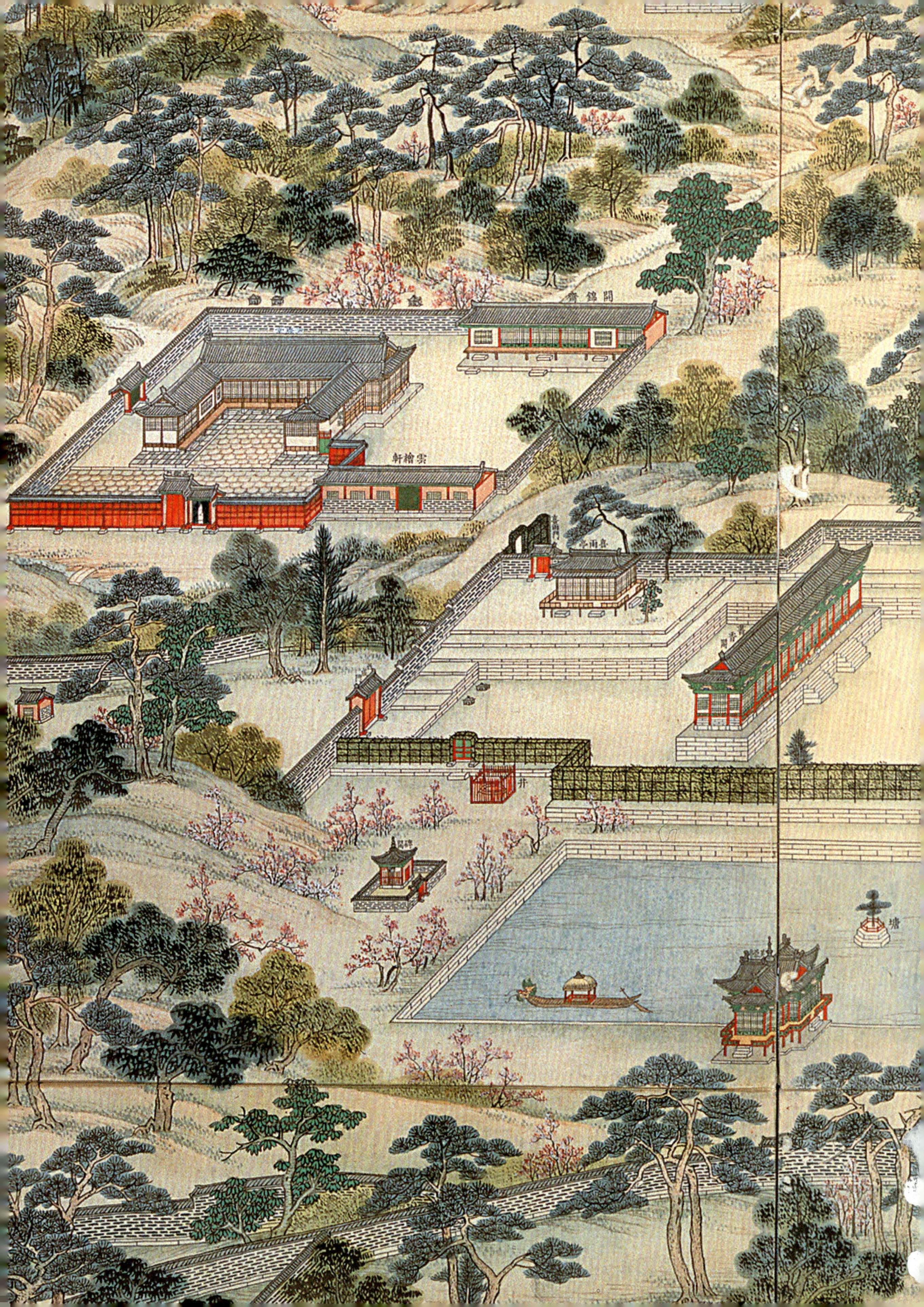

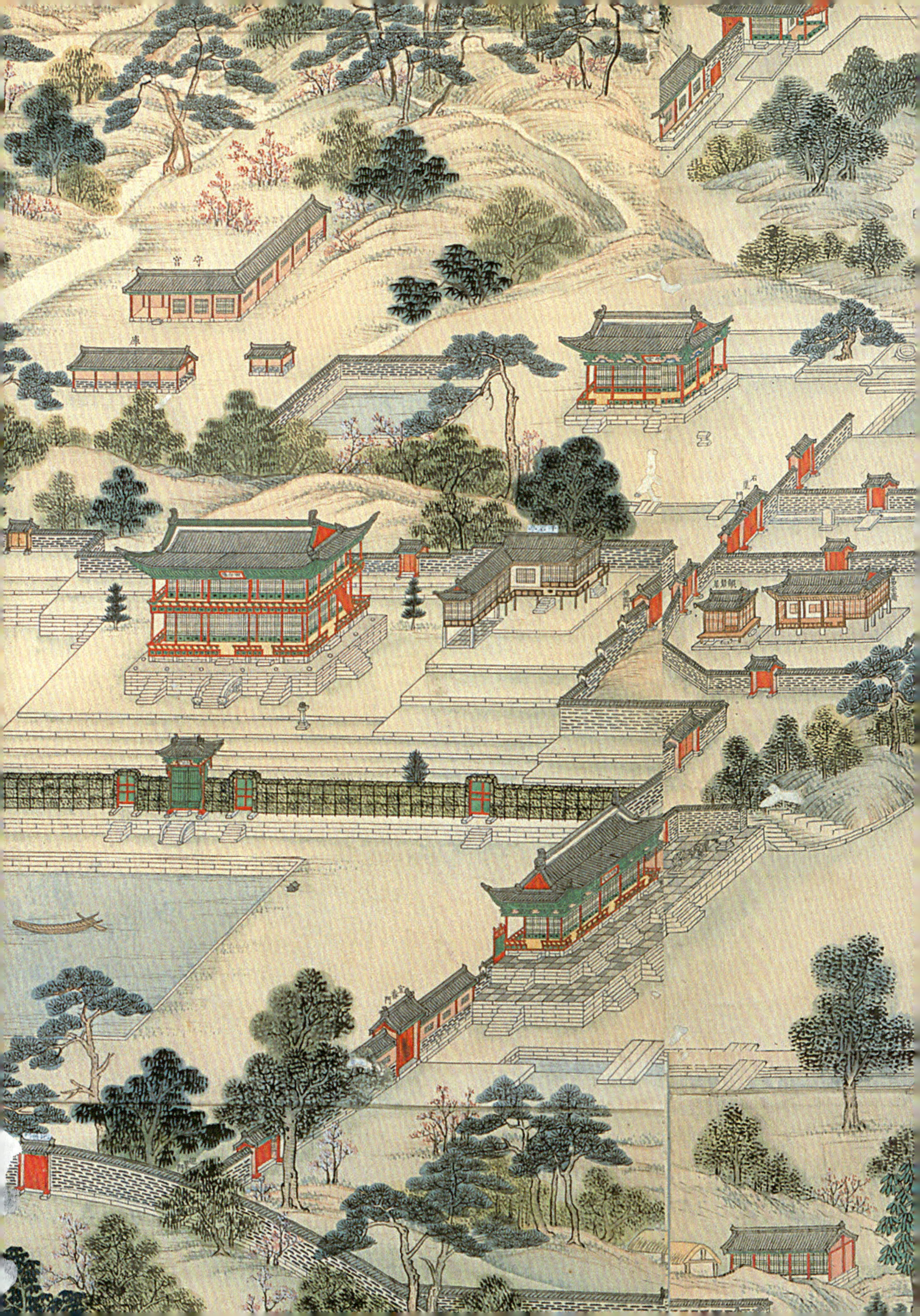

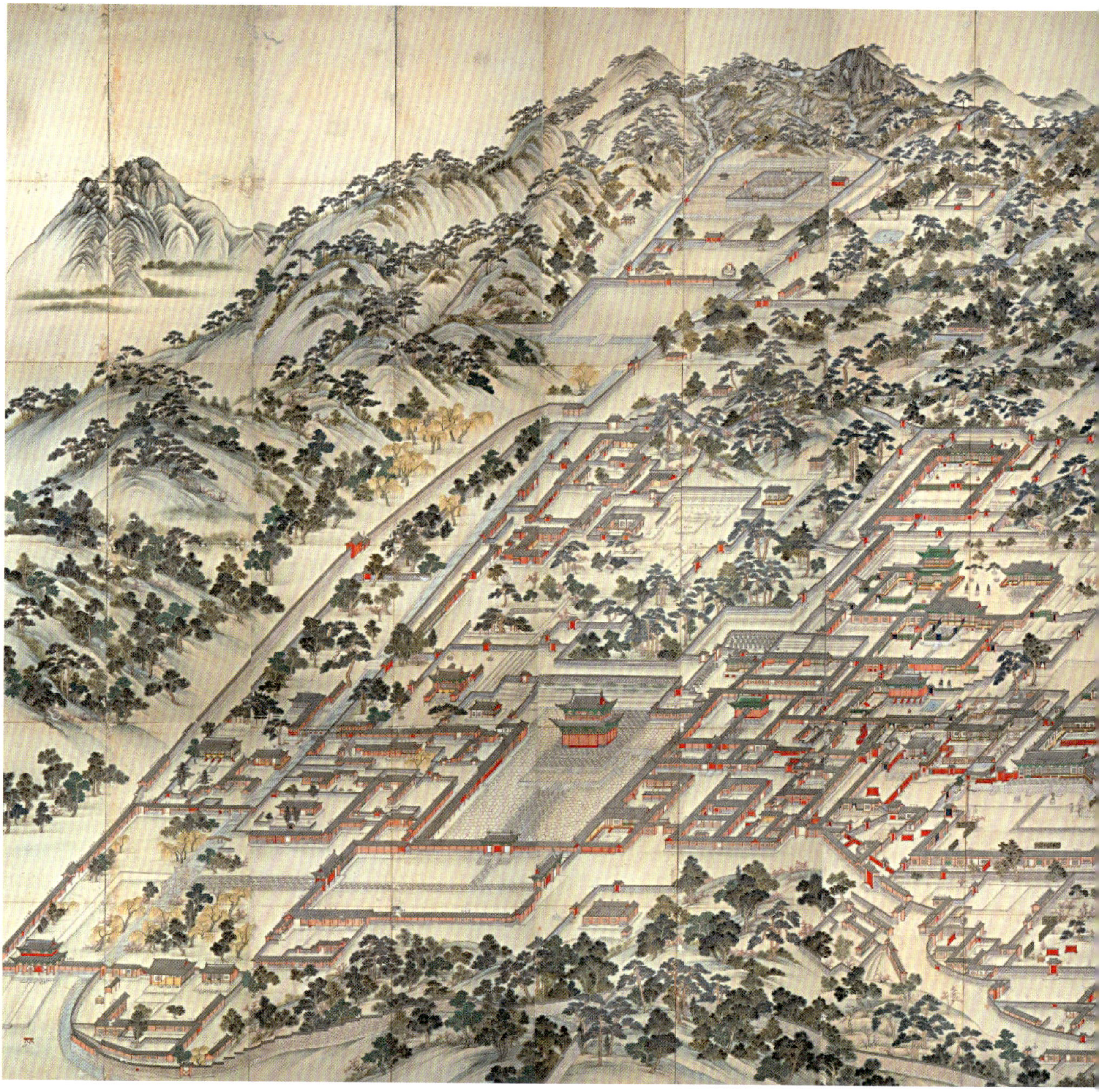

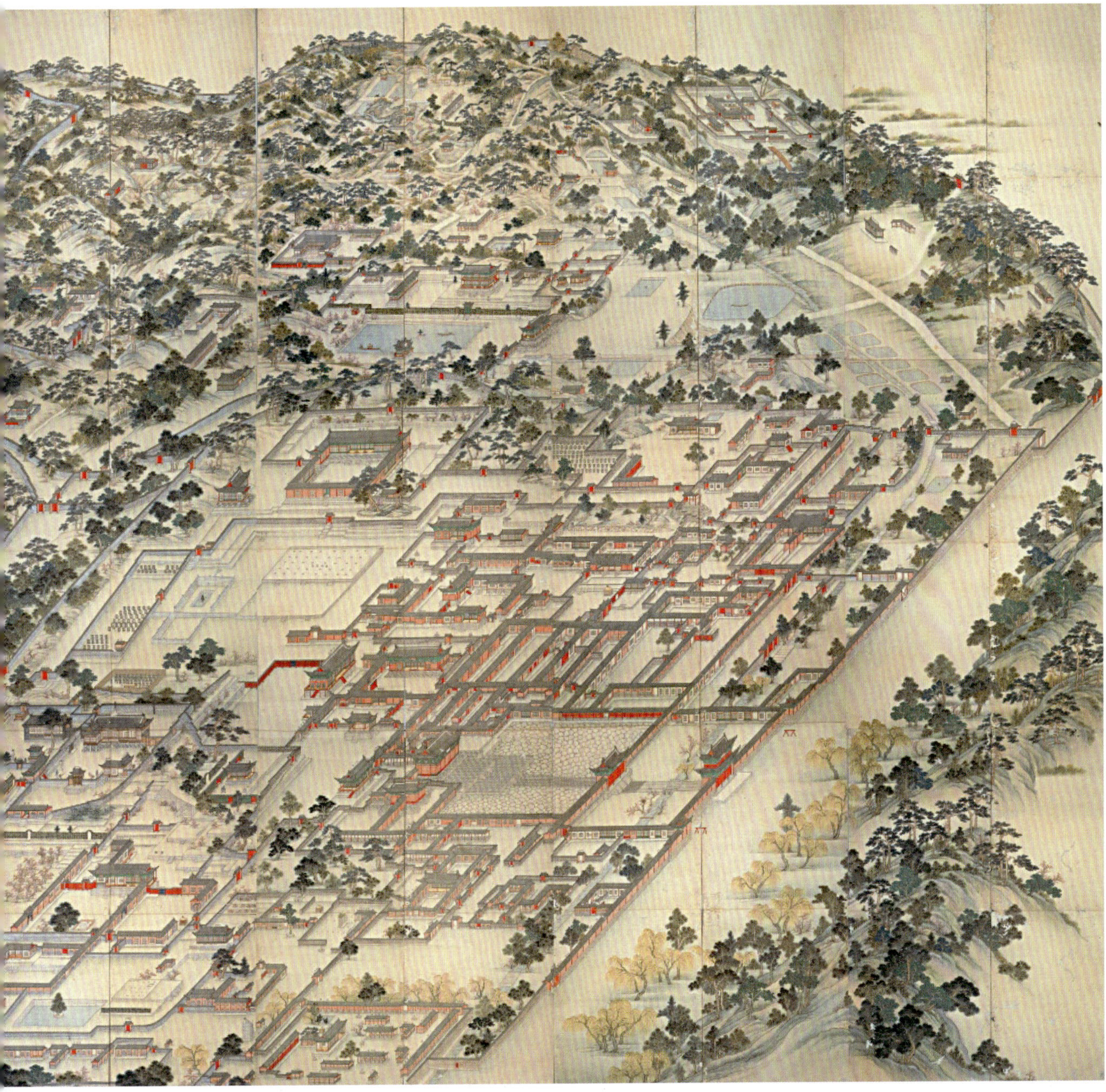

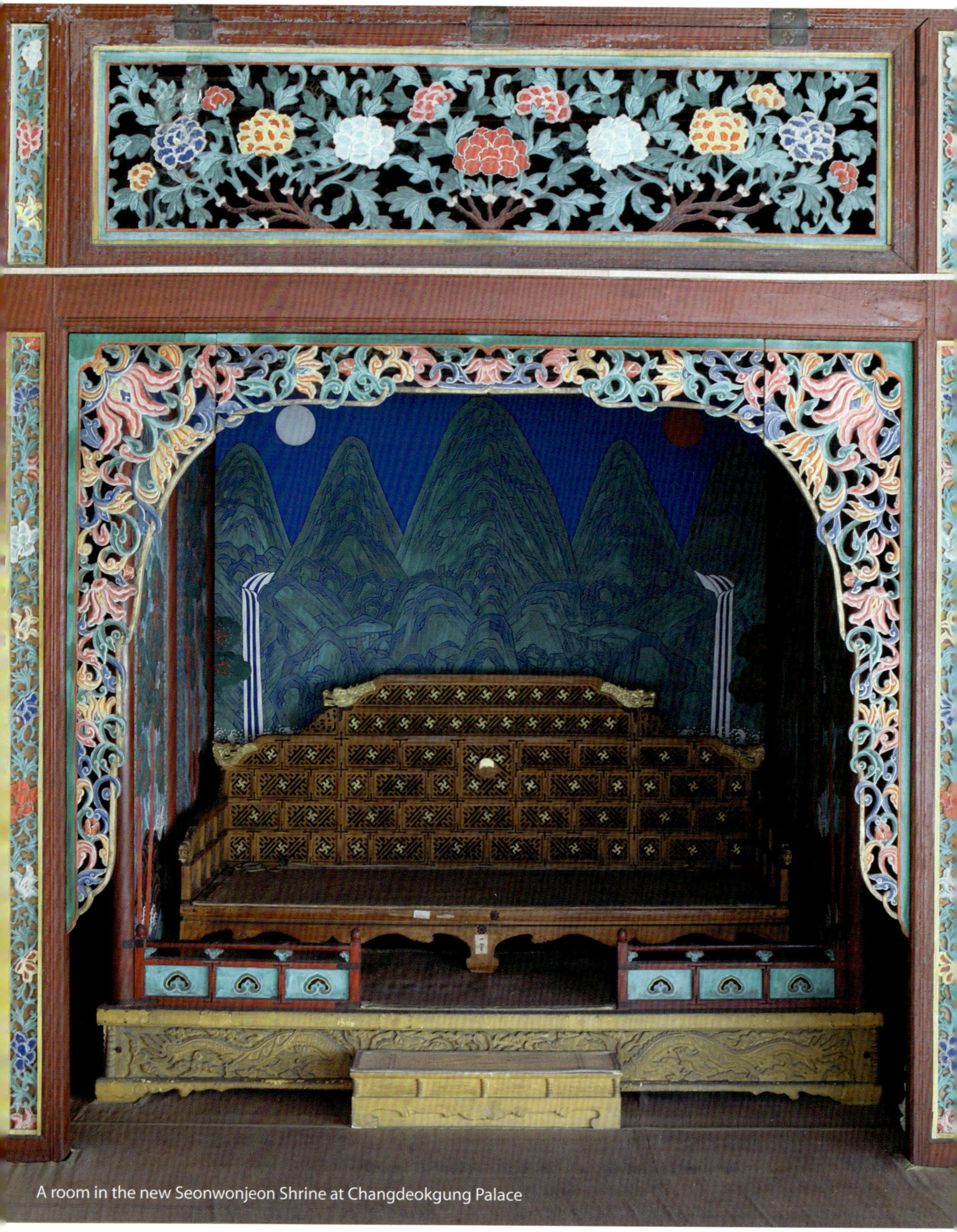

A room in the new Seonwonjeon Shrine at Changdeokgung Palace

Sun, Moon, and Five Peaks *Irwol Obongdo*

Late 19th to early 20th century / six-fold screen / ink and color on silk / 150.5 × 354.6 cm / National Palace Museum of Korea

Sun, Moon, and Five Peaks (*Irwol Obongdo*) is a screen painting that portrays natural elements such as the sun and moon, five steep rocky mountains, waves and water bubbles, two waterfalls, and pine trees, all of which symbolize eternity, perpetuity, and longevity. The simple subject matter, symmetrical composition, and flatness of the perspective all add to the geometric quality of the painting. Moreover, both the patterned scenery and the use of limited colors such as blue, green, red and white result in a strong visual impact.

It is difficult to define the exact origin of the iconography of the *irwol obongdo*. Some cite Daoistic yin-yang and Five Elements theory from the *Book of Changes* as the source, while others suggest it derives from the poem "Heaven Protects" from *Classic of Poetry*. Nevertheless, there is no documented evidence to clarify the iconographic significance of the sun, moon, and five peaks imagery, nor is there any record of the origin of its use. In all likelihood, the picture may be seen as a fusion of Confucian theory—including the yin-yang and Five Elements theory—and the indigenous culture of the Korean peninsula.

As a visual manifestation of royal authority and the presence of the king, *irwol obongdo* was always installed as the backdrop whenever the king was present at official occasions. It was also typically placed behind the king's portraits and spirit tablets. The manner in which *irwol obongdo* was typically installed can be seen in the new Seonwonjeon Shrine at Changdeokgung; in each of the twelve rooms, a royal portrait would have been enshrined with an architectural canopy, as shown at left, with an *irwol obongdo* painting covering the three walls of the enclosed space.

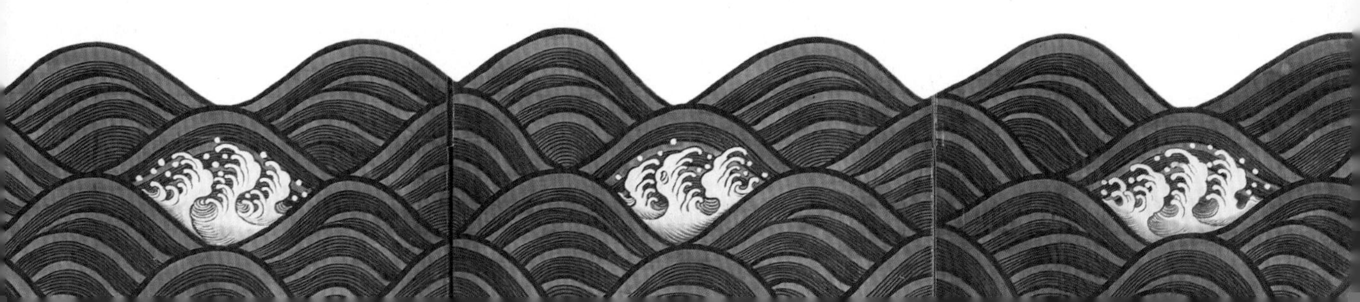

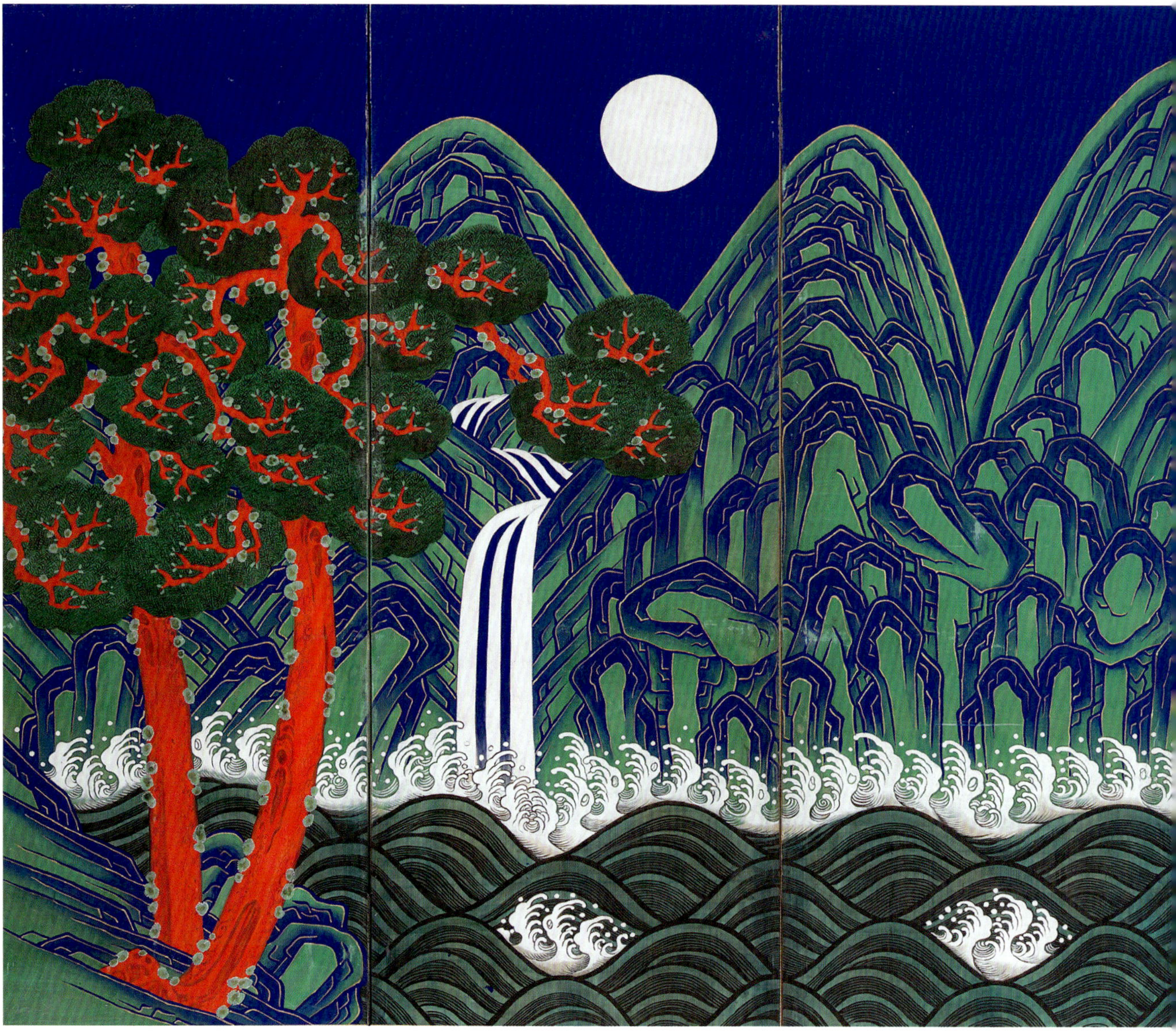

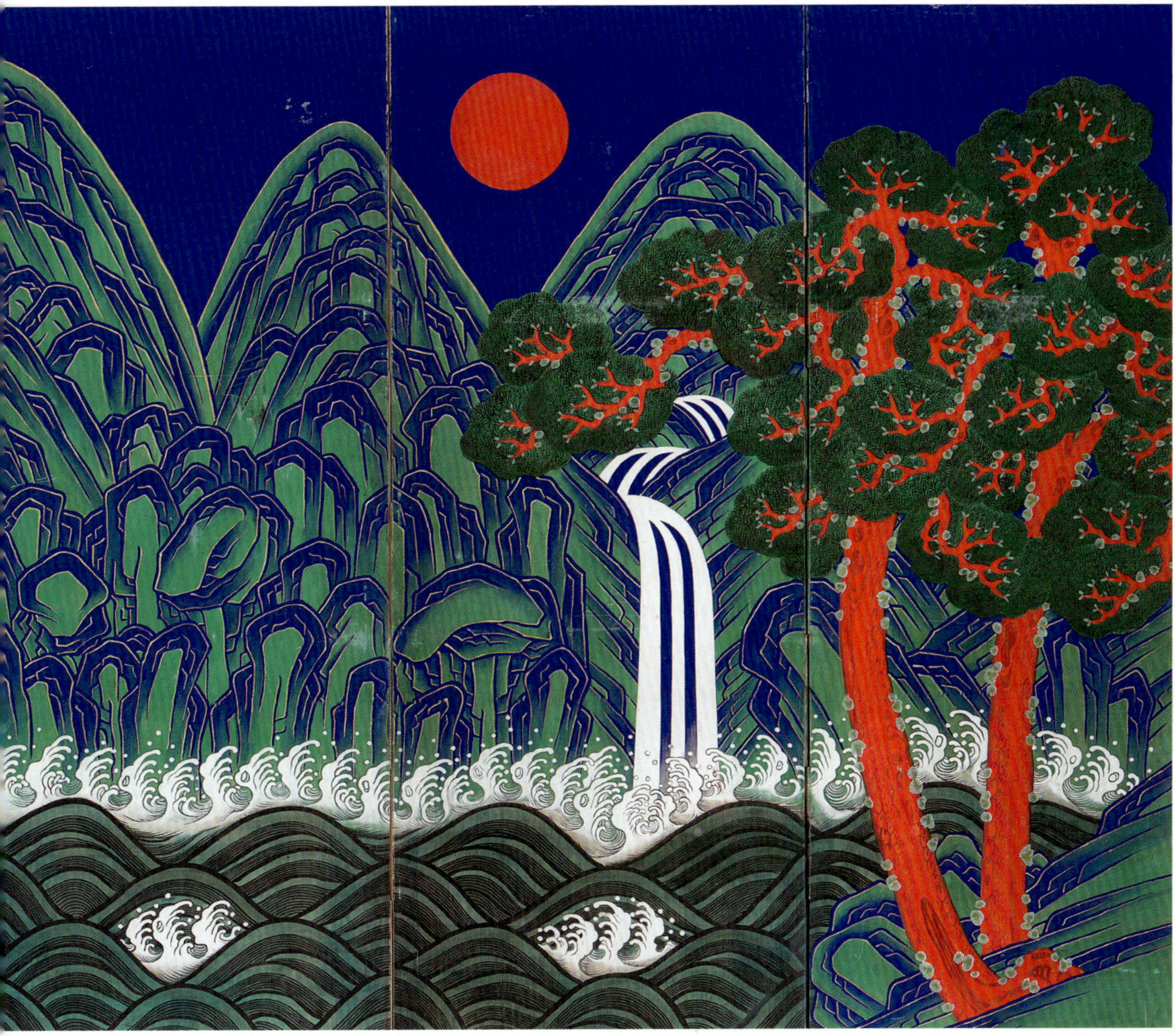

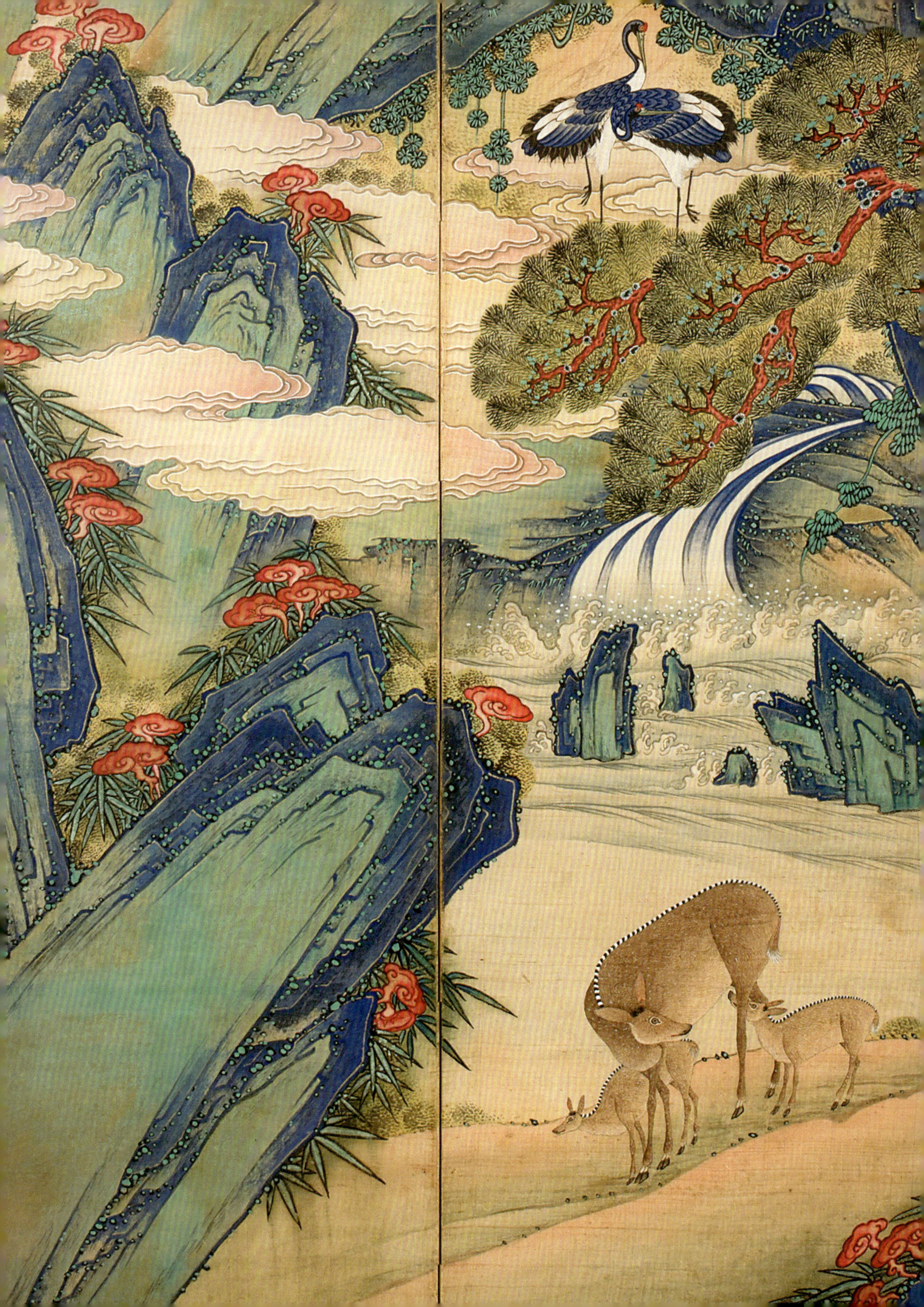

Ten Symbols of Longevity *Sipjangsaengdo*

1880 / ten-fold screen / ink and color on silk / each panel 201.9 × 52.1 cm / Jordan Schnitzer Museum of Art, University of Oregon

Ten Symbols of Longevity (*Sipjangsaengdo*), one of the many longevity paintings present in Korea's history of visual art, portrays ten different symbols of health and long life, a unique Korean tradition that emerged during the Goryeo Dynasty (918–1392). Not necessarily limited to ten subjects, the subject matter includes thirteen types of items in total—the sun, the moon, clouds, mountains, rocks, water, turtles, cranes, deer, pine trees, bamboo, peaches, and the fungus of immortality—ten of which were selected by the painter. These paintings were used as backdrops for ceremonial events, such as royal weddings and court banquets, or were attached to the sliding doors of palace walls.

This particular screen was commissioned to celebrate the then six-year-old crown prince's (later Emperor Sunjong, r. 1907–1910) 1879 recovery from smallpox. The list of names on the two left panels indicates that the painting was commissioned by the administrators at the Office of Medicine, which oversaw the health of the royal family. It is not surprising that they chose the ten longevity symbols as the subject matter as a means of praying for the long life of the royal heir.

In the foreground, a family of deer roams around the red pine trees, sniffing at the fungus of immortality. Beyond the deer, tortoises swim in the stream, while a group of cranes rests on the upper mountains, showing off their exquisite plumage. The cloudy red sky serves to further reinforce the auspiciousness of the scene. Overall, *Ten Symbols of Longevity* portrays a utopian landscape in which fortuitous animals of the land, water, and heavens harmonize with nature.

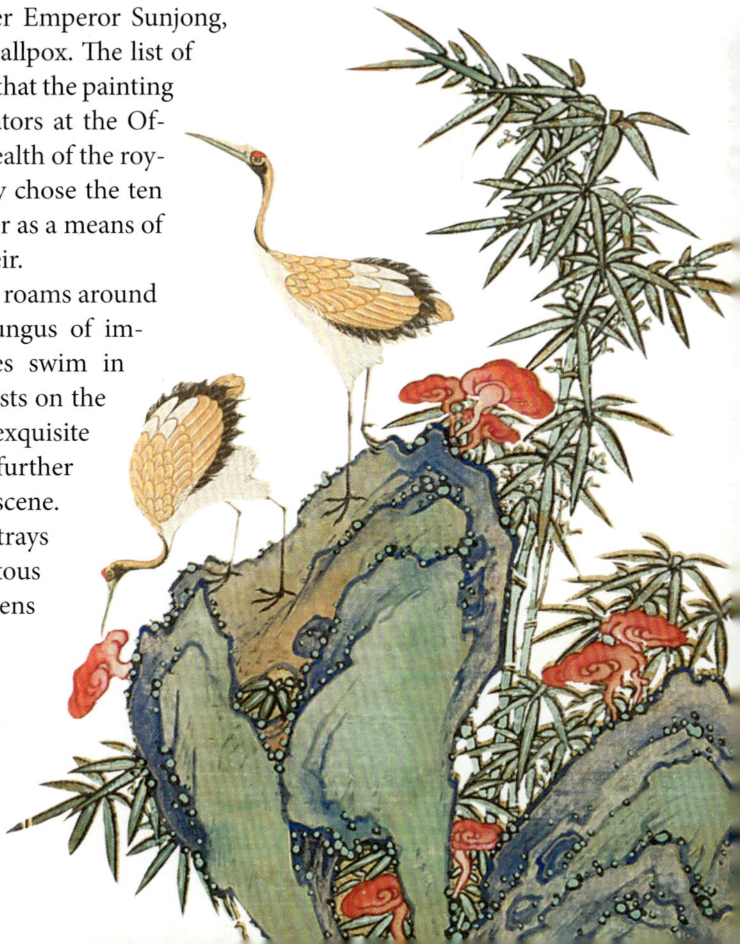

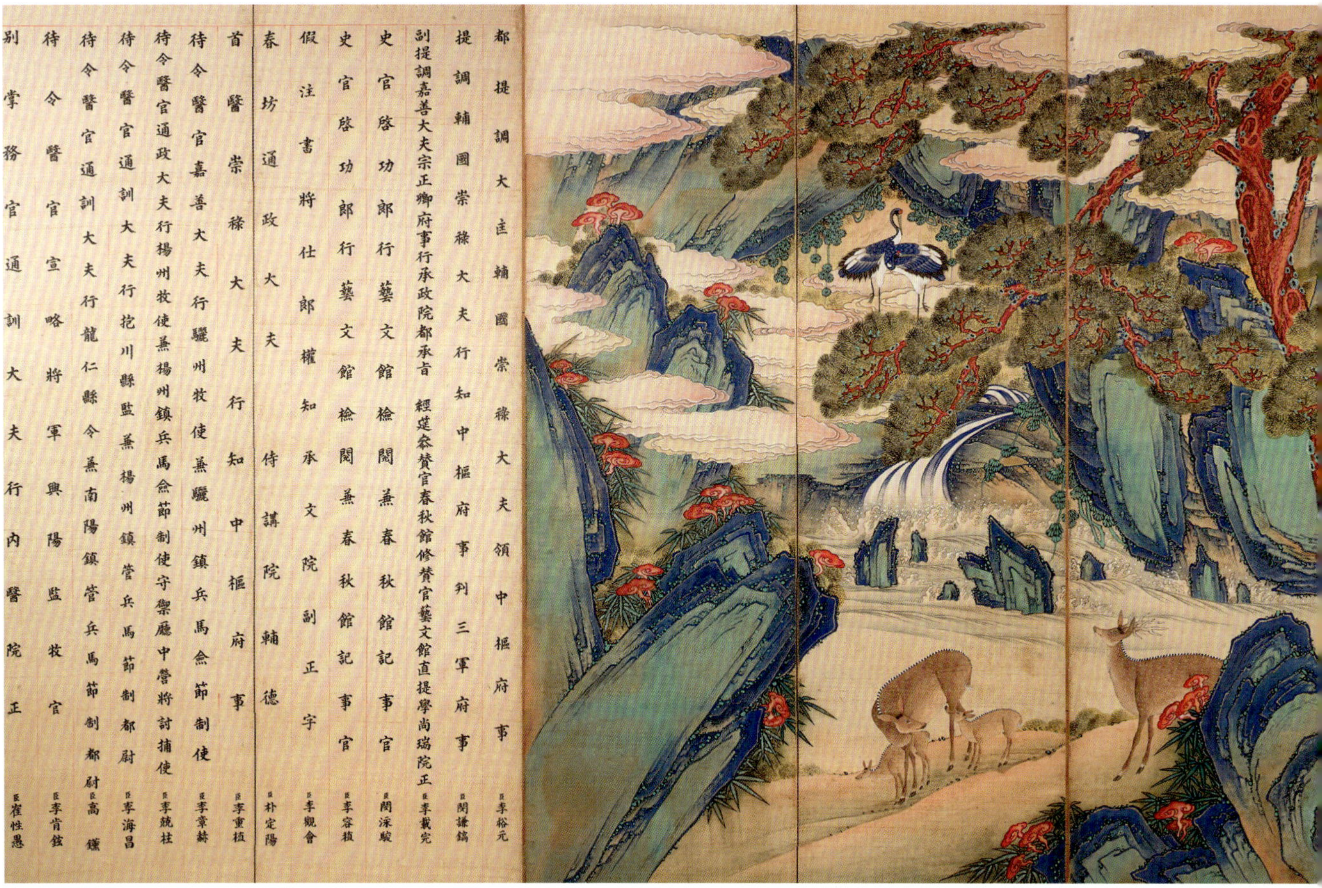

都提調大匡輔國崇祿大夫領中樞府事 臣李裕元
提調輔國崇祿大夫行知中樞府事判三軍府事 臣閔謙鎬
副提調嘉善大夫宗正卿府事行承政院都承旨 經筵叅贊官春秋館修賛官藝文館直提學尚瑞院正 臣李載完
史官啓功郎行藝文館檢閱兼春秋館記事官 臣閔泳駿
史官啓功郎行藝文館檢閱兼春秋館記事官 臣李容稙
假注書將仕郎權知承文院副正字 臣李觀會
春坊通政大夫侍講院輔德 臣朴定陽
首醫崇祿大夫行知中樞府事 臣李重植
待令醫官嘉善大夫行驪州牧使兼驪州鎮兵馬僉節制使 臣李章爀
待令醫官通政大夫行楊州牧使兼楊州鎮兵馬僉節制使守禦廳中營將討捕使 臣李兢柱
待令醫官通訓大夫行抱川縣監兼楊州鎮管兵馬節制都尉 臣李海昌
待令醫官通訓大夫行龍仁縣令兼南陽鎮管兵馬節制都尉 臣高鑛
待令醫官宣略將軍興陽監牧官 臣李肯鉉
別掌務官通訓大夫行內醫院正 臣崔性愚

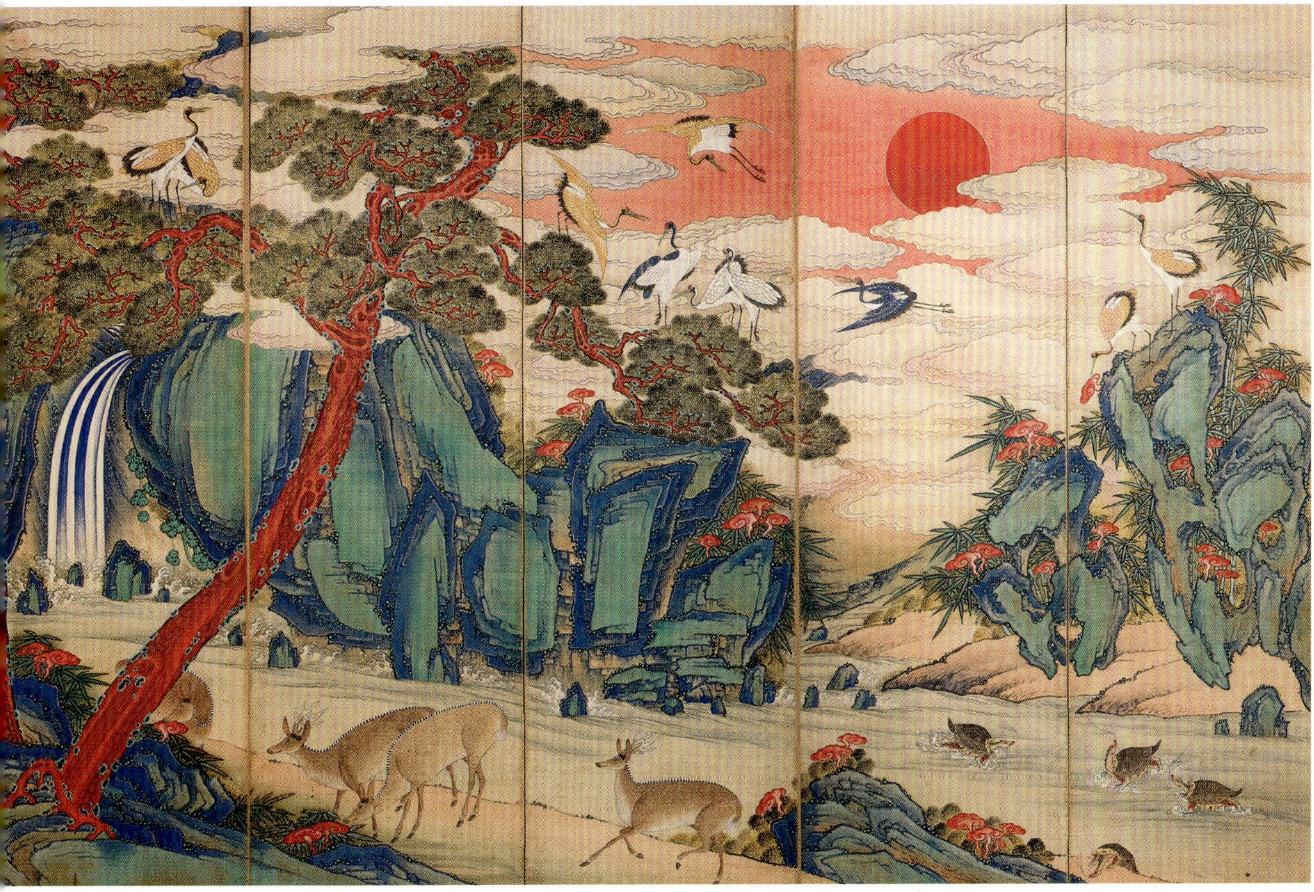

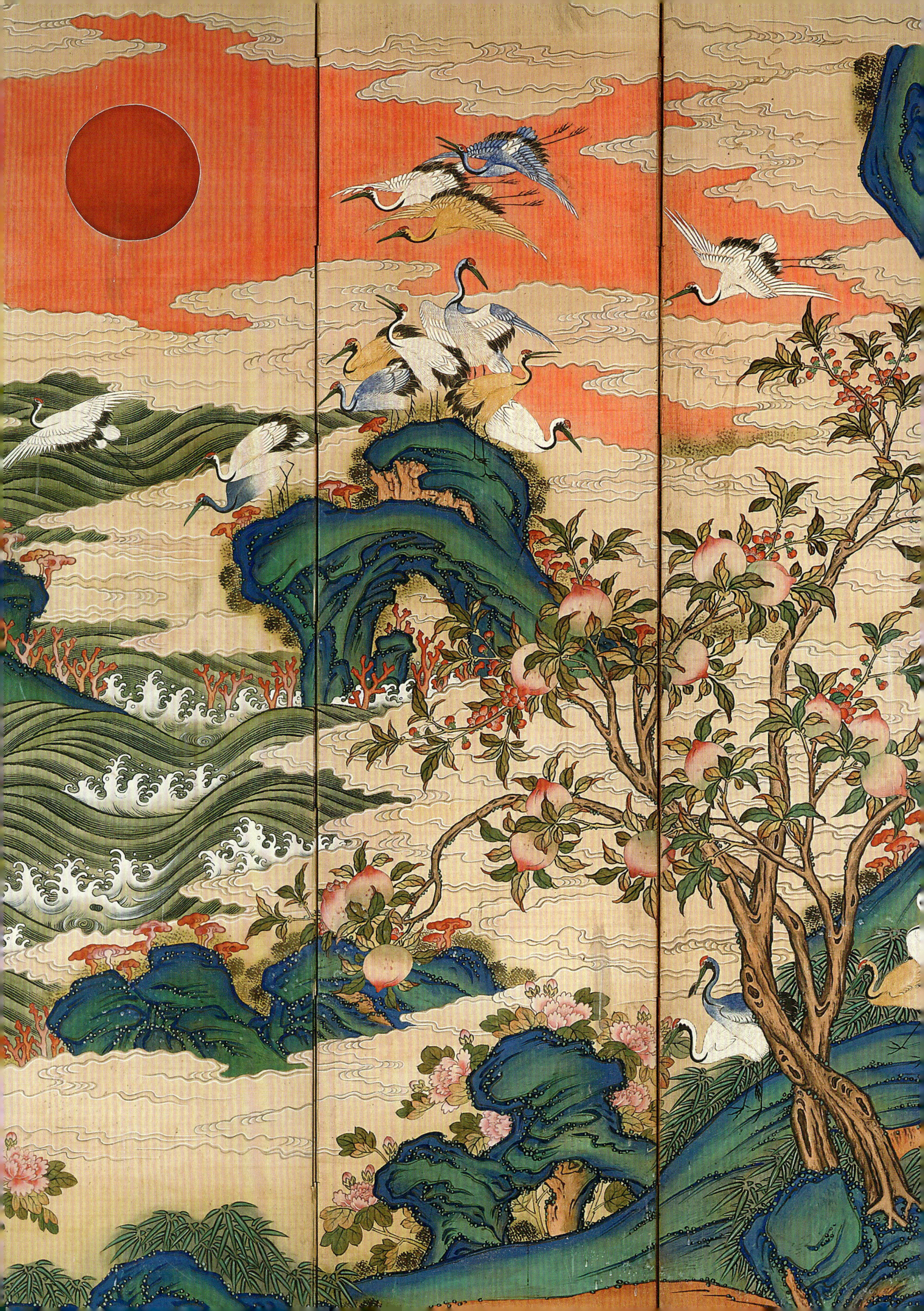

The Cranes and Peaches of Immortality by the Sea | *Haehak Bandodo*

19th century / ten-fold screen / ink and color on silk / 166 × 416 cm /
Ewha Womans University Museum

The Cranes and Peaches of Immortality by the Sea (*Haehak Bandodo*), another type of longevity painting, depicts the same motifs of long life as the *sipjangsaeng* works, excluding pine trees, deer, and tortoises. Instead, it focuses on cranes and peach trees in the sea. Unlike other longevity paintings, the background of this screen is filled with the billowing sea and sky whose boundaries are blurred by the auspicious clouds, imbuing the picture with a sense of fantasy and impermanence.

A group of cranes flies over the oddly shaped rocks in the sea. According to traditional folklore found throughout East Asia, cranes were capable of living for a thousand years, making them one of the strongest symbols of longevity. Cranes that live for longer than a thousand years were thought to turn blue, a belief that is portrayed in the painting.

In the foreground are two large peach trees—displacing the typical pine tree imagery—that provide a sense of central balance to the composition. Peaches also served as the representative fruits to signify long life, stemming from the Chinese myth of the Queen Mother of the West (Xi Wangmu), a matriarch who had a peach tree at her abode (瑤池, or Yoji in Korean) in the Kunlun Mountains. According to legend, her tree would bloom once every three thousand years and take another three thousand years to bear fruit.

The Feast of Yoji Pond (p. 41, p. 47), another popular subject among Joseon court paintings, depicts the party held by the queen to enjoy an elixir made from this fruit.

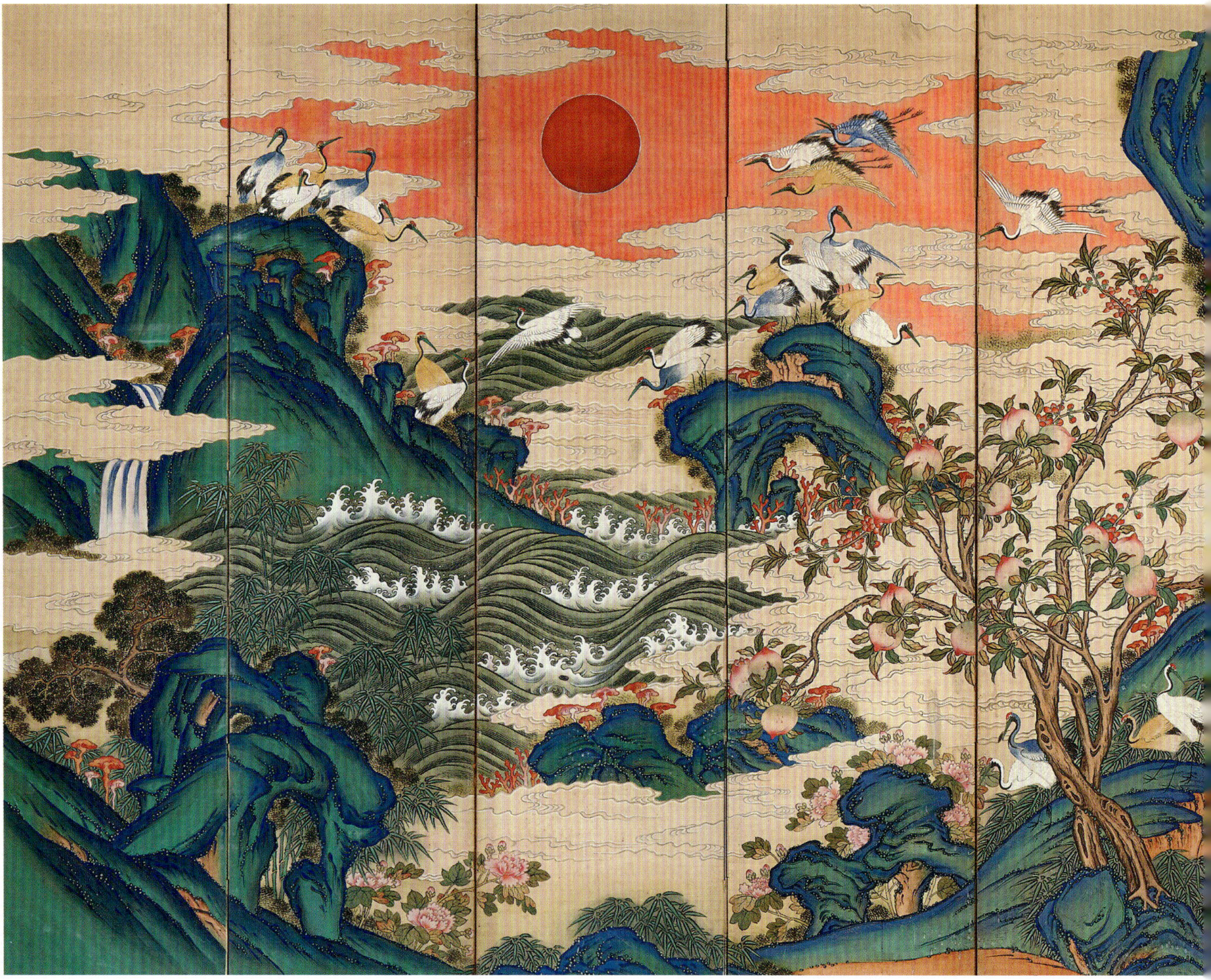

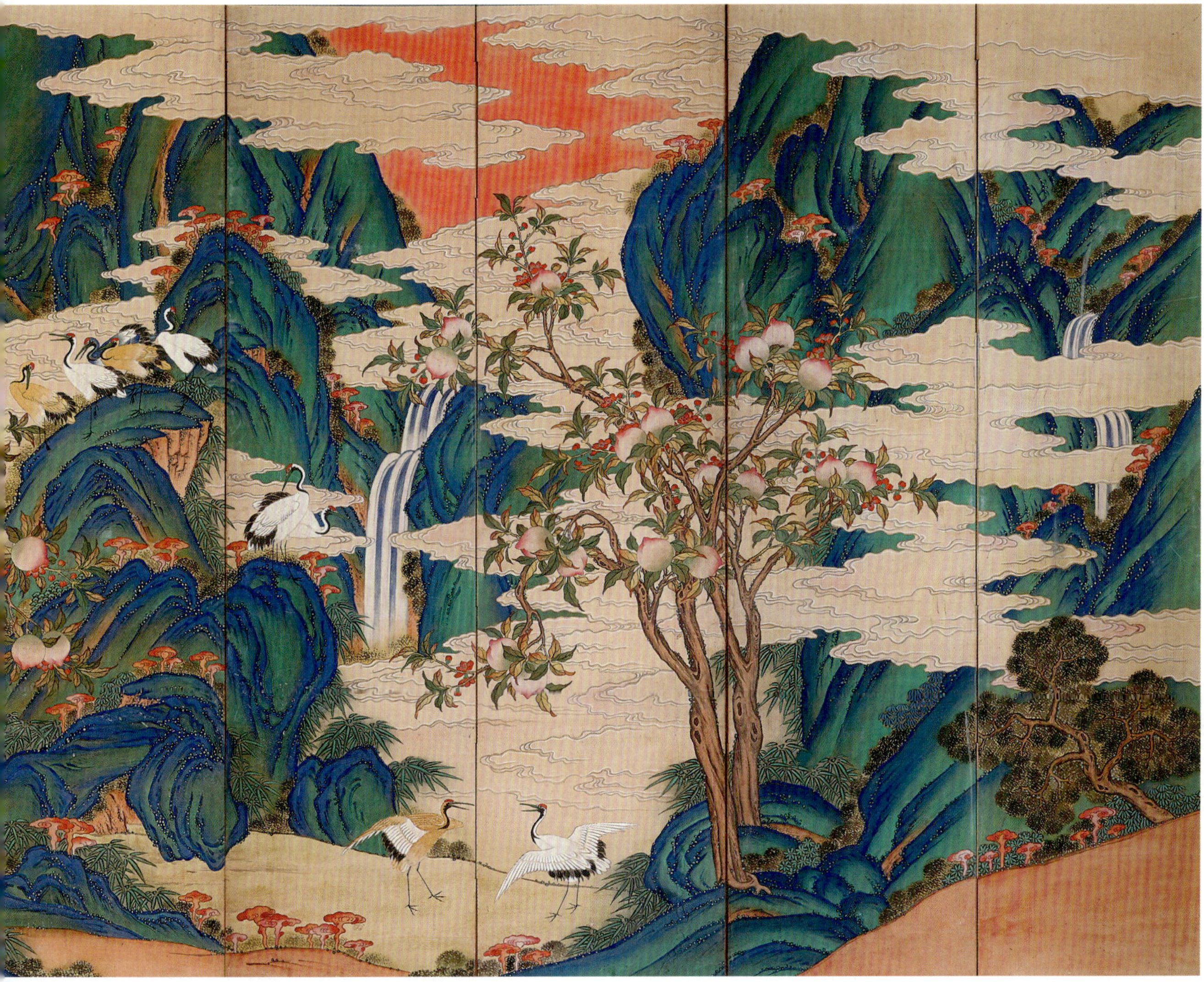

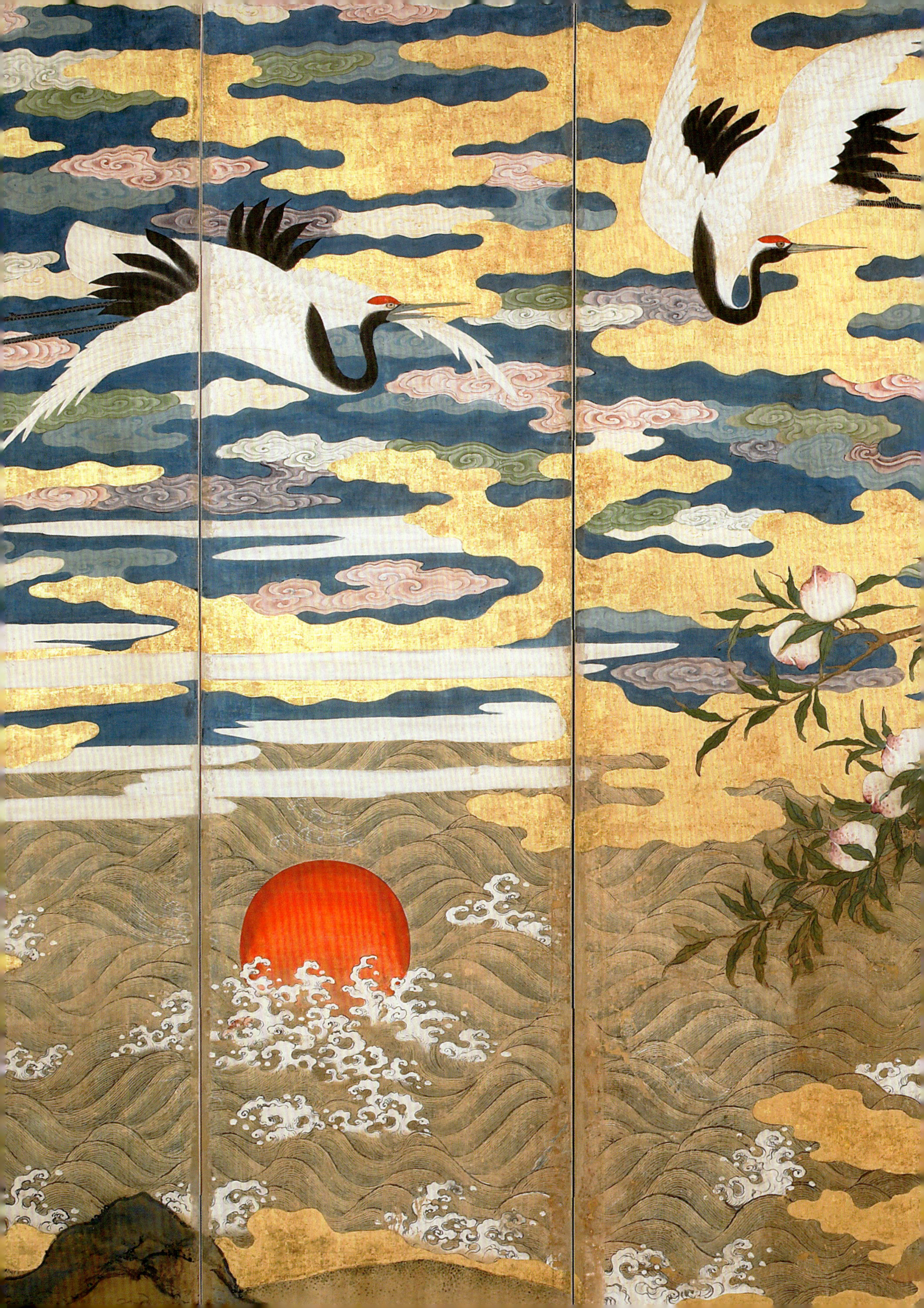

The Cranes and Peaches of Immortality by the Sea II *Haehak Bandodo*

Late 19th century / twelve-fold screen / ink, color, and gold on silk / 227.7 × 714 cm / Honolulu Academy of Arts

Seen in the foreground are a group of cranes and a peach tree growing toward the sea. Another peach tree protrudes from the large rock in the upper right corner of the frame. While the sun lingers over the sea in the lower left corner, golden decorative clouds overwhelm the rest of the screen, making it difficult to distinguish between the sea and sky. The flattened clouds shown in pink, light green, sky blue, white, and gold contribute to the painting's distinctive character.

Throughout Korean history, clouds were considered to be spiritual matter that connects heaven and Earth. In particular, multicolored clouds came to signify auspiciousness. Clouds in court paintings served as emblems of the king's virtues and peace-filled reign, rather than signifying a mere natural phenomenon. Whereas the clouds are emphasized with more abstract, decorative patterns, the image's other elements—cranes, peaches, wild plants, families of mandarin ducks, and the fungus of immortality—are painted in a more realistic, natural manner.

The writing in gold on the upper right corner suggests that the screen was produced around 1902, when King Gojong (r. 1863–1907) turned fifty-one. The inscription reads as follows: "The immortals wrote this, wishing, with hands clasped and much respect, for the long life in the summer of the Year Imin."

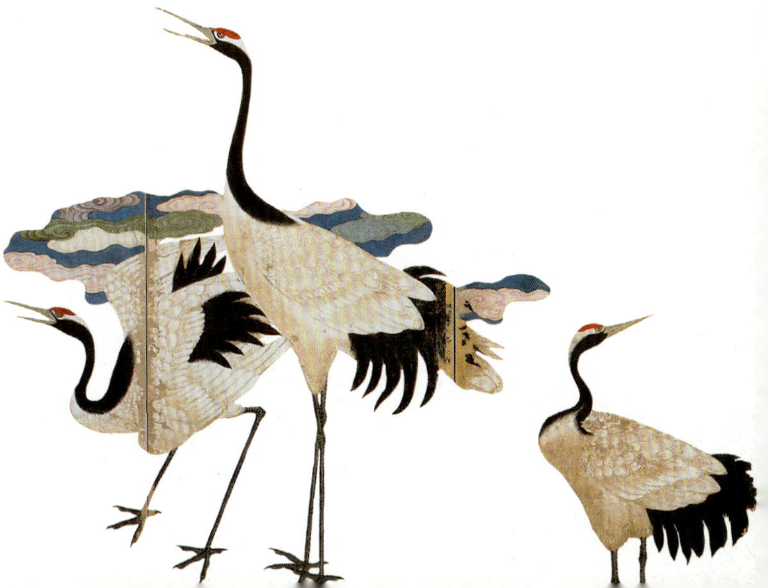

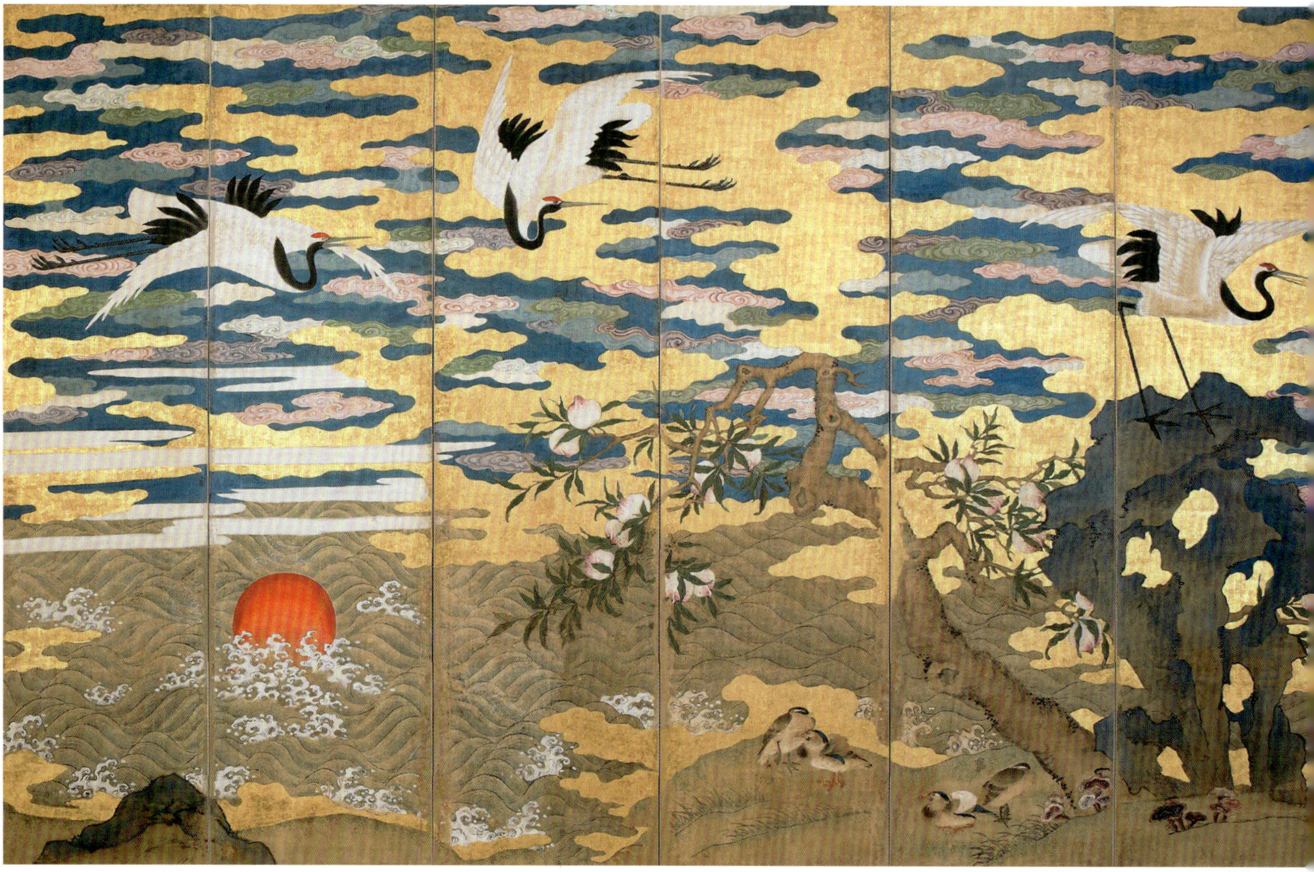

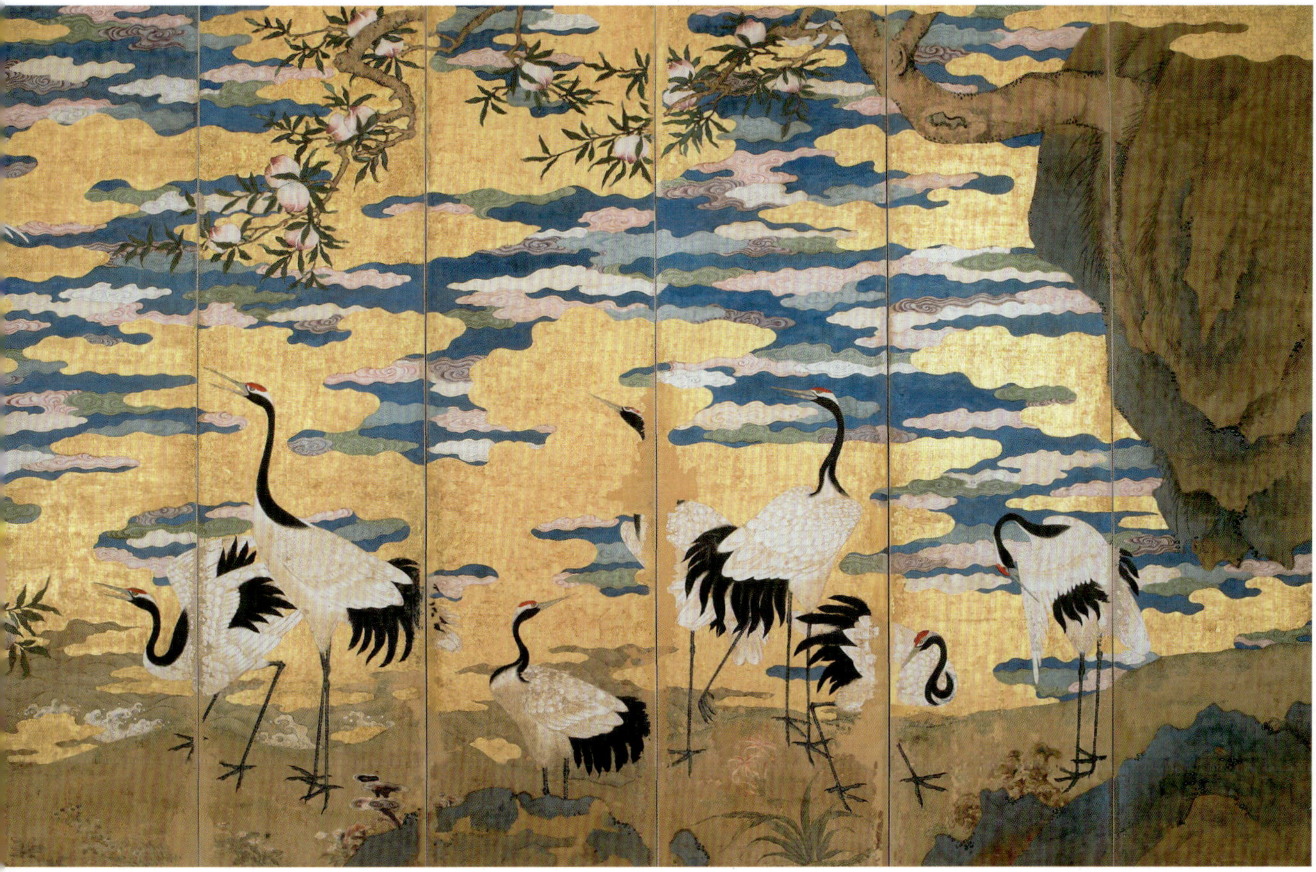

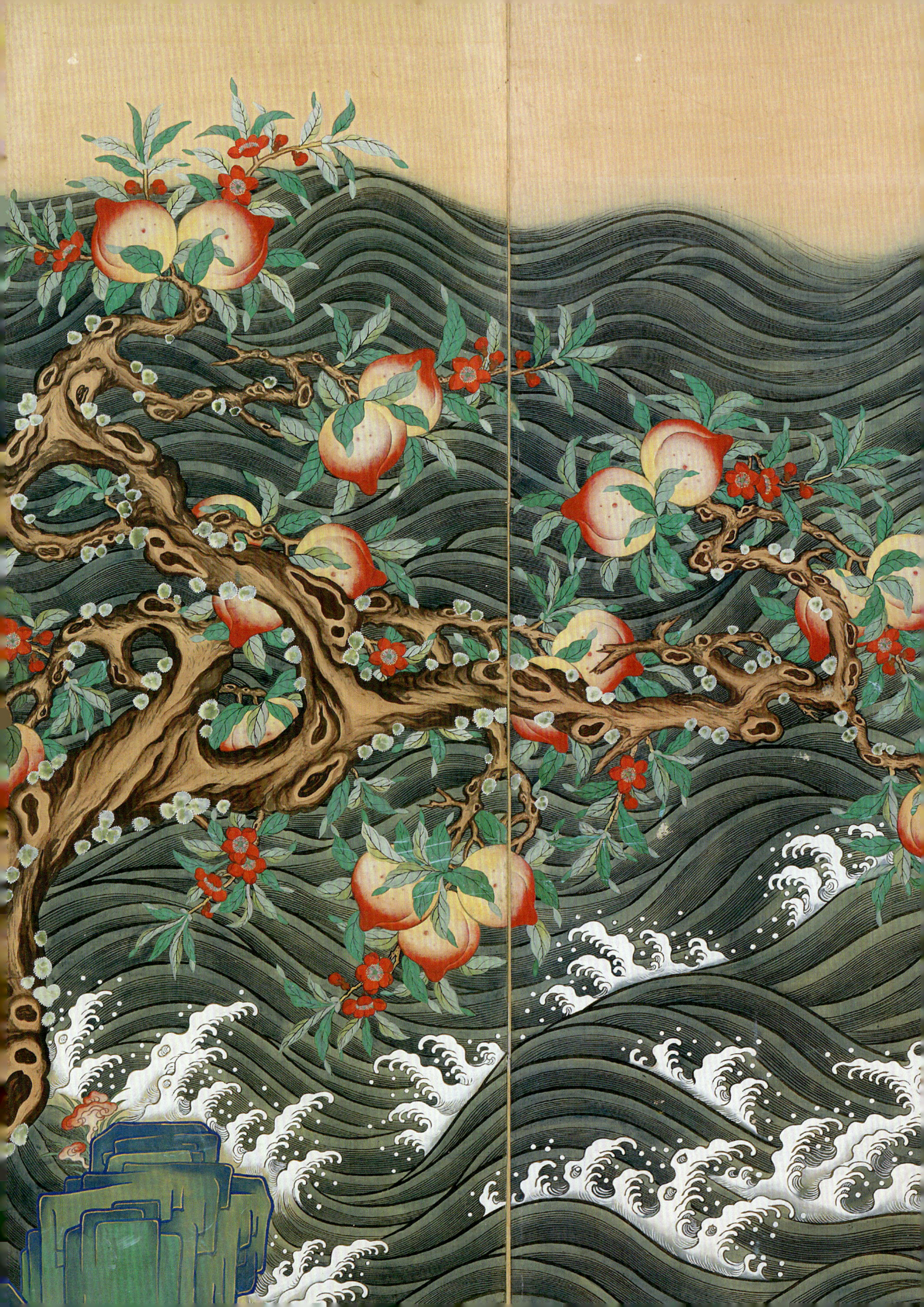

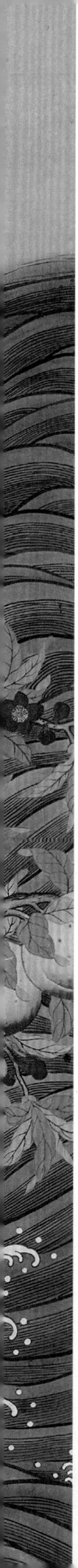

The Sun, Moon, and Peach Trees of Immortality *Irwol Bandodo*

19th century / a pair of four-fold screens / ink and color on silk / left screen, 317 cm × 257.2 cm; right screen, 317 × 259.4 cm / National Palace Museum of Korea

This painting consists of a pair of four-fold screens featuring the sun and moon, sea waves with surf, peach trees, and a mountain range in the background, with rocks in the lower corners. These simple, natural motifs bring some of the ten longevity symbols to mind, as if an enlarged detail of the water section of the aforementioned longevity painting (*Ten Symbols of Longevity* on p. 25).

When aligned, the pair of screens makes a larger picture that is nearly symmetrical. Each diagonally positioned peach tree takes up nearly half of its respective screen, exhibiting a burgeoning vitality that makes it the focal point of the work. The complete painting's geometrical composition—characterized in the horizontal sea, two circular orbs, and triangular mountain peaks and rocks—reinforces its subdued aesthetics. While the isolated sun and moon and the defined mountain peaks remain static, it is the billowing waves crashing against the rocks that add movement, creating balance in the work.

Despite the screens' simple composition, the full image delivers a visual impact that is stronger than any other paintings of the sun, moon, and peach trees. Its imposing size—reaching over three meters in height—also adds to its powerful visual message. It is highly plausible that this pair was produced with the intention of being the backdrop of a shrine. *Uigwe*, or the book of court rites, records that a pair of four-fold screens were installed in the Seonwonjeon, a royal portrait hall at Changdeokgung Palace.

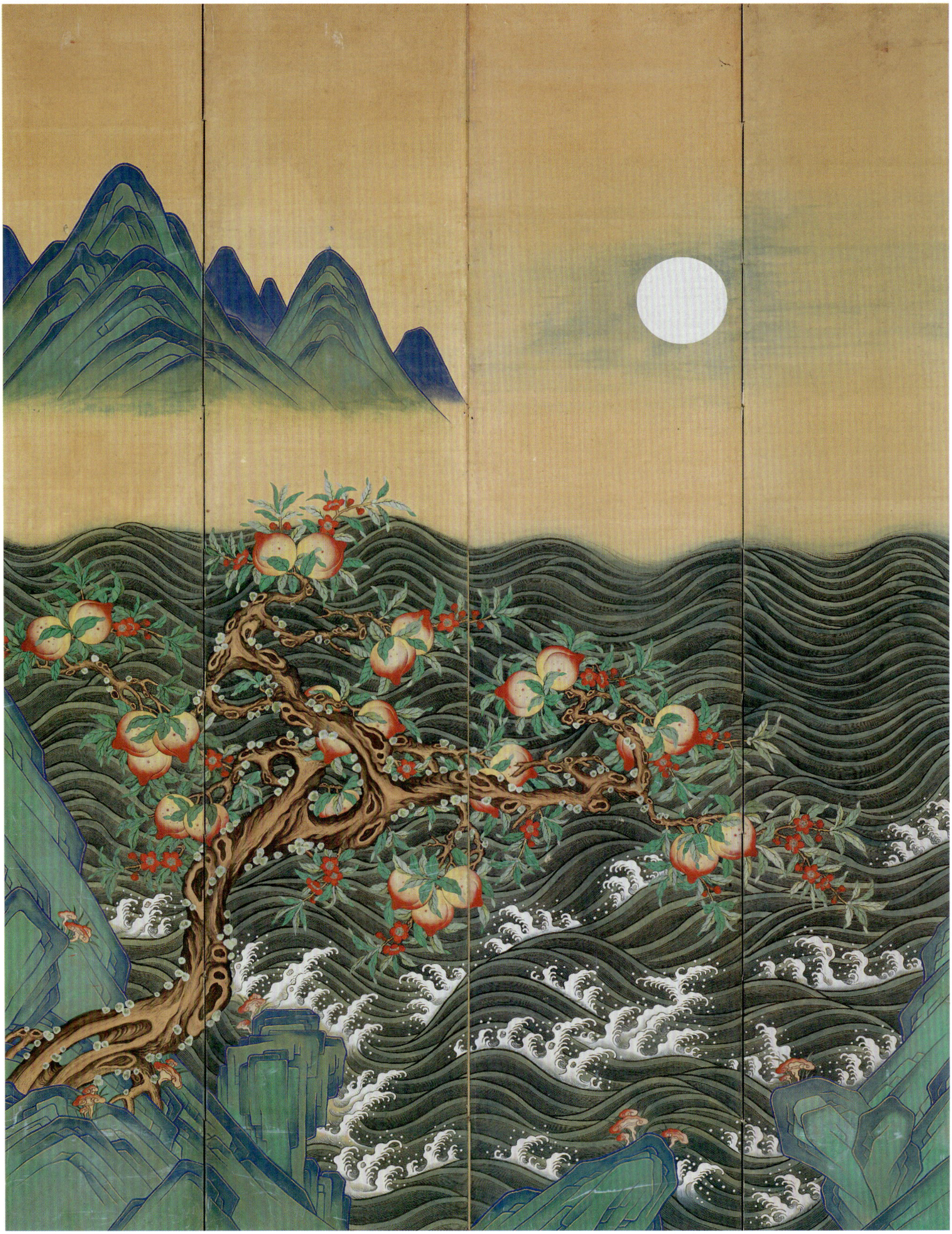

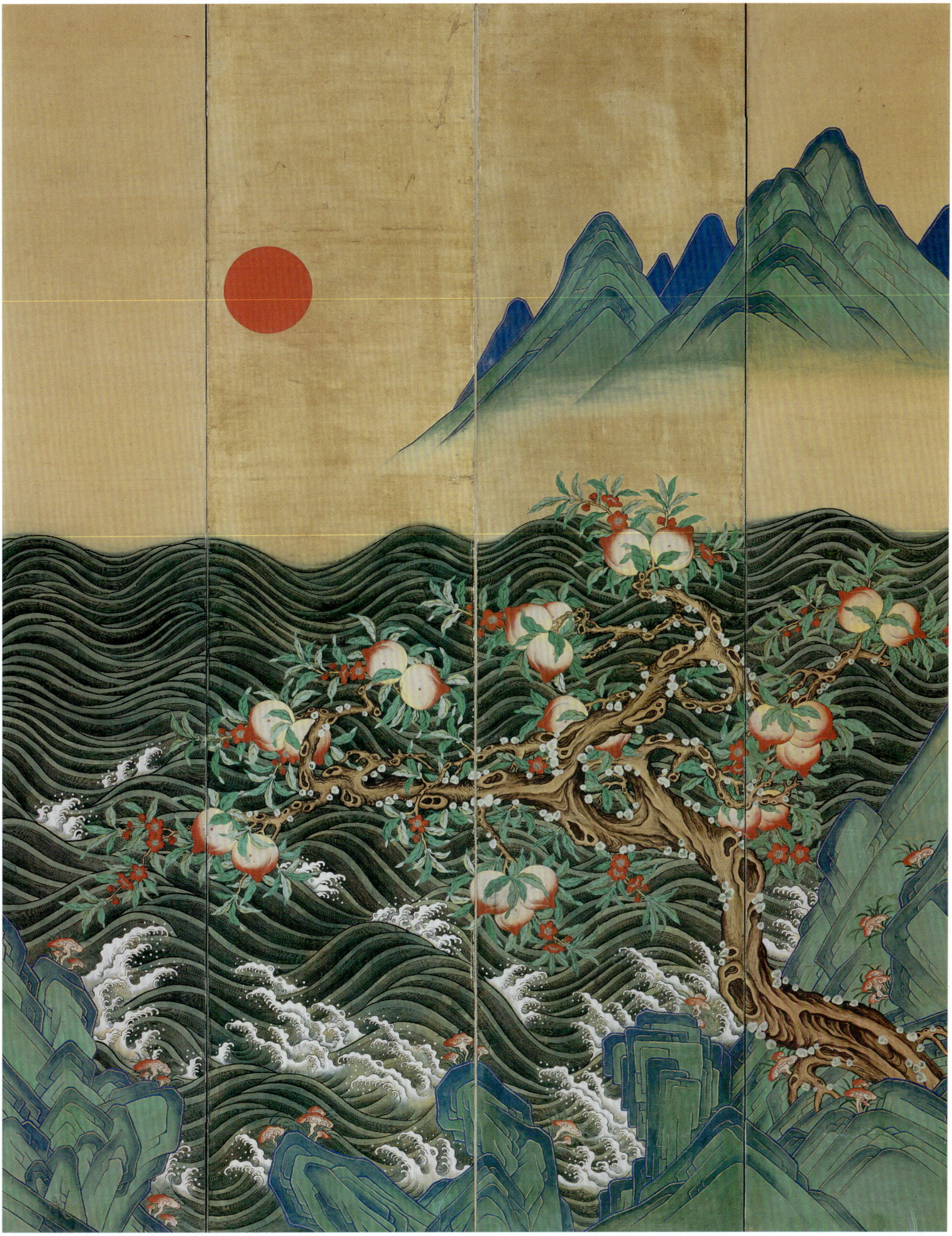

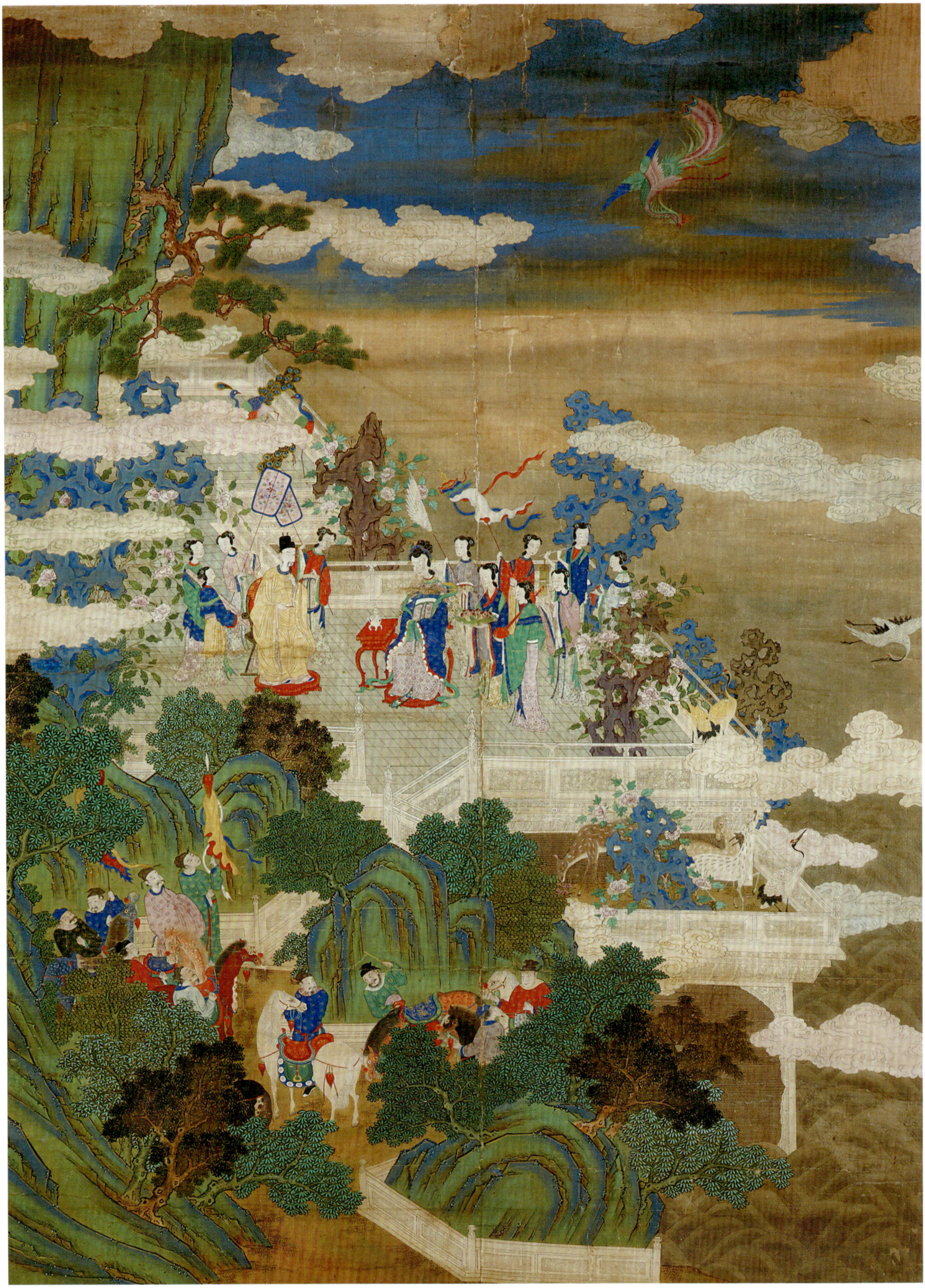

The Feast of Yoji Pond | *Yojiyeondo*

Late 18th century / ink and color on silk / 151.5 × 122.7 cm / National Museum of Korea

Yojiyeon, or the Feast of Yoji Pond, refers to the legendary party held by Xi Wangmu (Queen Mother of the West) in celebration of the peach harvest, an event that included the presence of King Mu (r. 976–922 BCE) of the Zhou Dynasty (1046–256 BCE) at her residence in the Kunlun Mountains. The painting portrays Xi Wangmu receiving the king at a palatial terrace in the deep, secretive valleys of Kunlun that overlook the ocean. Waiting on the ground under the multi-floored terrace is the king's entourage.

Though the painting recounts the famous story of Xi Wangmu and King Mu, a closer look at the background reveals that the pictorial emphasis is on the portrayal of the imaginary world that surrounds them. A phoenix looks over the meeting of the king and queen while pairs of peacocks, cranes, and deer absentmindedly rest on the terrace, details that suggest that the painting represents a very auspicious world. The landscape is drawn in a highly decorative manner, as seen in the presence of flat clouds, oddly shaped blue rocks, peonies, angled pine trees, the patterned rail of the terrace, the flags, and the decorated saddle. In contrast, the brushstrokes are much less rigid and formalized.

This painting reflects the tendency for early Yojiyeon paintings to focus on the meeting of the queen and king, a popular theme imported from China. Over time, however, the theme and pictorial style of Yojiyeon paintings became more tailored to Korean tastes, especially during the late eighteenth century when Joseon painters were at their most bold and creative.

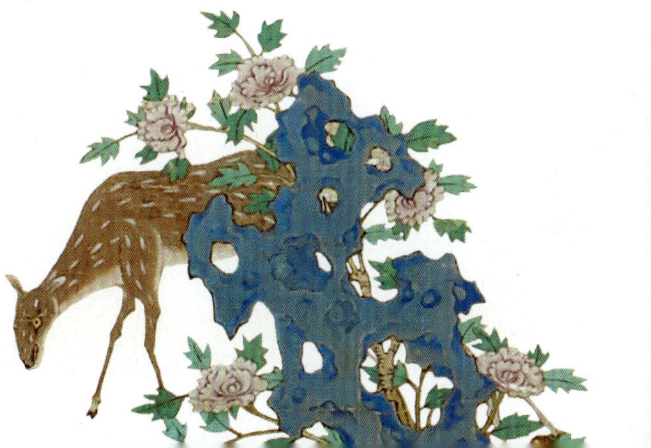

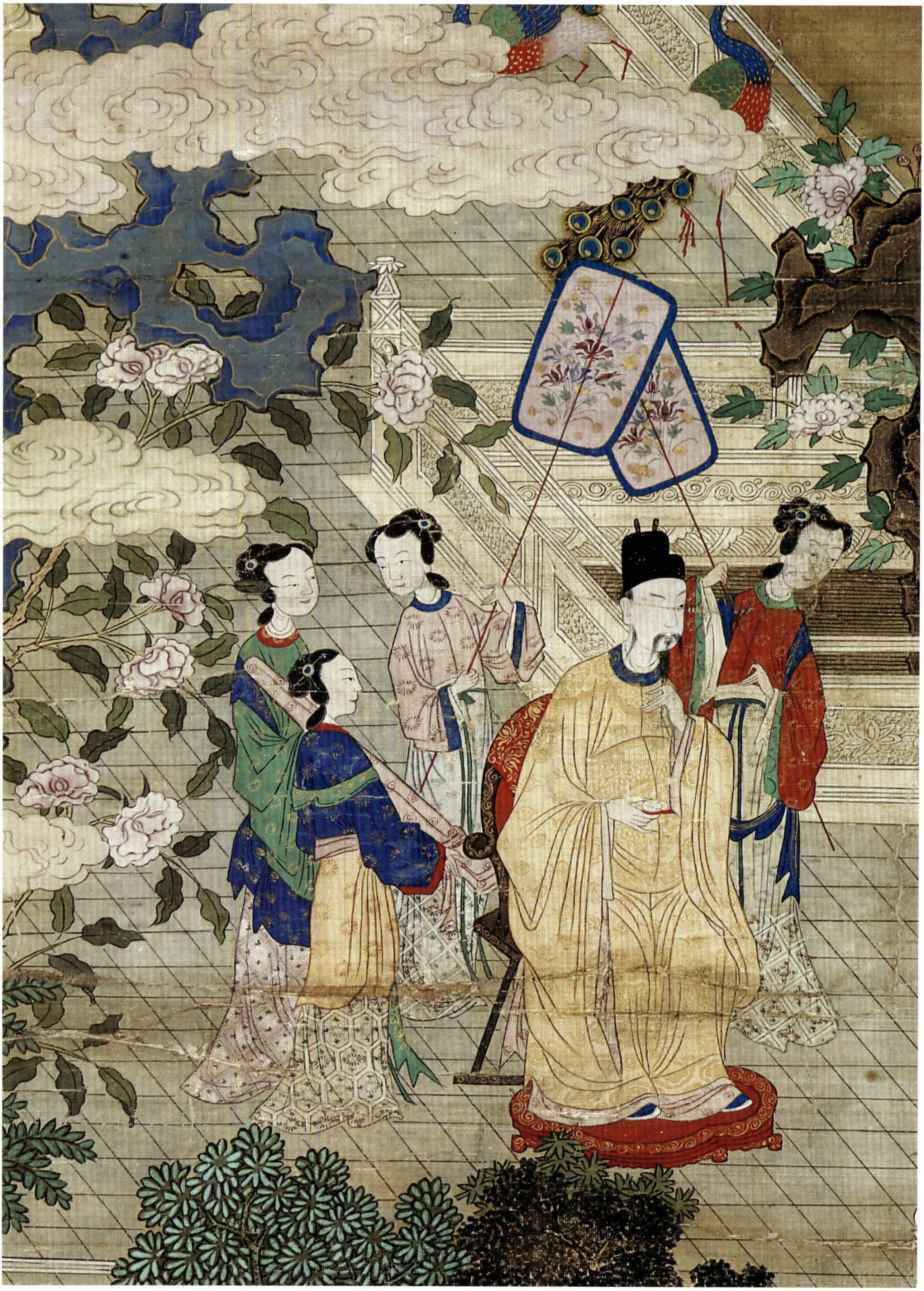

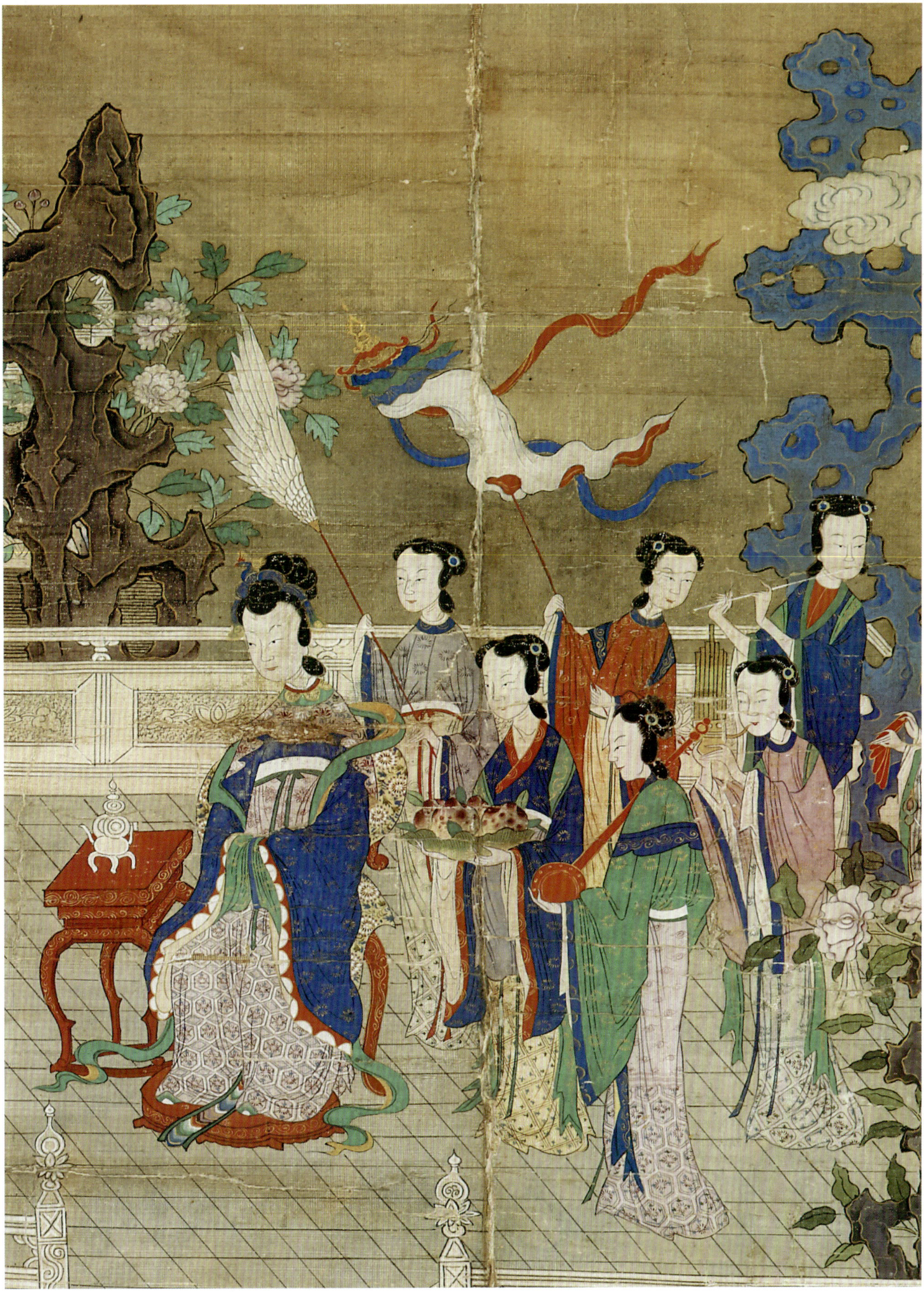

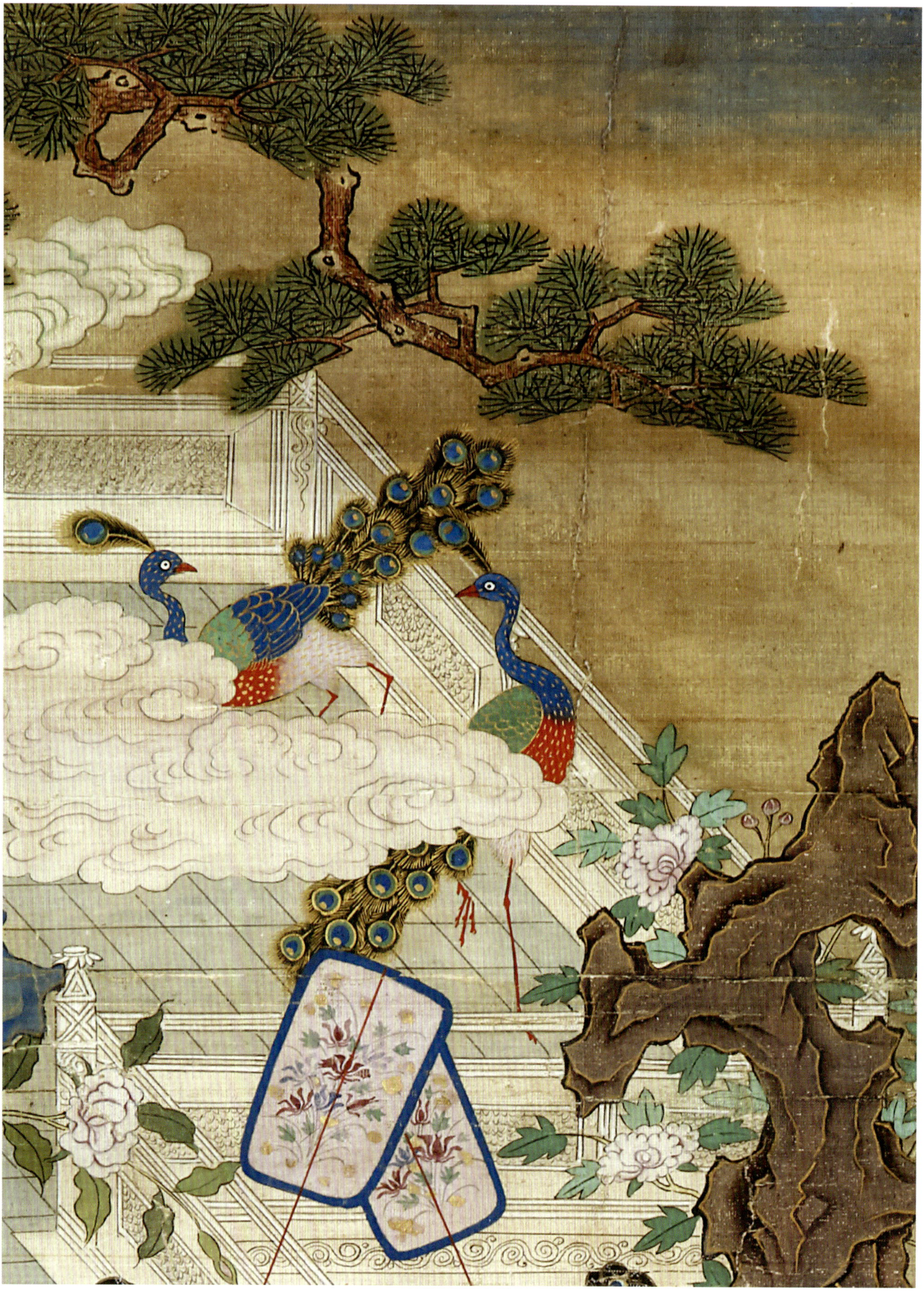

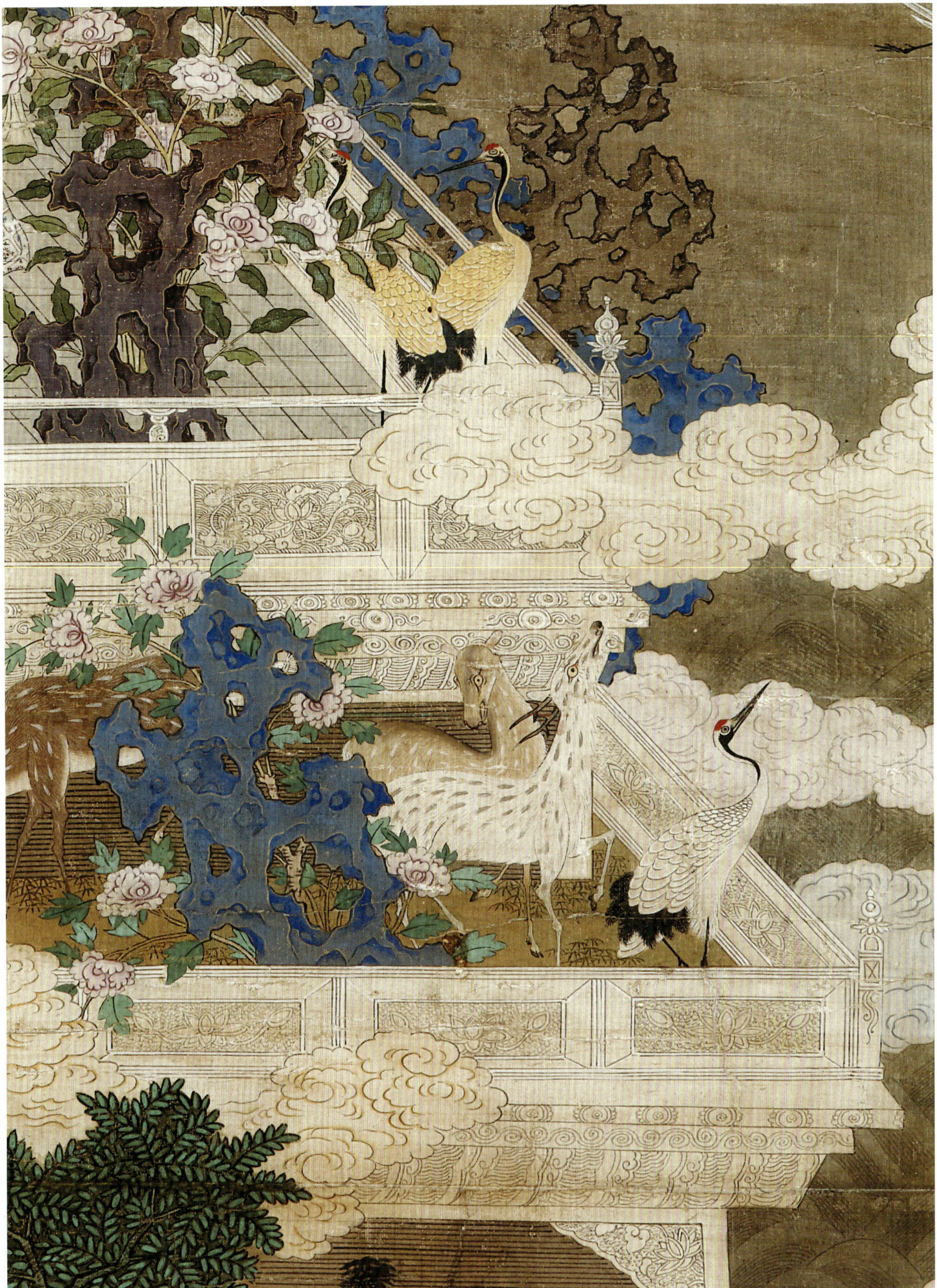

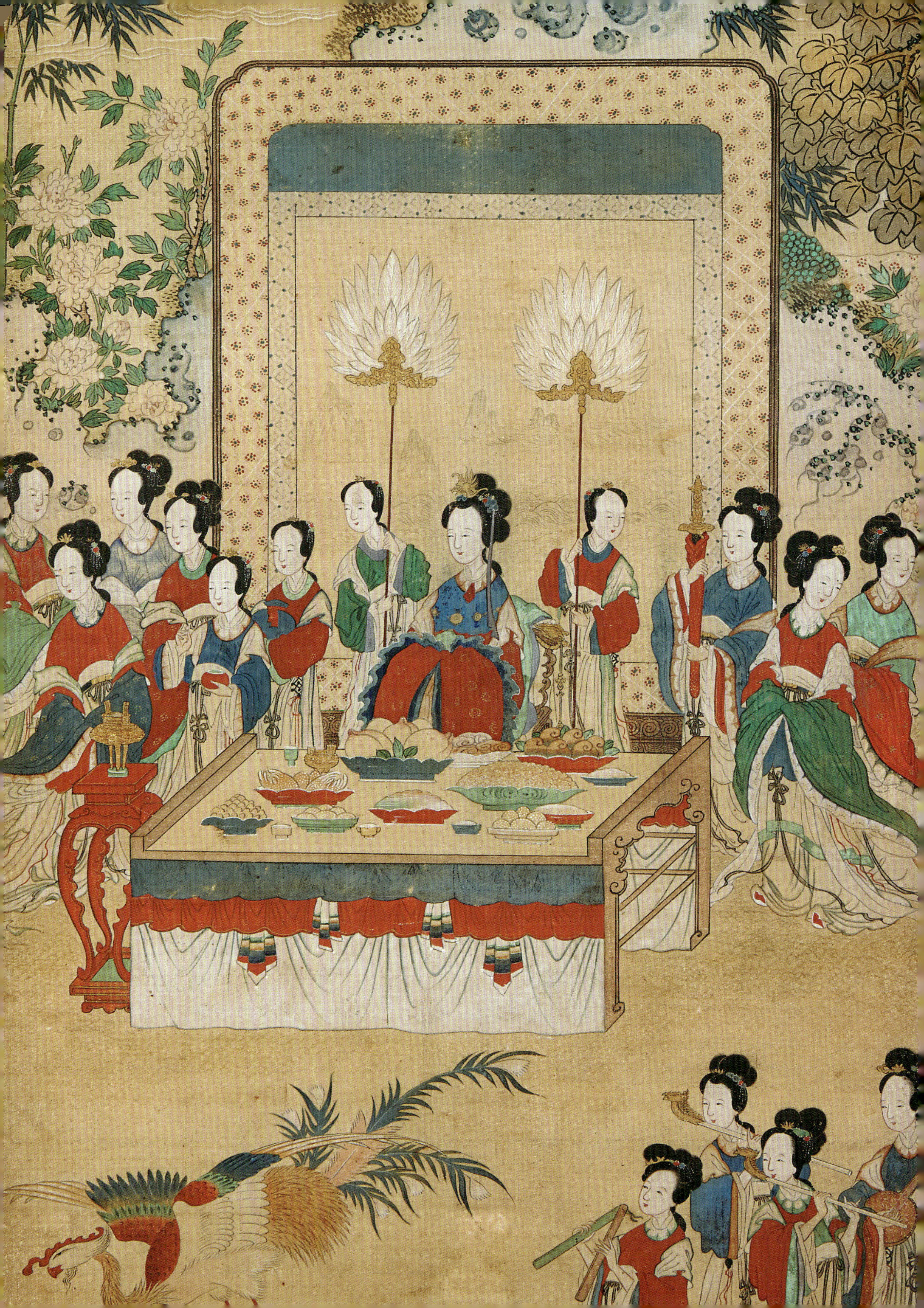

The Feast of Yoji Pond II *Yojiyeondo*

19th century / eight-fold screen / ink and color on silk / each panel, 115.5 × 43 cm / National Museum of Korea

This screen painting demonstrates the typical style of the nineteenth-century Yojiyeon paintings, which are known to combine two popular themes regarding Xi Wangmu: a scene of the feast hosted by Xi Wangmu, to which King Mu of the Zhou Dynasty was invited, and a scene in which the immortals invited to the celebration gather around.

A group consisting of the Buddha, bodhisattvas, lohans, and the Four Heavenly Kings on the clouds, as well as the Old Man of the Southern Celestial Pole boarding a crane, flies down from the sky, while other immortals arrive riding on waves or walking over the mountain peaks. In the foreground, Laozi riding an ox and Suxian Gong riding a deer appear out of the mountain to join the feast at the queen's abode.

The painting represents the ideal world of immortality as imagined by the people of Joseon, and also characterizes the blending of Buddhist and Daoist iconography with traditional Asian folklore.

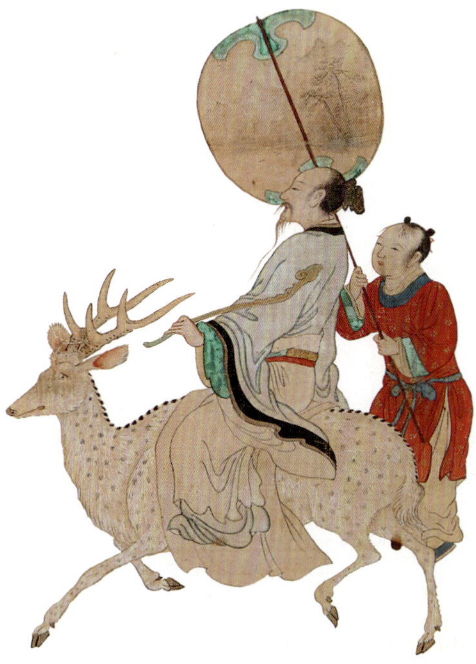

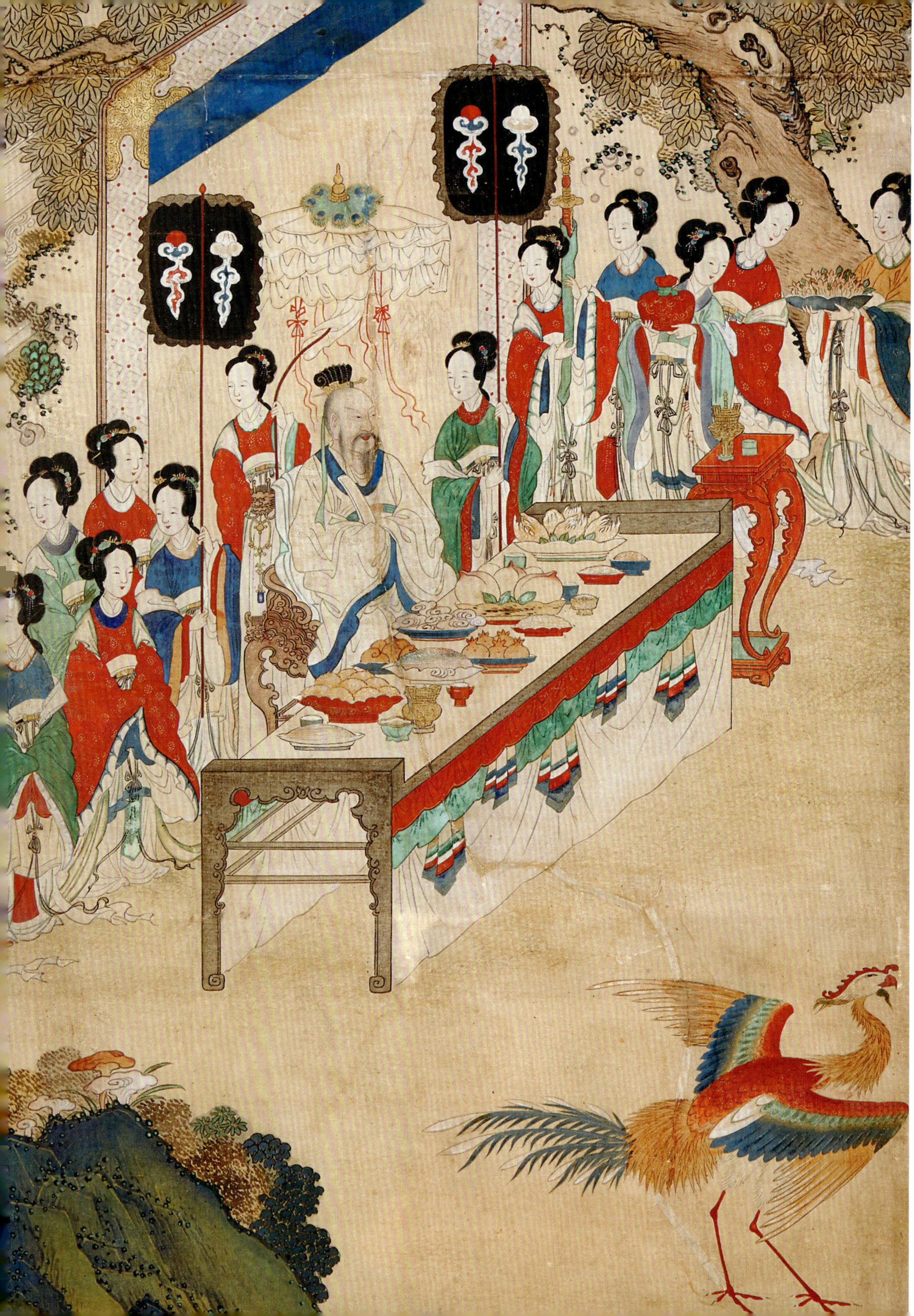

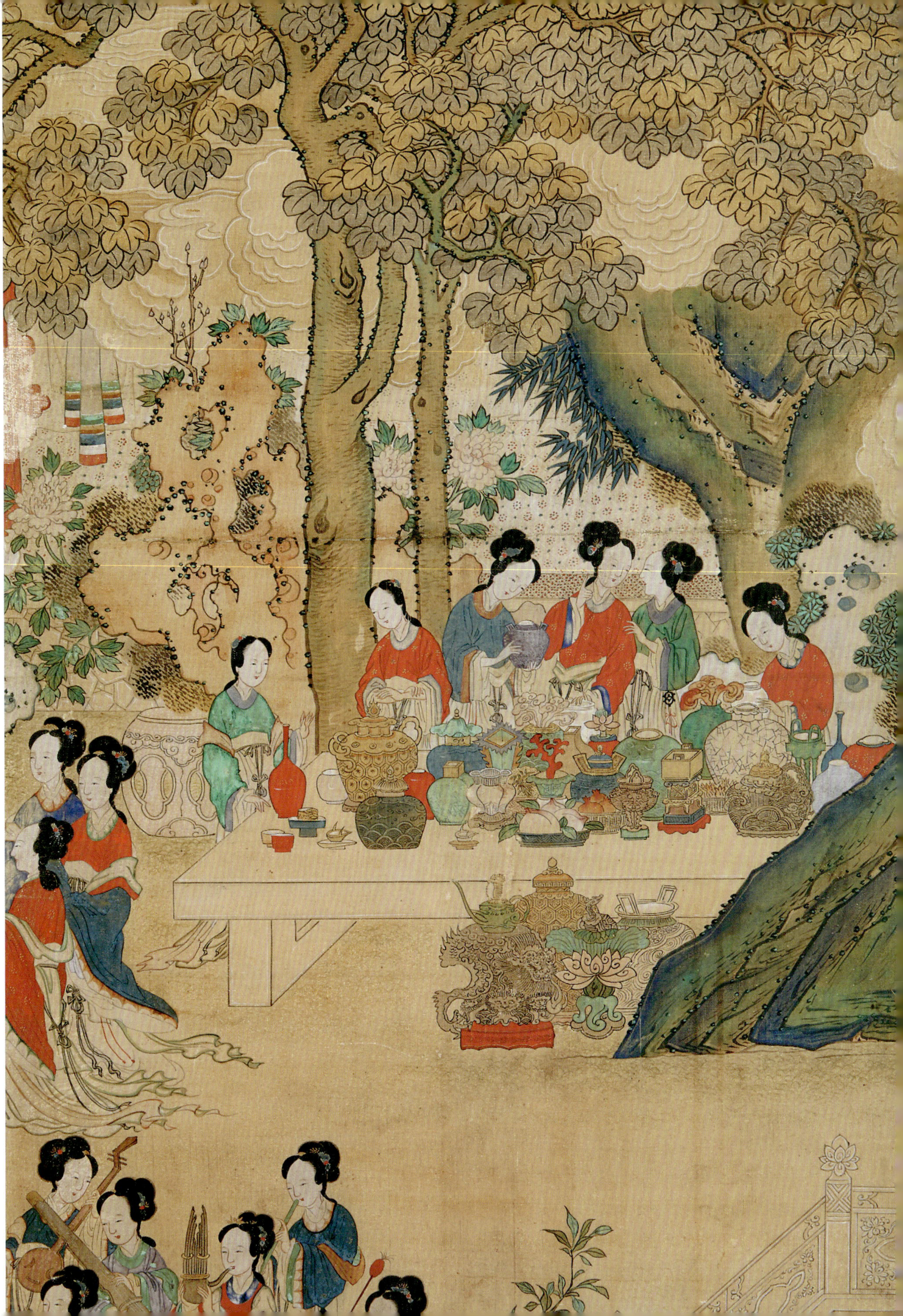

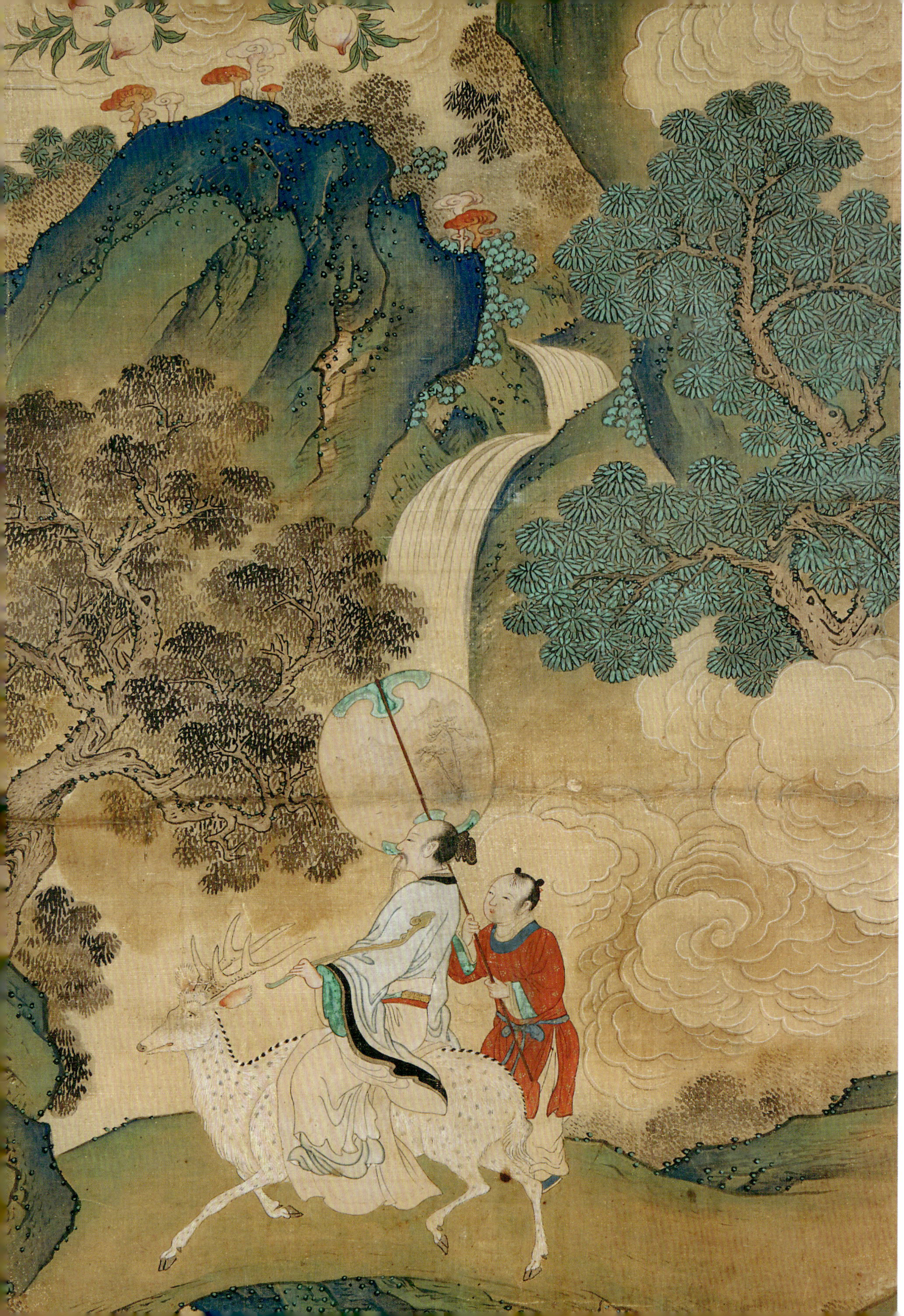

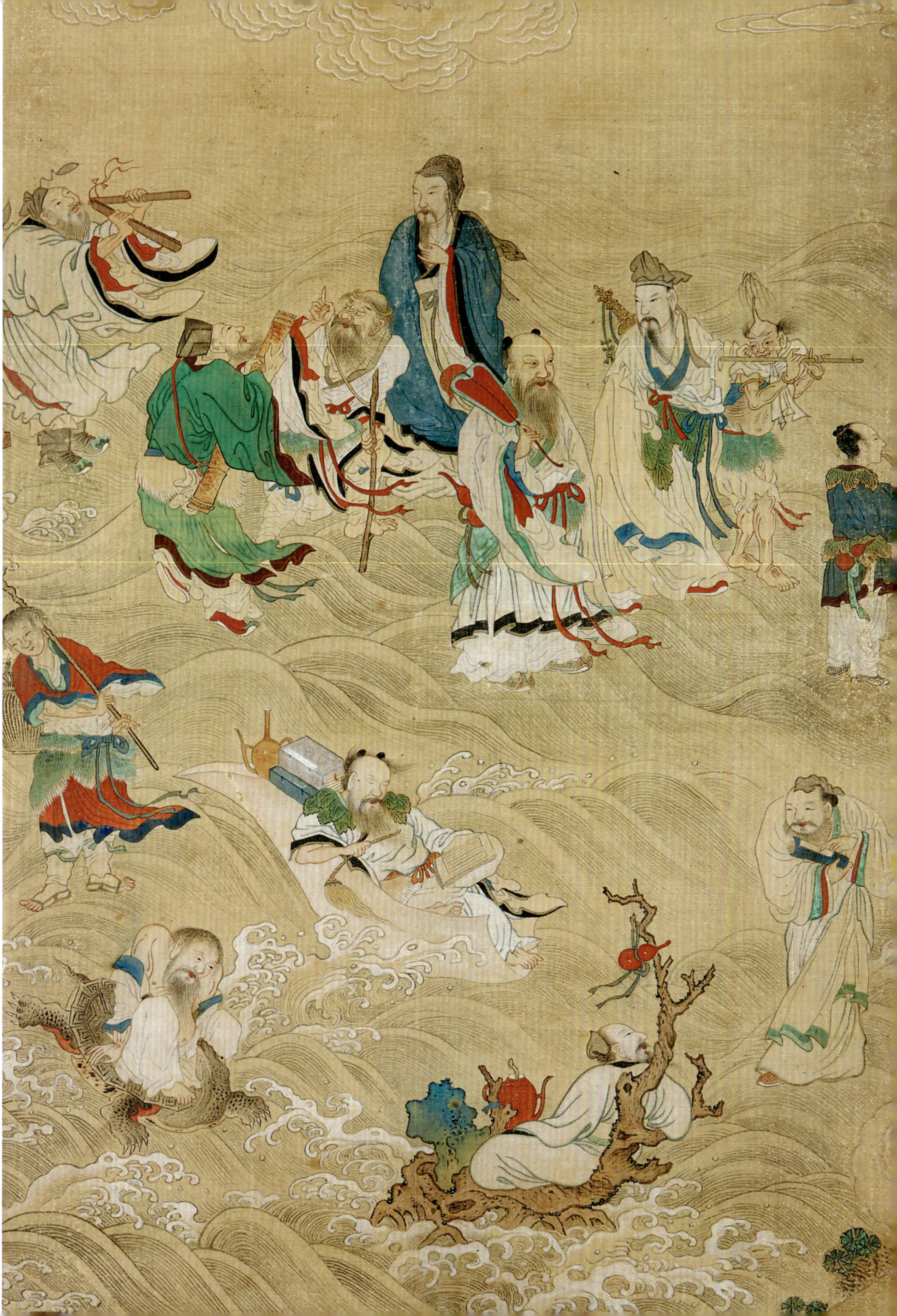

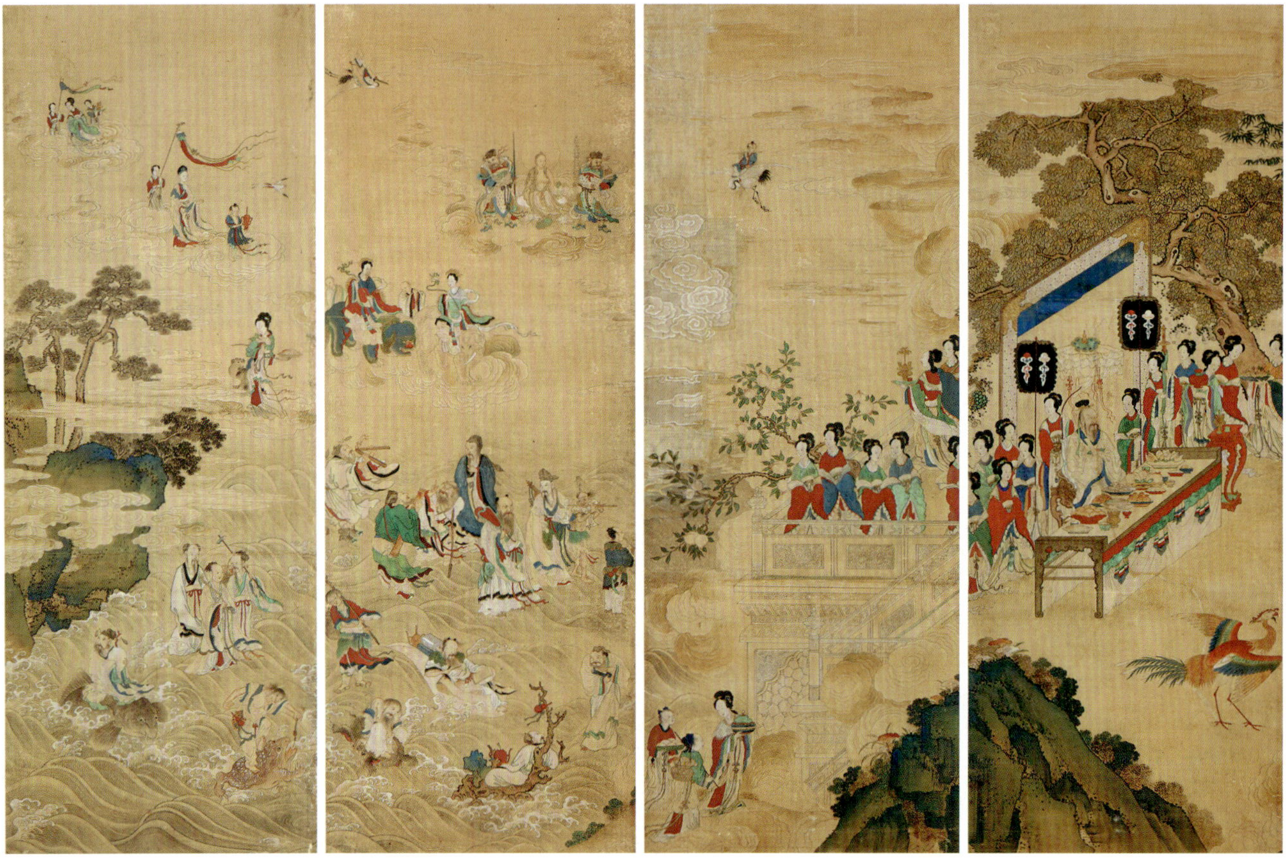

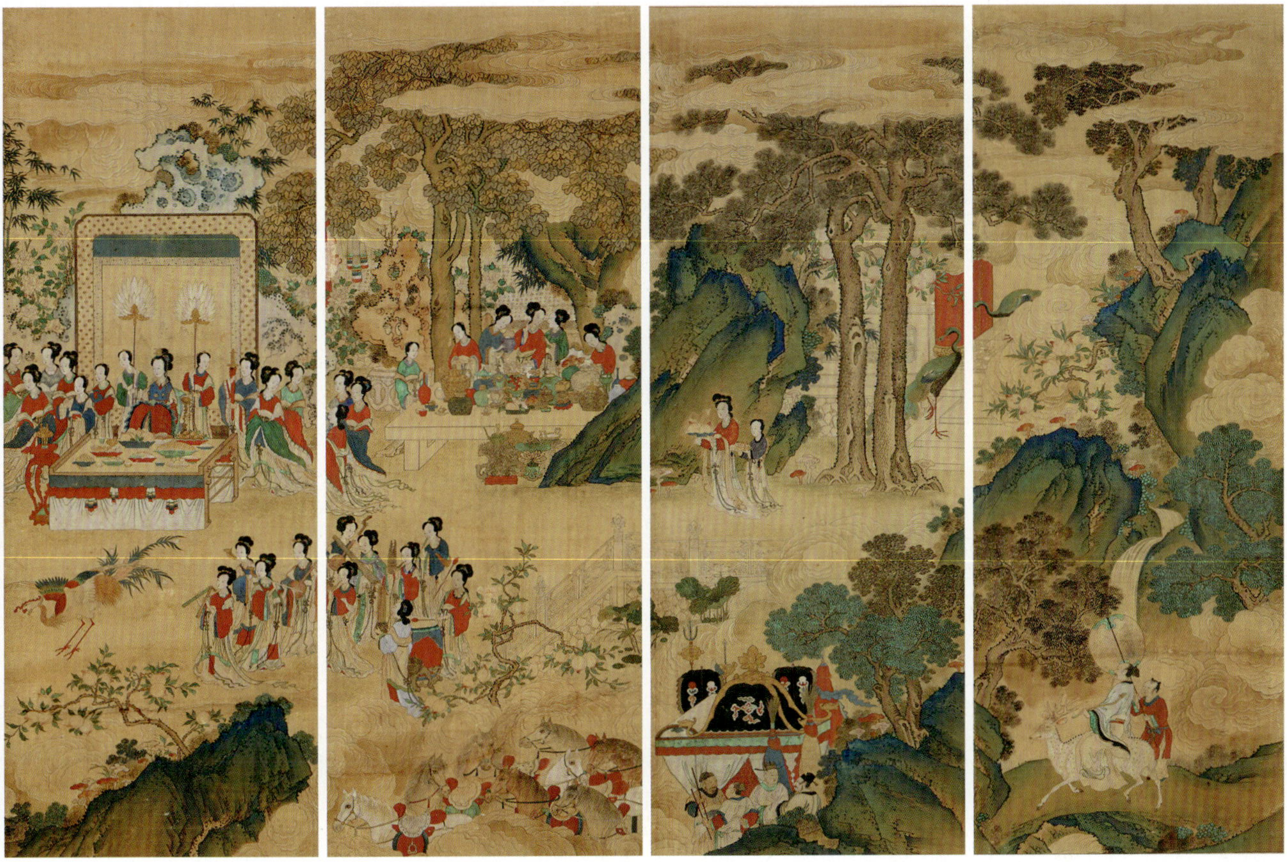

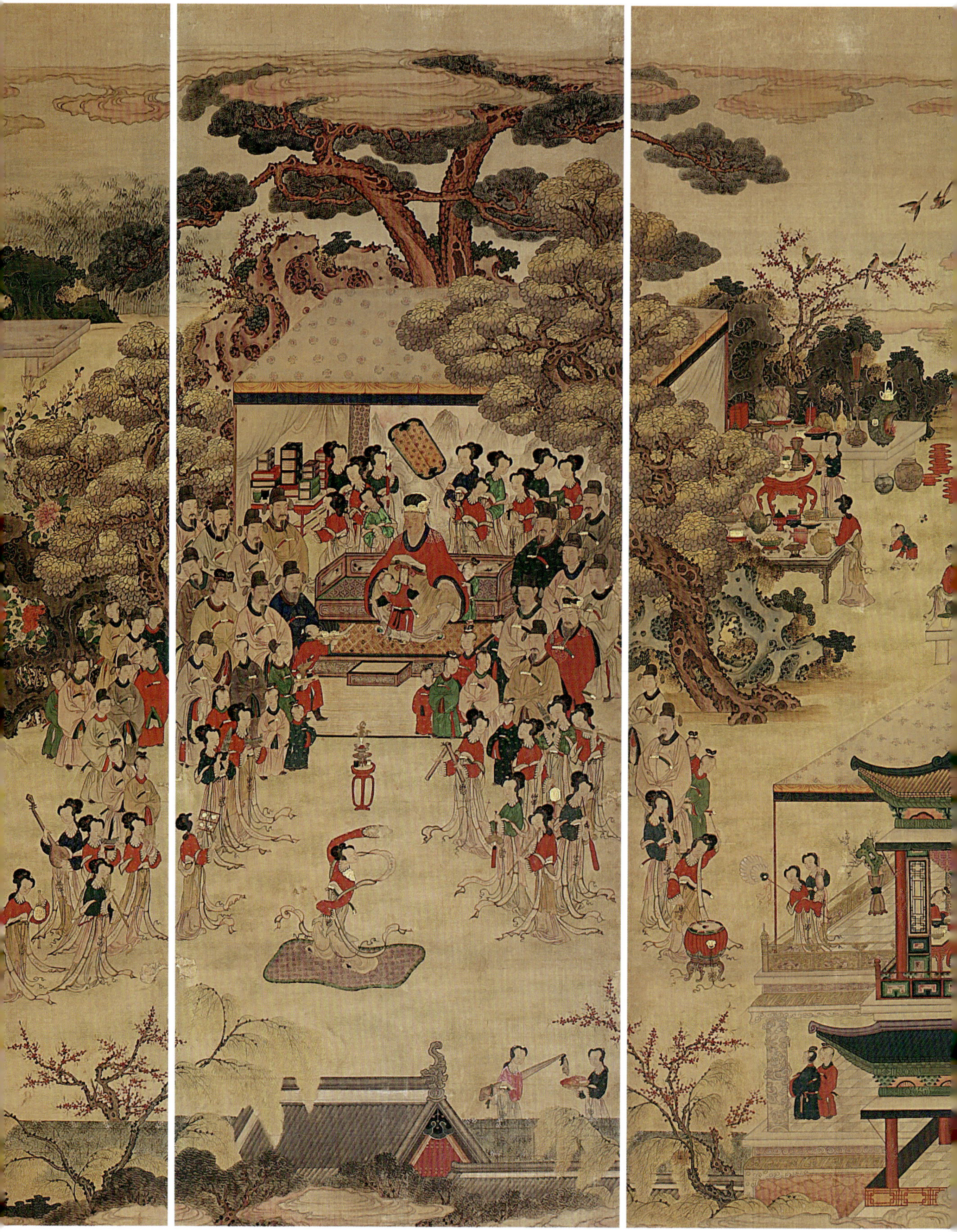

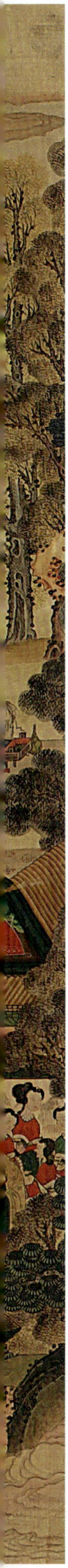

The Happy Life of Guo Ziyi

Gwakbunyang Haengrakdo

19th century / eight-fold screen / ink and color on silk / each panel, 144.5 × 53 cm / National Museum of Korea

The Happy Life of Guo Ziyi depicts a lavish party held in the garden of Guo Ziyi's grand residence. Guo Ziyi (697–781) was a great general known to have achieved all blessings possible throughout his life during the reign of Emperor Xuanzong (r. 712–756) of the Tang Dynasty (618–907). In recognition of his achievement during a national crisis, Guo was honored with being named as prince of the Fenyang region, a position that later brought him the popular nickname "Guo Fenyang."

During the Silla era, Guo was initially known to the Korean people as a military general and a loyal servant; in eighteenth-century Joseon, however, the perception of Guo began to expand. Among the Korean people, he slowly evolved into an icon of good fortune, longevity, wealth, and prosperity. His most admired achievement was to have led a family that included eight sons and seven sons-in-law, all of whom became successful.

Unlike many other Chinese versions, this Joseon-era painting is largely divided into three different parts: The middle part shows Guo surrounded by his successful male descendants as he enjoys a female dancer's performance under the large tent in his garden; on the left, men enjoy checkers in the garden's pavilion over a pond; and on the right, Guo's wife watches the performance from her pavilion. The daily activities of women of nobility—from doing their hair and embroidering to chatting, going on walks, taking care of birds and cats, and nursing children—are illustrated in detail.

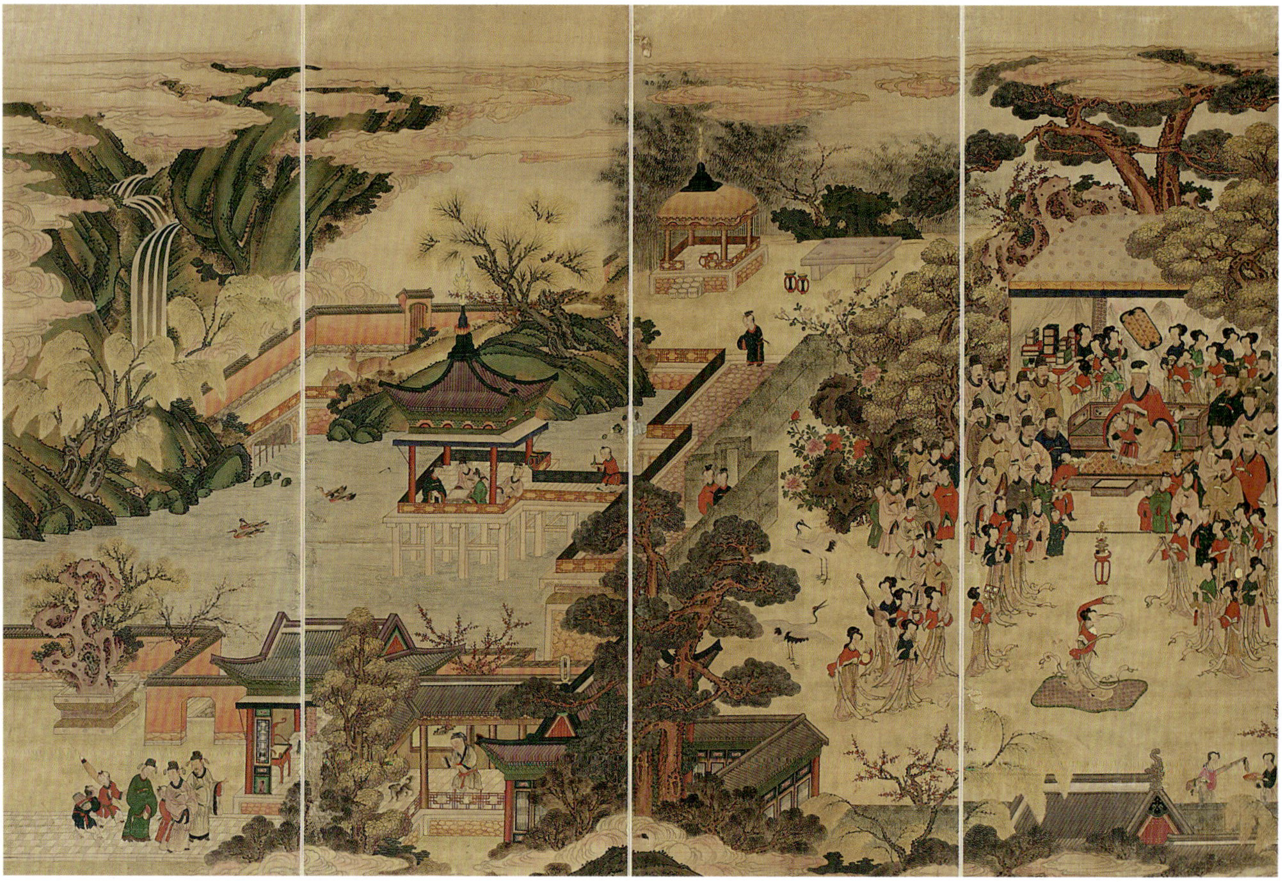

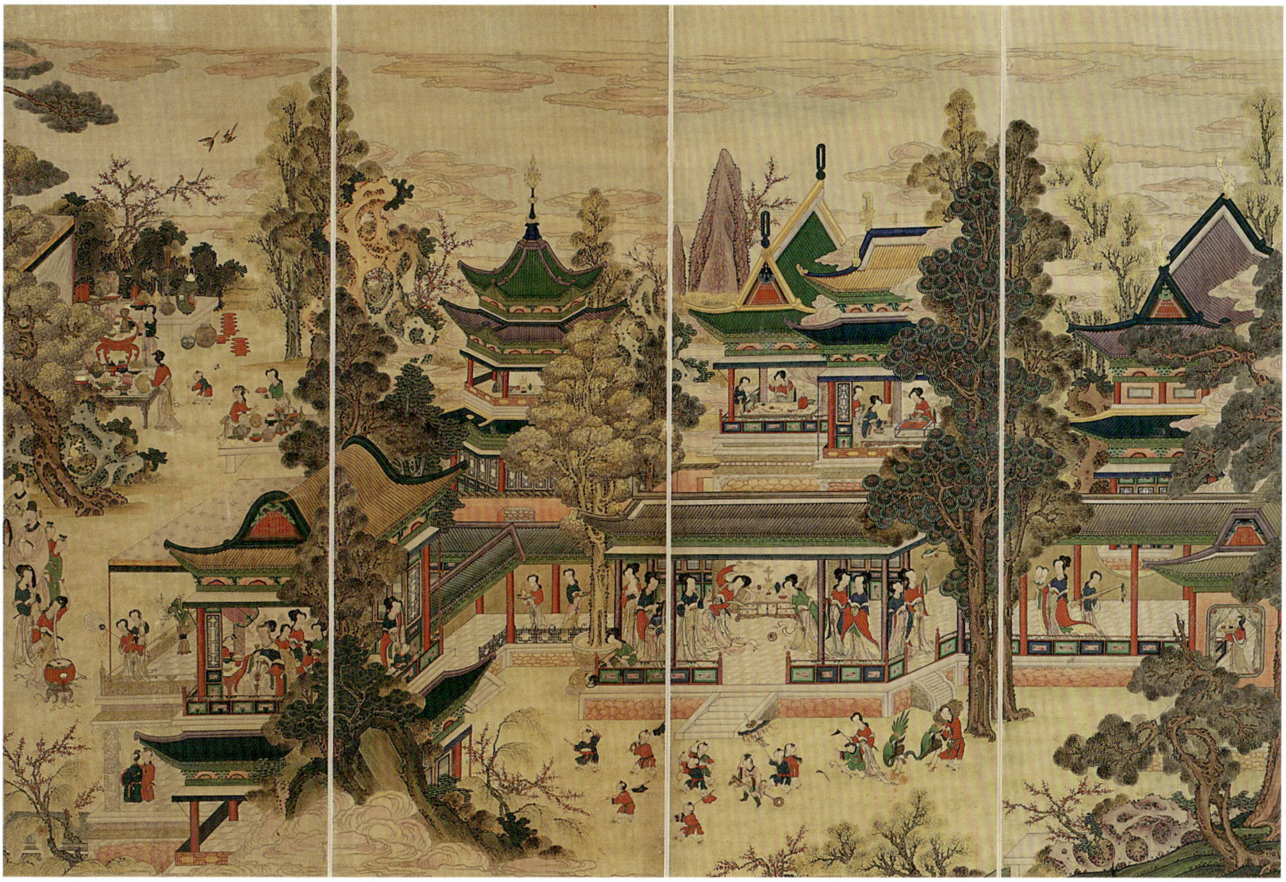

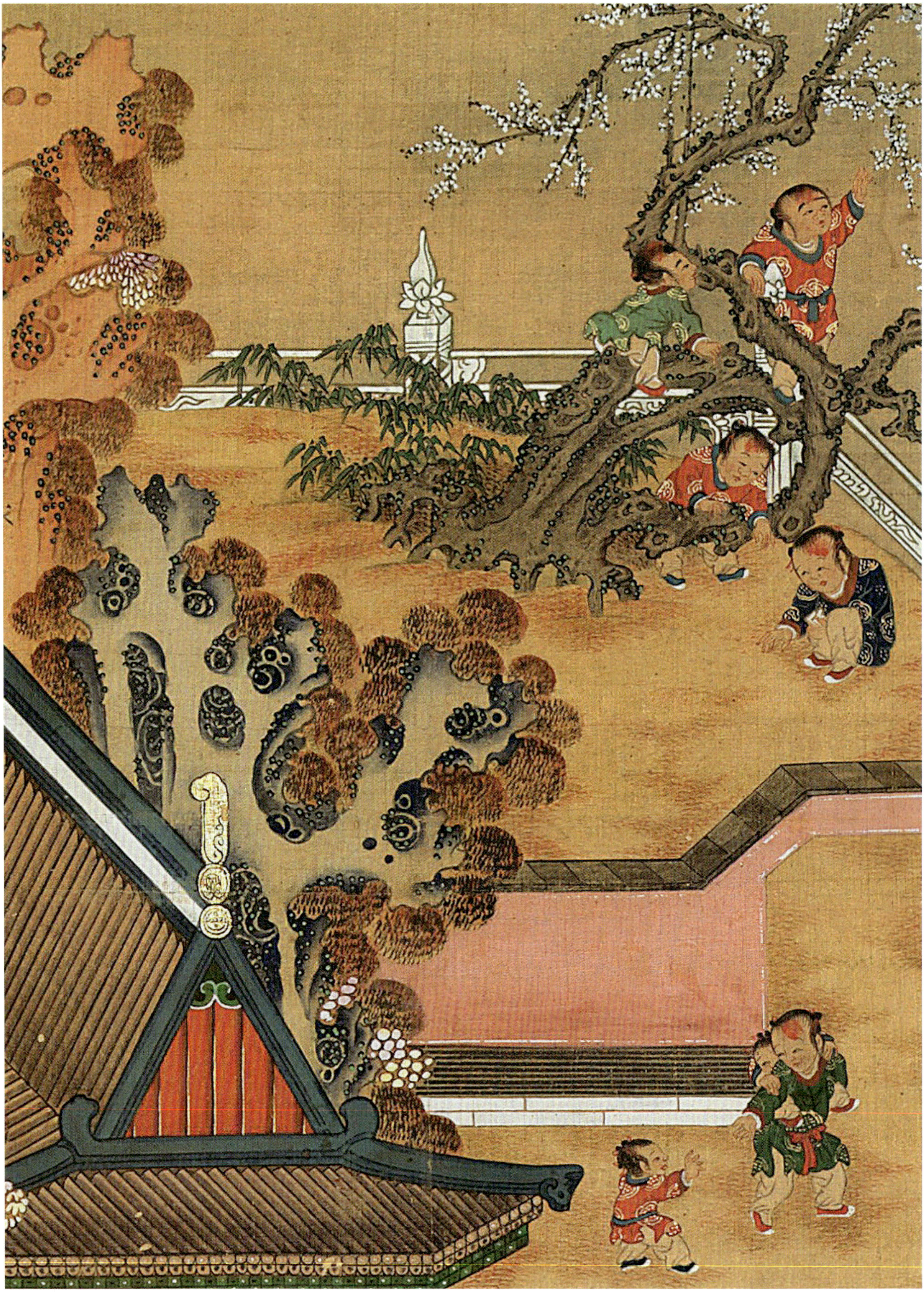

One Hundred Children *Baekjado*

19th century / six-fold screen / ink and color on silk /
each panel, 74.8 cm × 46.3 cm / National Palace Museum of Koera

The term *baekjado* refers to the painting of groups of children at play. The title, *baekja*—in Chinese, *baek* (a hundred, or abundant) and *ja* (children)—refers to the presence of large groups of children, which symbolized good fortune for a family. During the Joseon Dynasty, images of *baekjado* always served a symbolic purpose, promoting the continuous bearing of noble sons. Hence, such images were placed in the temporary residence of a queen-to-be or in the quarters of the crown princess as they learned rules of the palace.

In this screen painting, multiple children play at a palatial garden where a pavilion rests on a pond full of blossoming lotus flowers. This painting represents a rare case of *baekjado* because the picture is painted across the entire screen, without any divisions between the panels. It also boasts splendid imagery of nature, architecture, and individual children in great detail.

Though the theme of the painting was borrowed from China and both the dress style and architecture reflect Chinese design, the games that the children play clearly reflect Korean tastes. On the far right under the willow tree, a group of youths entertain themselves with strips of grass; the child on the far left must have won, for he holds the other's arm and is ready to slap him on the wrist. Below, another group of children is immersed in fishing in the pond. Next to them, a child holds a large lotus flower high in the air while others playfully struggle to take it away from him. In the center of the image, children imitate the procession of a deputy of county, and to their left, another group teases a monkey. Behind them, a pavilion reveals its room filled with books in their cases and an incense burner, a reference to Korean society's hope that the children will be equipped with scholarly virtue.

Meanwhile, the screen also contains references to the four seasons, starting from the far right panel in which a willow stands tall and continuing to the last panel where a plum tree blooms. The panels also include animals that signify bliss and good fortune, such as mandarin ducks and goats.

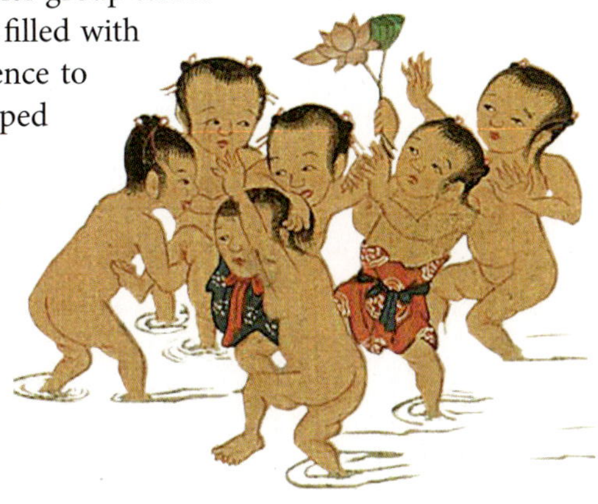

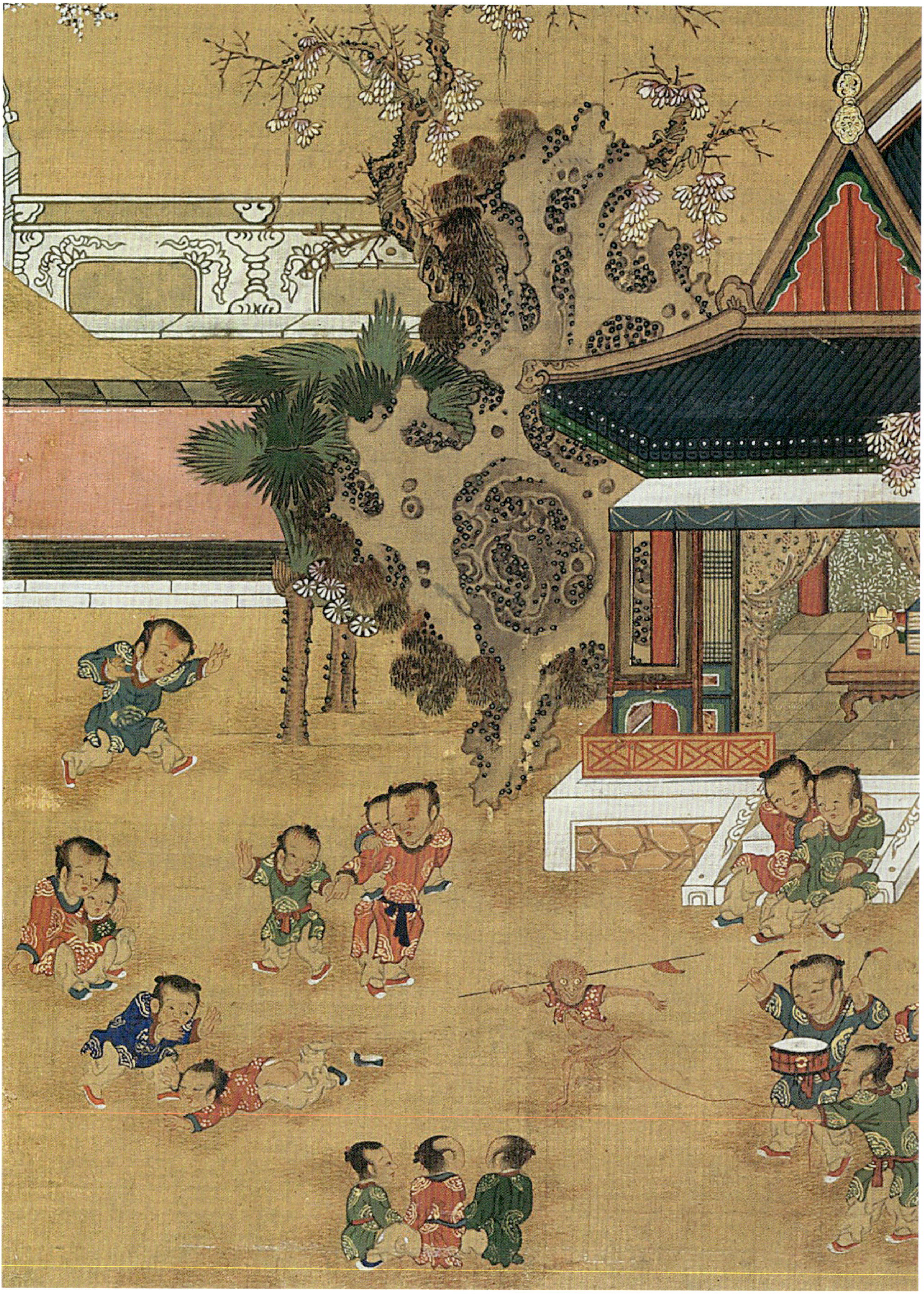

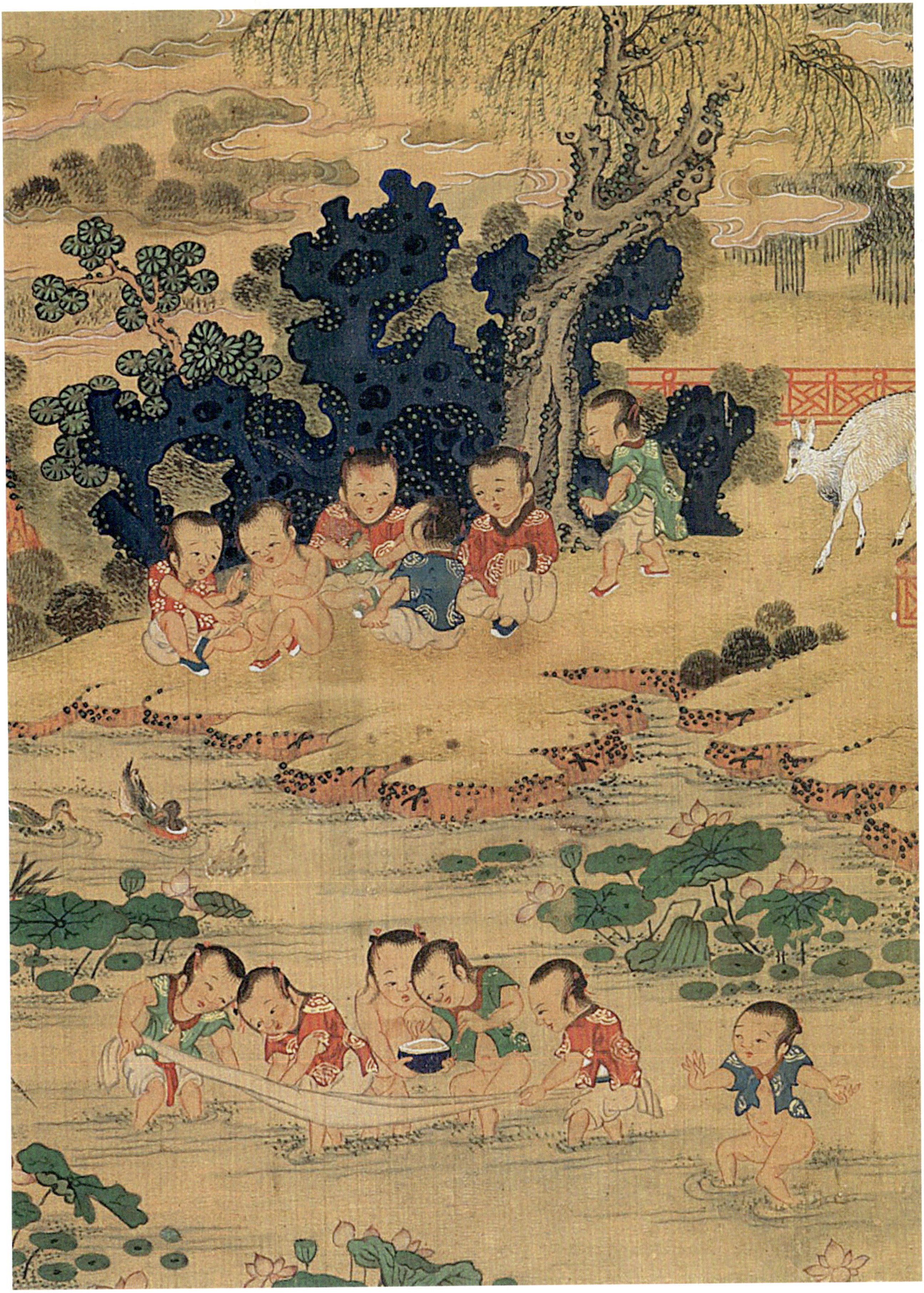

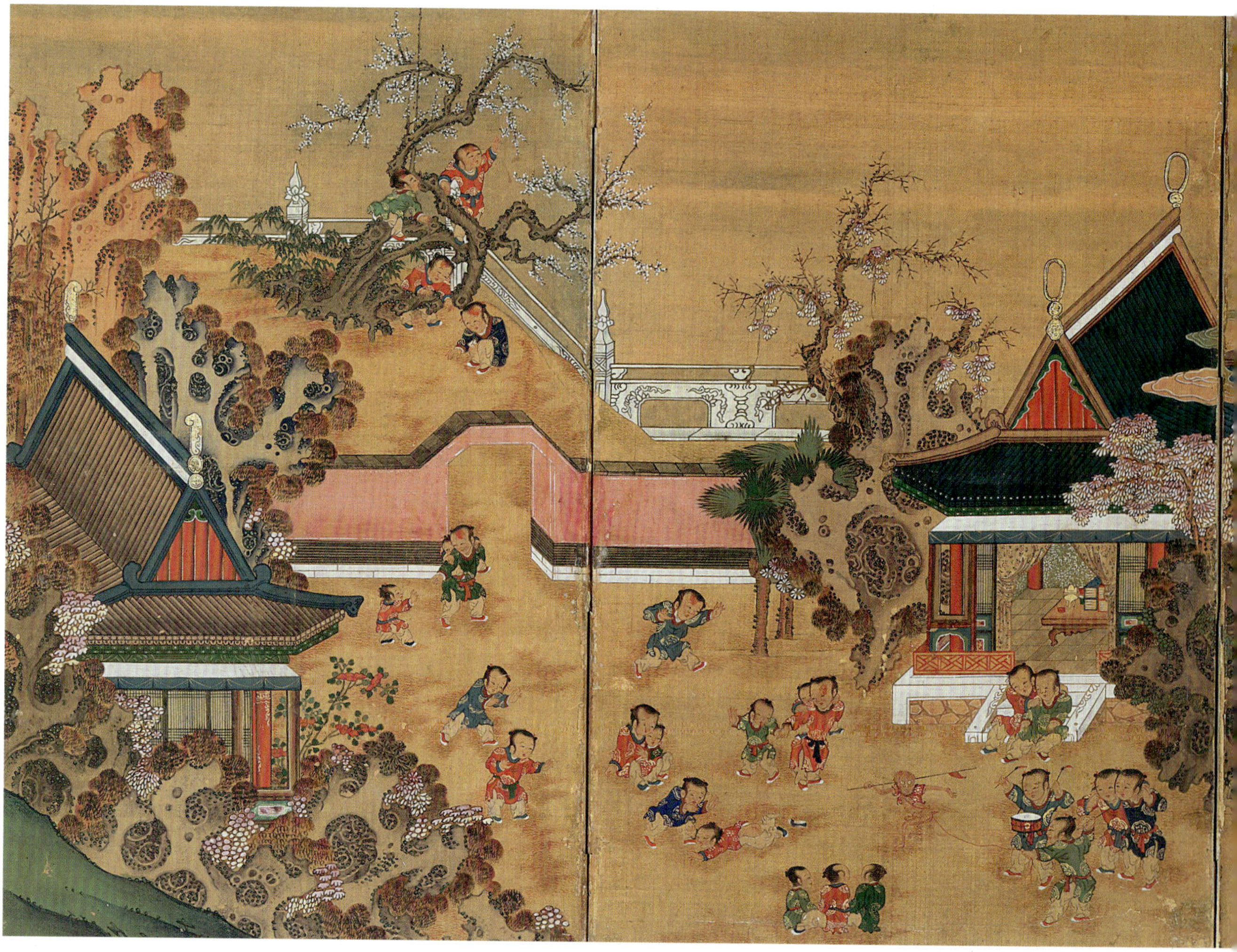

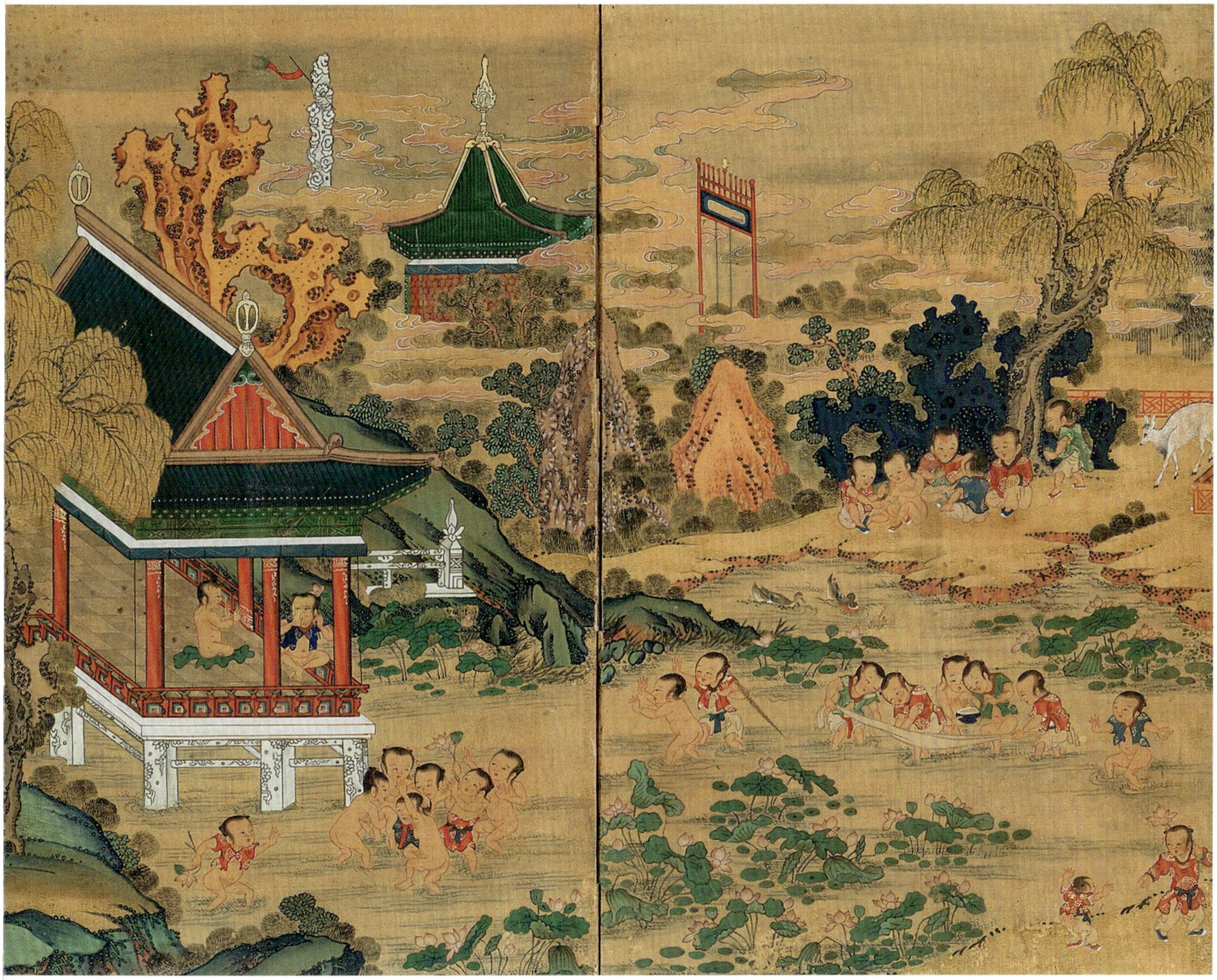

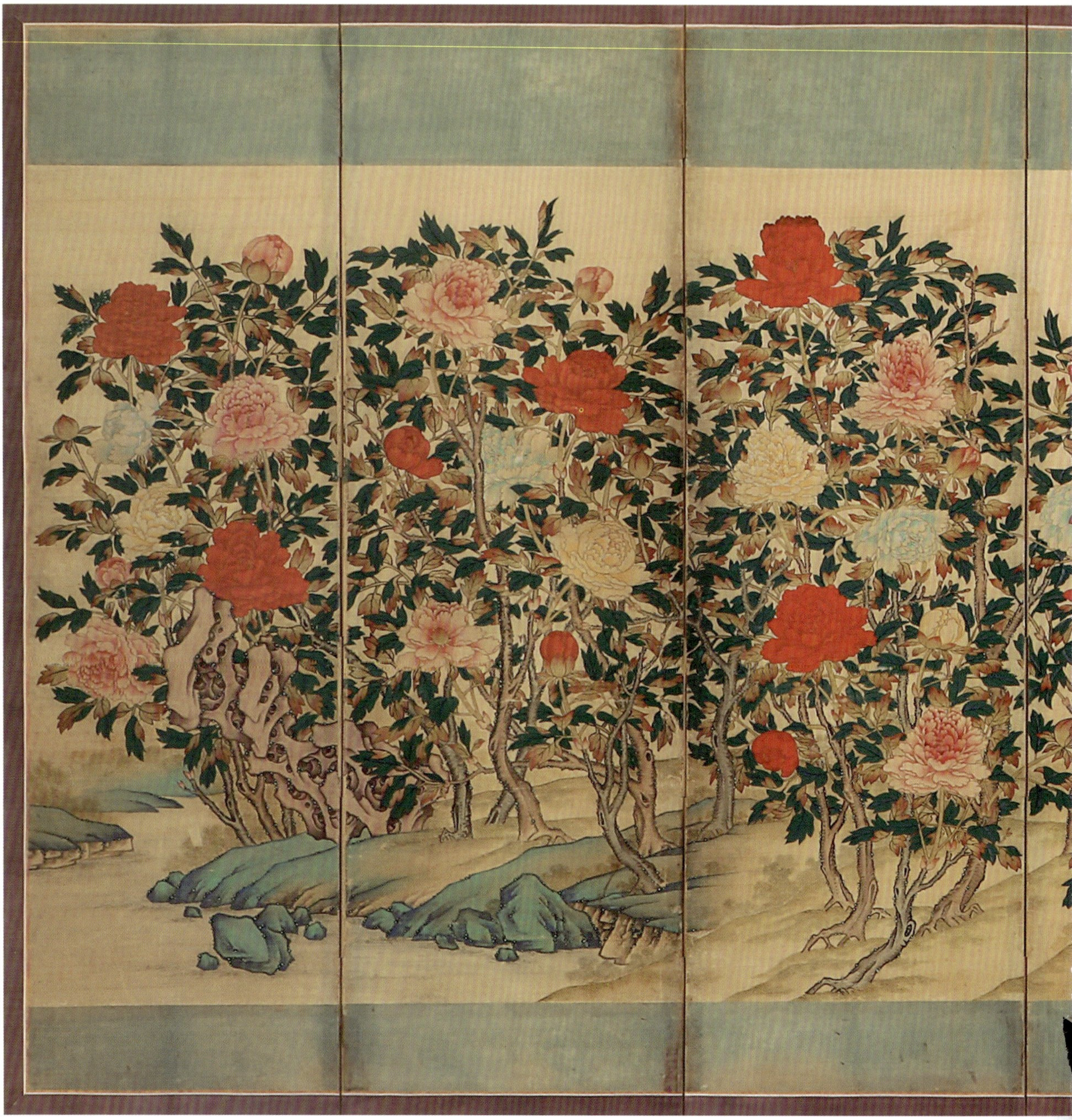

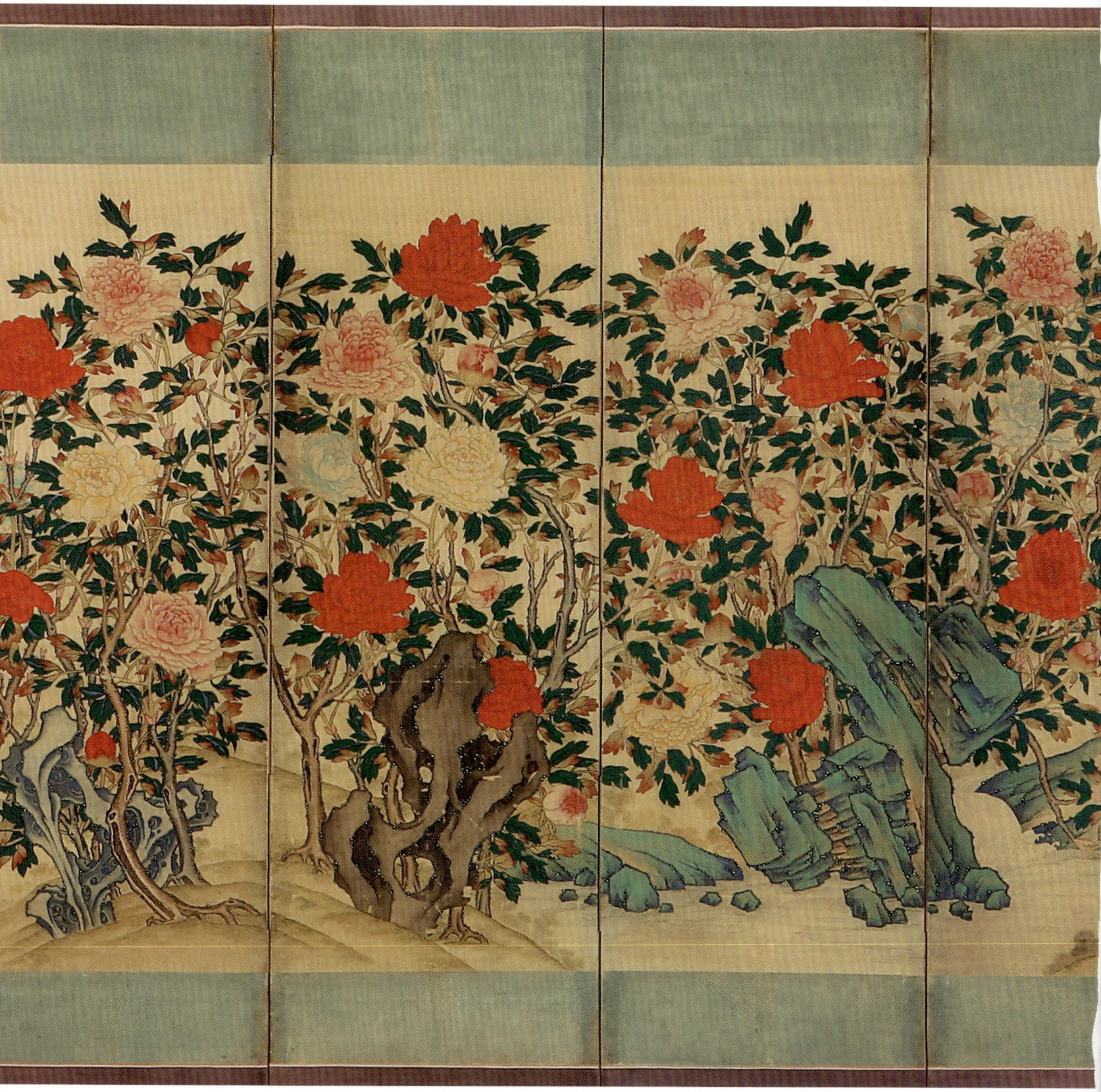

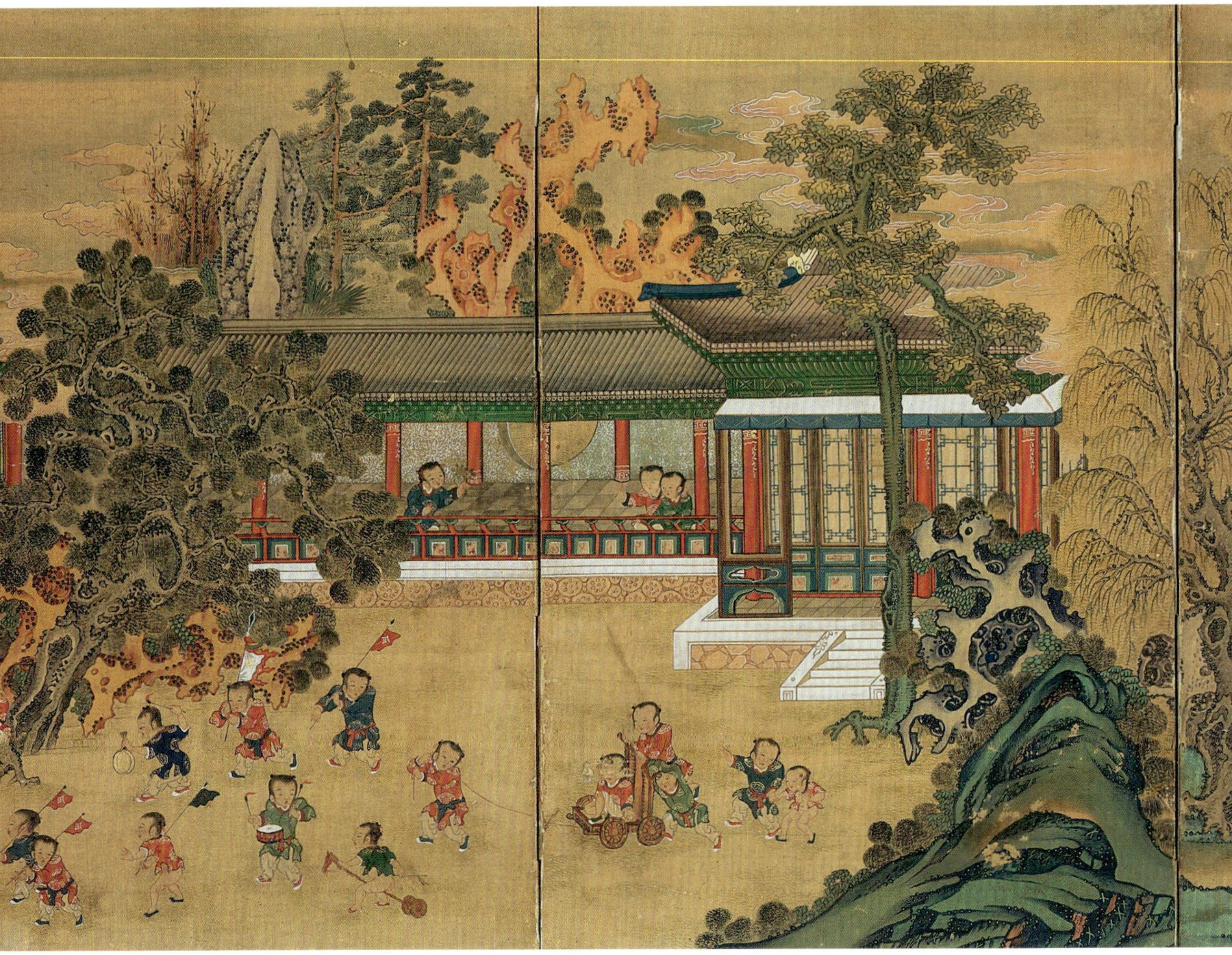

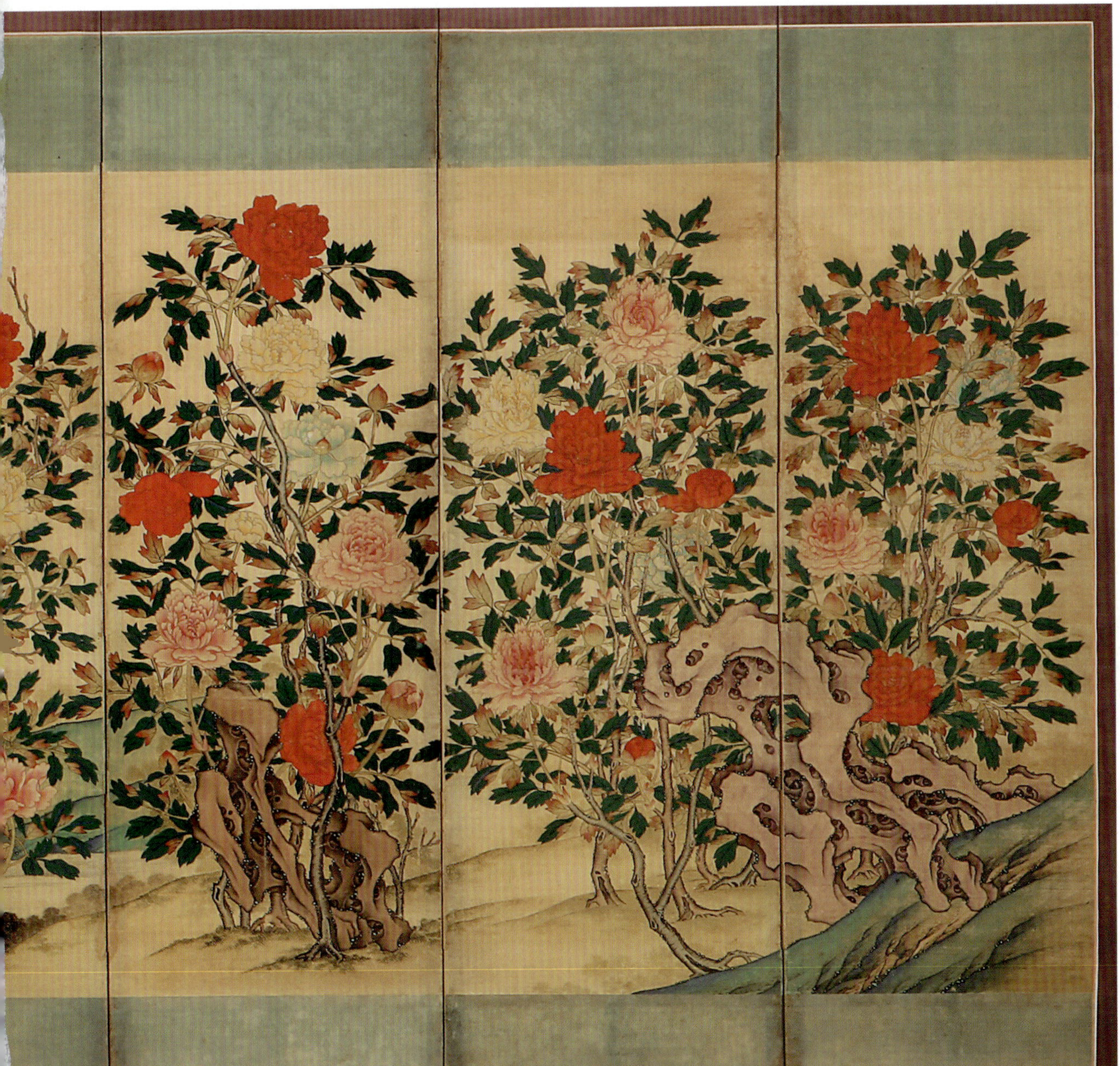

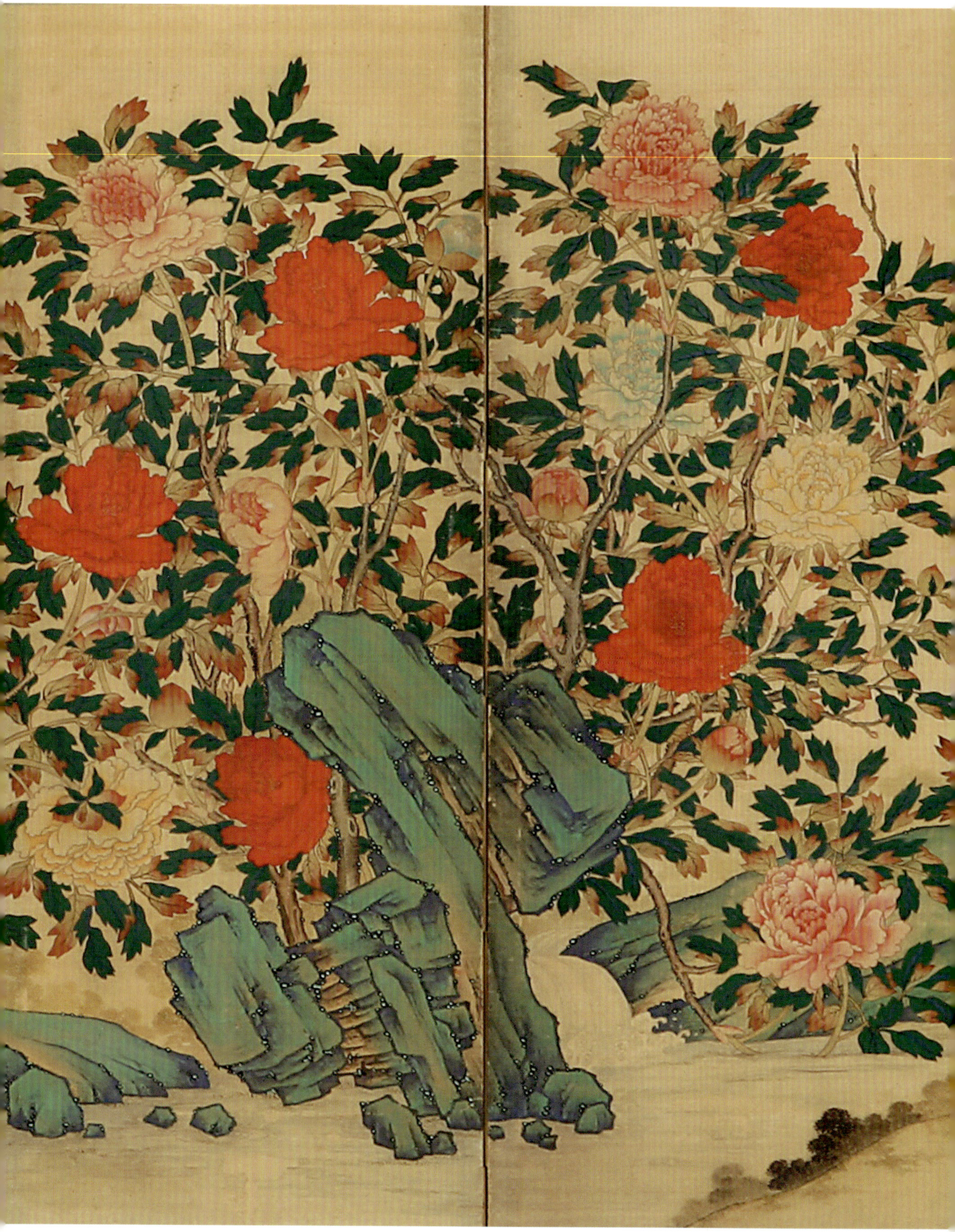

Peonies | *Morando*

Early 19th century / ten-fold screen / ink and color on silk / 194 × 580 cm / National Museum of Korea

Of the folding screens that decorated the rooms and halls of the palaces, those depicting peony blossoms were most commonly used. Often referred to as the king of flowers, peonies were symbols of wealth and prosperity. Consequently, peony screens were used for important state ceremonies as an auspicious sign for the age of peace. While the peonies on albums or hanging scrolls were painted for personal appreciation, those drawn on folding screens were intended to decorate ceremonial spaces.

Due to the ornamental and regal nature of fully unfolded screens, they were widely used for various purposes at palace events. According to the record of Joseon-era court rites, a book known as the *uigwe*, peony folding screens were an essential part of the formal marriage bow during royal weddings. The screens were also used alongside the main screens at royal funerals, coming-of-age ceremonies, reproductions of royal portraiture, palace constructions, and enshrinements of the spirit tablets at the Jongmyo Shrine.

This particular *morando* screen is significant because there are few remaining screens whose entire scene extends uninterrupted across the ten panels. Placed on the low mounds beside the two small streams of water is a peony grove whose naturalistic depiction is unlike any other peony screens produced in the later years. The peonies blossom in all different shapes and directions, while the leaves grow and curve without much stylization. The three-dimensional quality of the foliage is enhanced by the shading used on the flower petals and the odd, curving rocks. Lastly, on the fourth panel from the right, note the flower with the bulging stem that dips under the mini waterfall, an unexpected detail for such a scene.

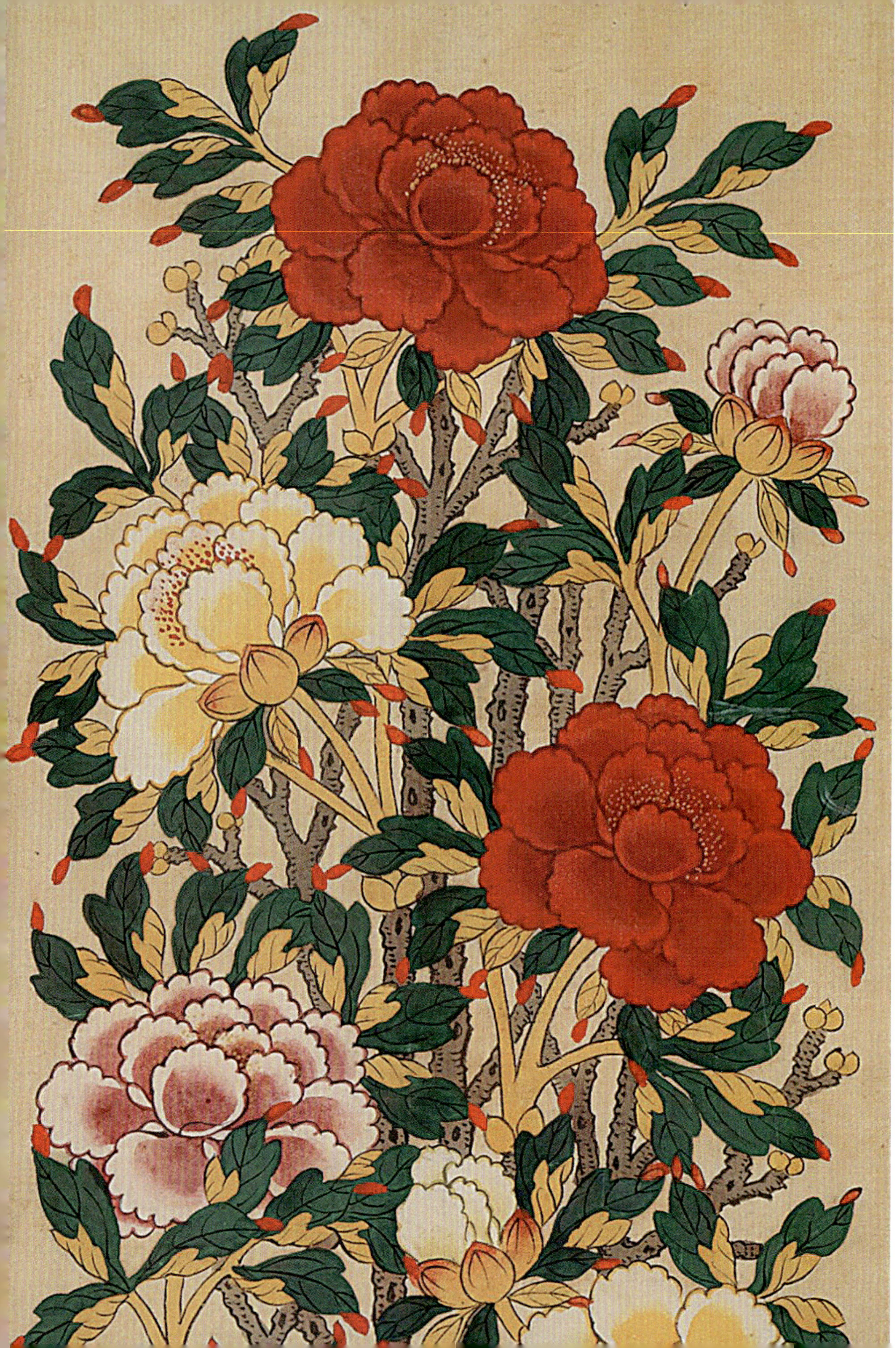

Peonies II *Morando*

19th century / eight-fold screen / ink and color on silk / each panel, 166 × 45.4 cm / National Palace Museum of Korea

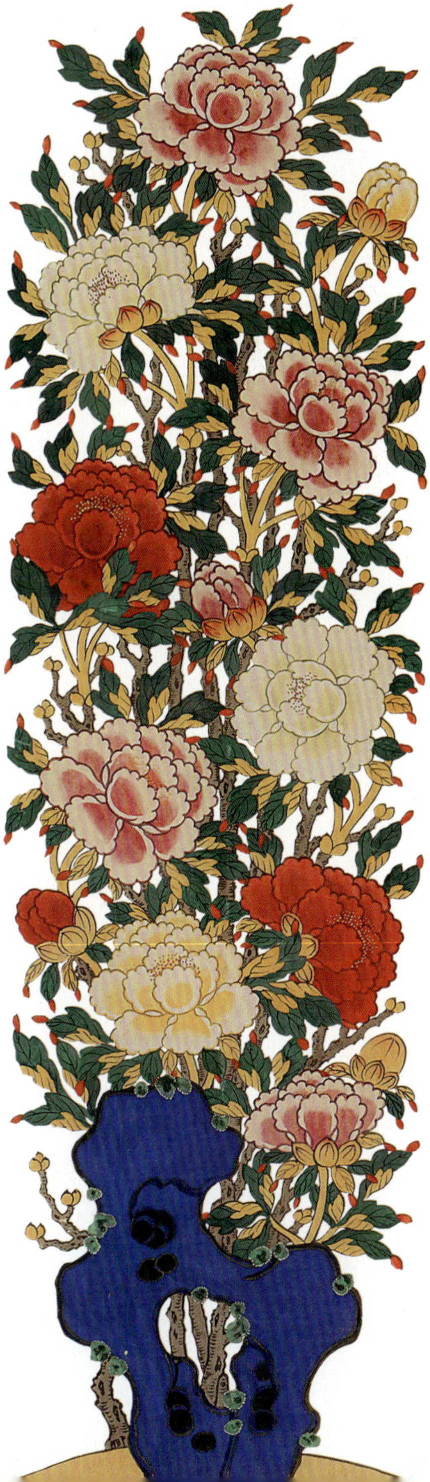

In some *morando*, or peony screens, the composition extends across the panels as a single canvas, while in others, the peony trees are confined to the column of each panel. The latter type, which is more stylized and less naturalistic, became very popular during the late Joseon era and comprises most of the peony screens that remain today.

The folding screens made during this time would occasionally reach over two meters in height, as they were meant to occupy the entire wall of a ceremonial space. The images of peonies repeated over multiple panels with an emphasis on vertical orientation are considered to be a unique motif of Korea.

In this work, the peonies vary both in their color—red, pink, yellow, and white—and in their state of maturity—in full or half blossom or bearing buds. More often, peonies were drawn together with rocks, presenting an ideal synthesis of the most popular blessings of the time: wealth and longevity. The simple peony images repeat over each panel; colored in different pigments, they give the work a formal consistency as well as a dynamic quality.

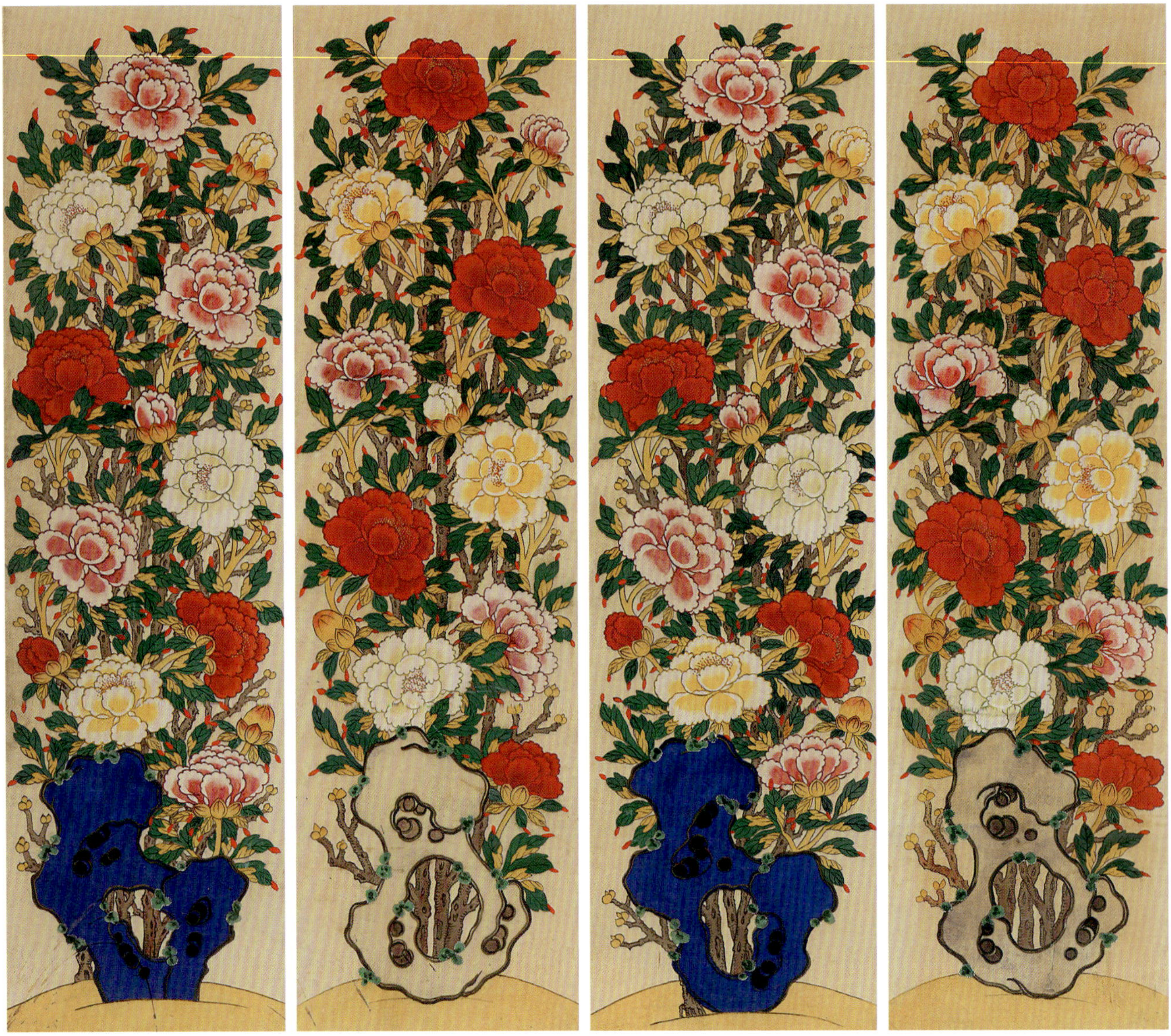

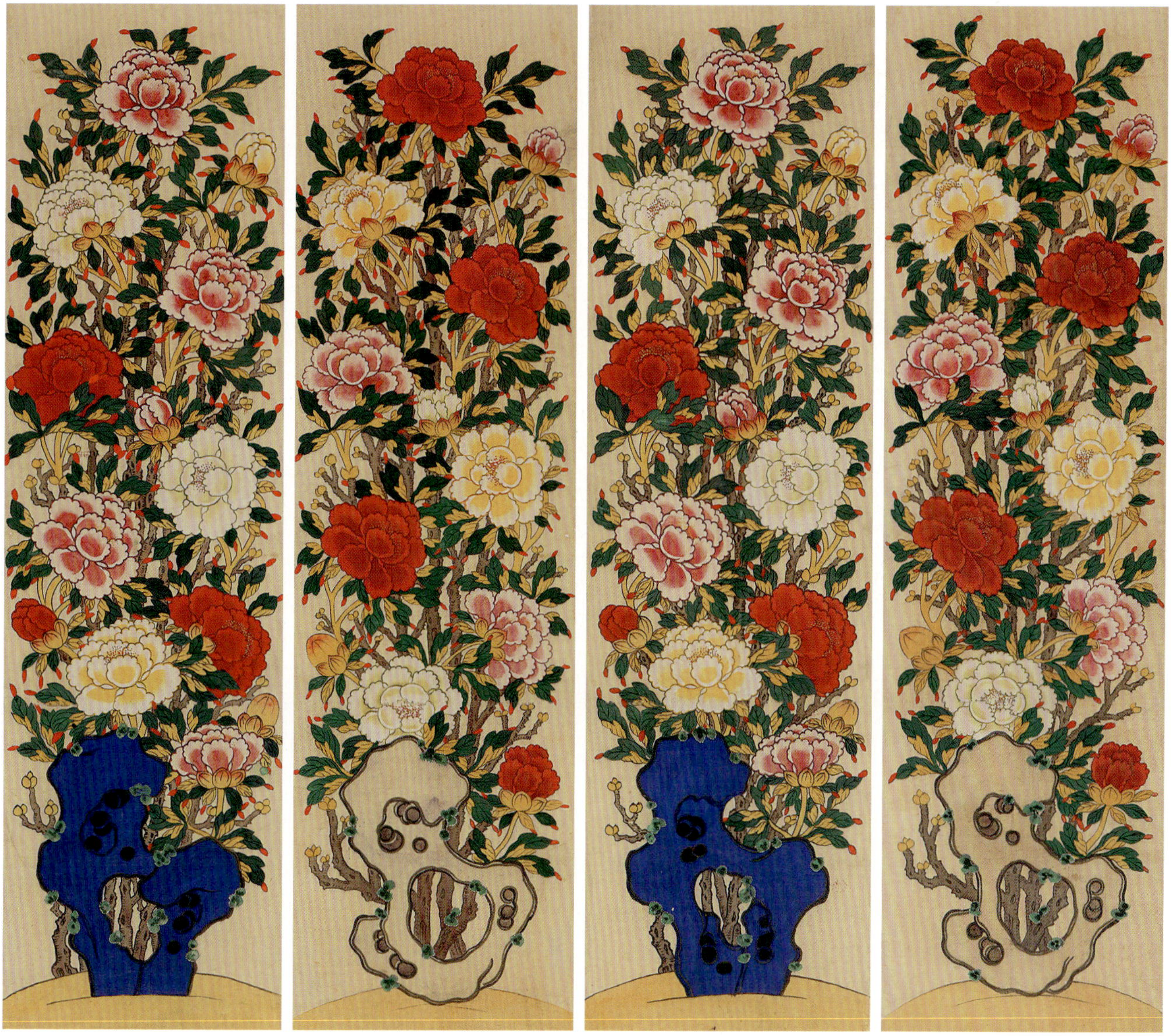

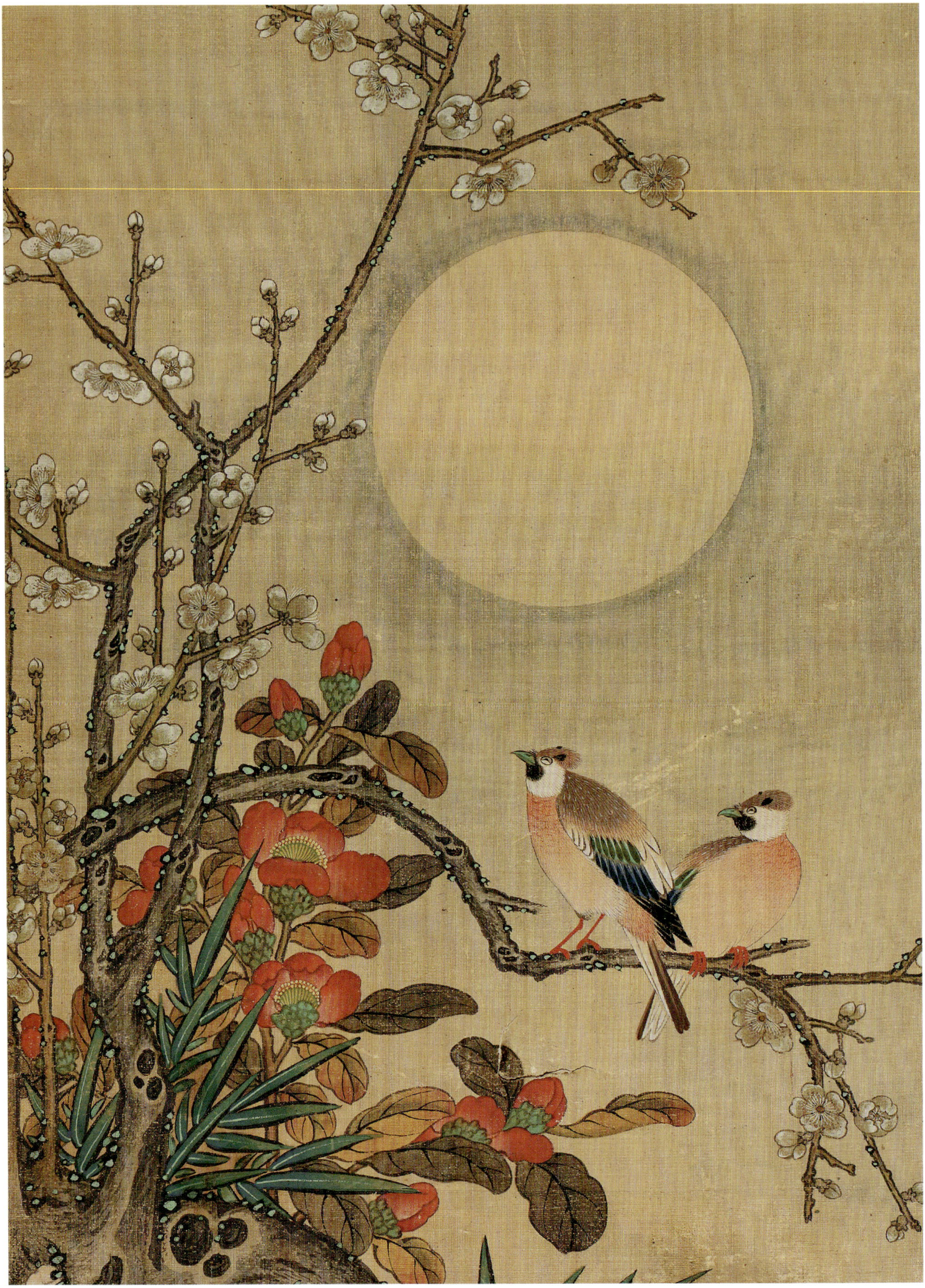

Birds and Flowers *Hwajodo*

19th century / eight-fold screen / ink and color on silk / each panel, 123.9 × 42.4 cm / Tongdosa Museum

Folding screens featuring birds and flowers, which were a common form of furniture in royal palaces, are characterized by the use of fine, rigid lines and rich colors. Colored *hwajodo*, or paintings of birds and flowers, were used as popular gifts to the envoys of China or the Ryukyu Kingdom, in addition to decorating the *byeolgung*, or temporary residence of the bride during royal weddings.

Laden with natural motifs such as tree blossoms, wildflowers, mountain and water birds, butterflies, and bees, *hwajodo* works were considered suitable for women's living spaces. Also *hwajodo* were known to display a wide range of positive symbols, from wealth and prosperity to eternal youth, the bearing of many sons, and social success.

As seen in this version, such paintings were usually themed in accordance with the four seasons. The first panel shows a pair of golden pheasants with their offspring, settled among the rocks from which azaleas and violets have bloomed (p. 79, right). The final panel features some of the most popular motifs to denote winter: plum blossoms, camellias, and pheasants. Moreover, the full moon gently reinforces the crispness of the cold season (p. 80, left).

Overall, the highly refined qualities of this painting correspond to its royal audience; the brushstrokes are neat and smooth while the colors are clear and vivid. The high caliber of technique is also visible in the exquisite details, such as the softness of the bird down, miniscule bumps on claws, intricate flower stamen, delicate leaf veins, rough texture of plant stems, and so on.

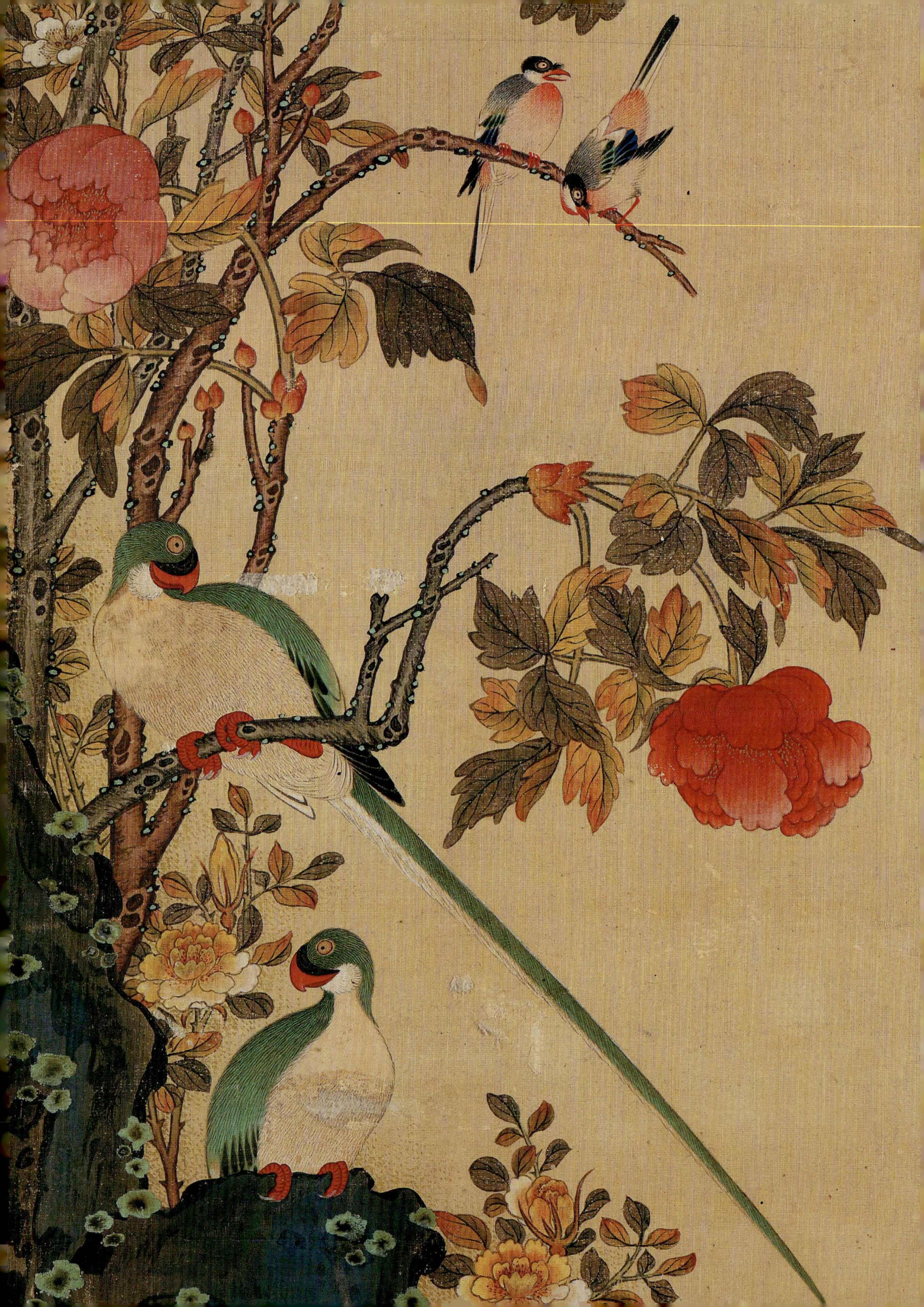

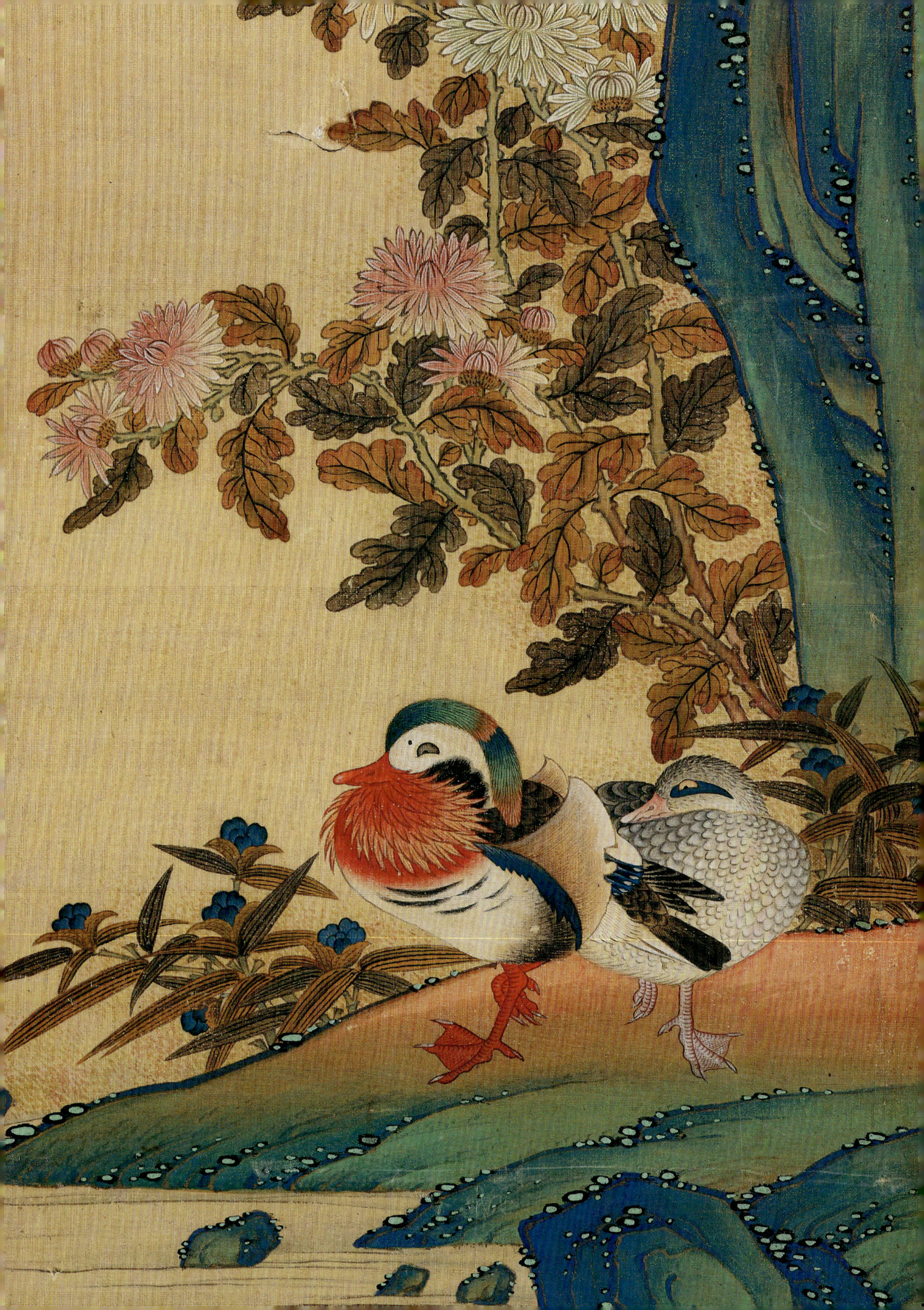

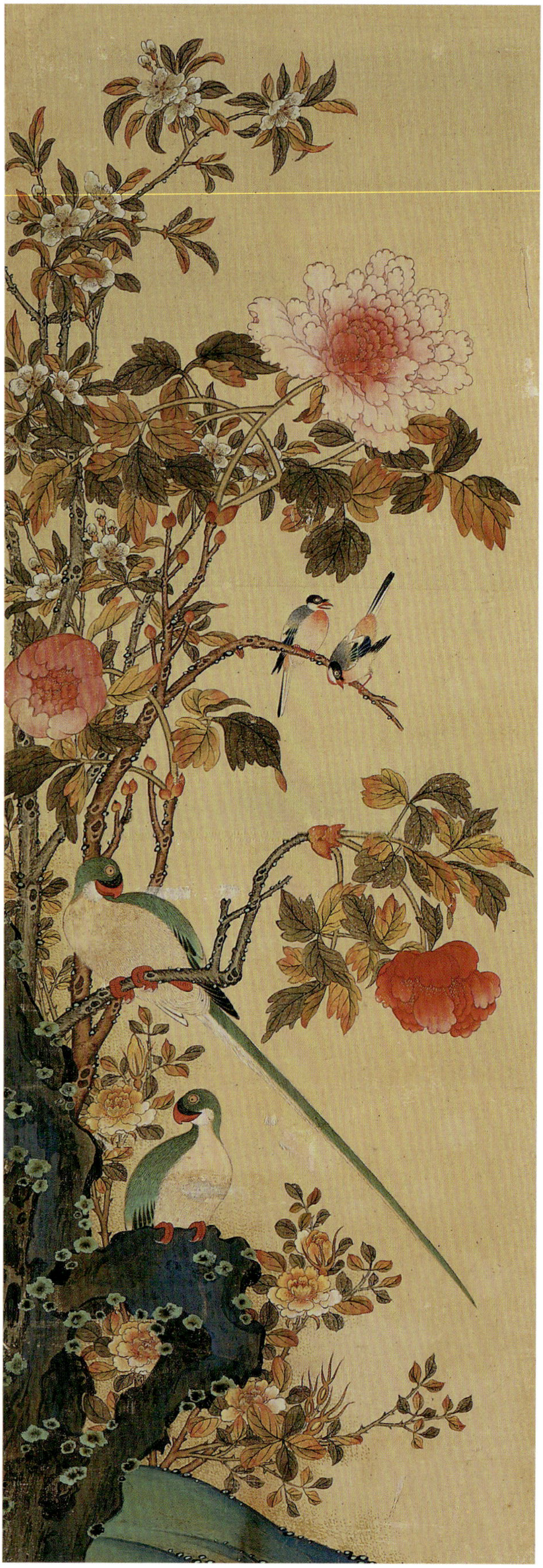

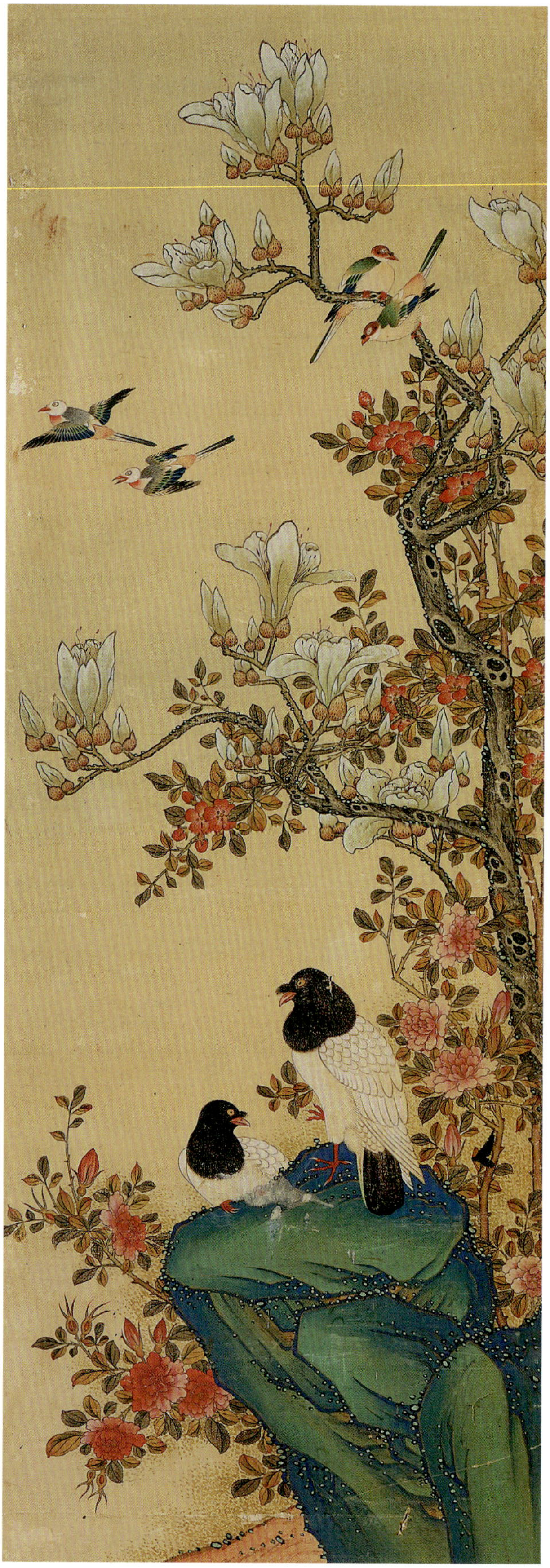

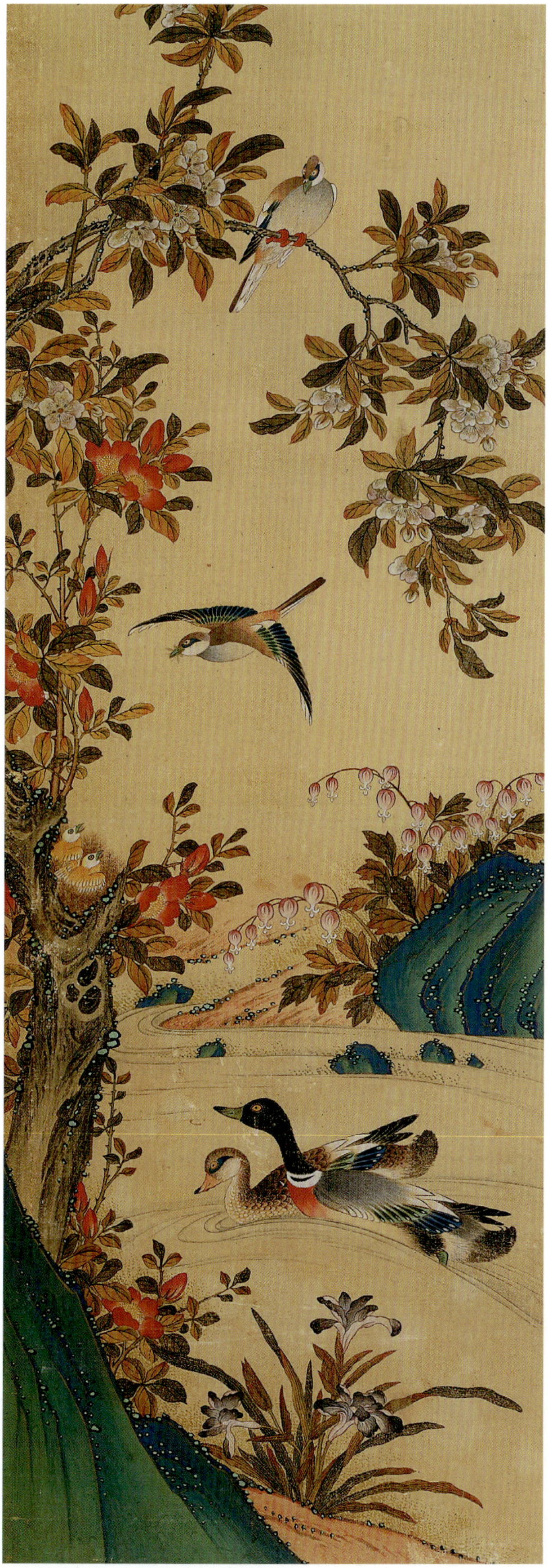
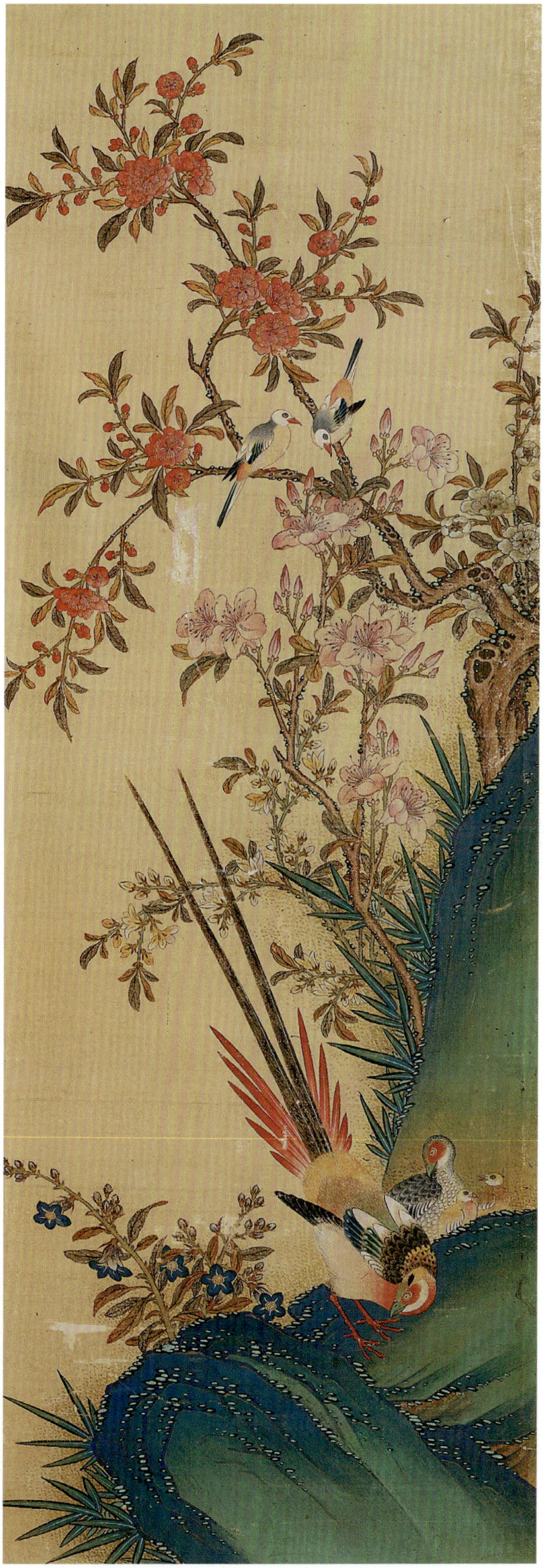

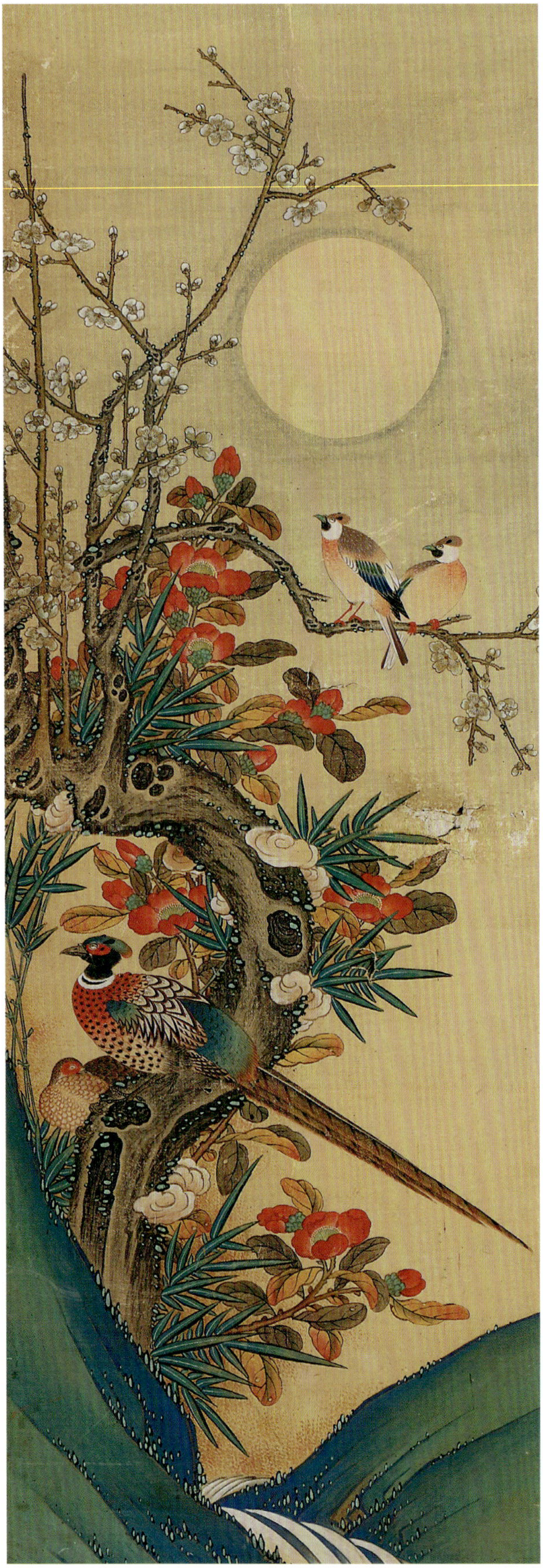

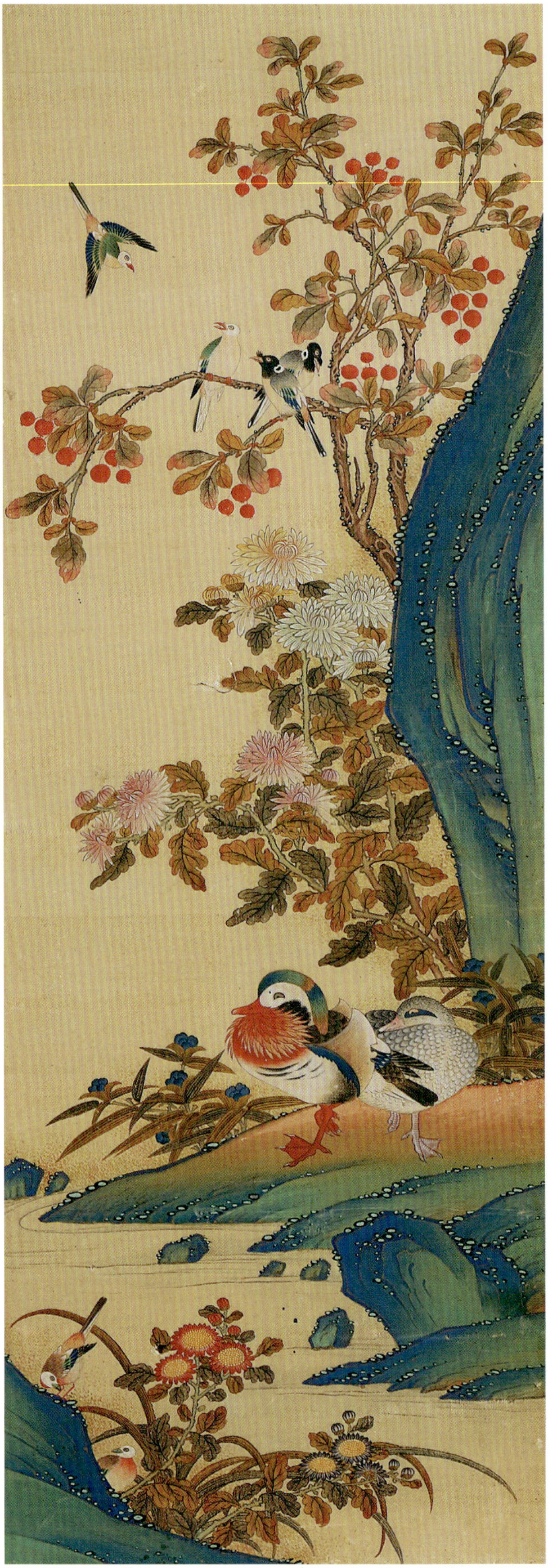

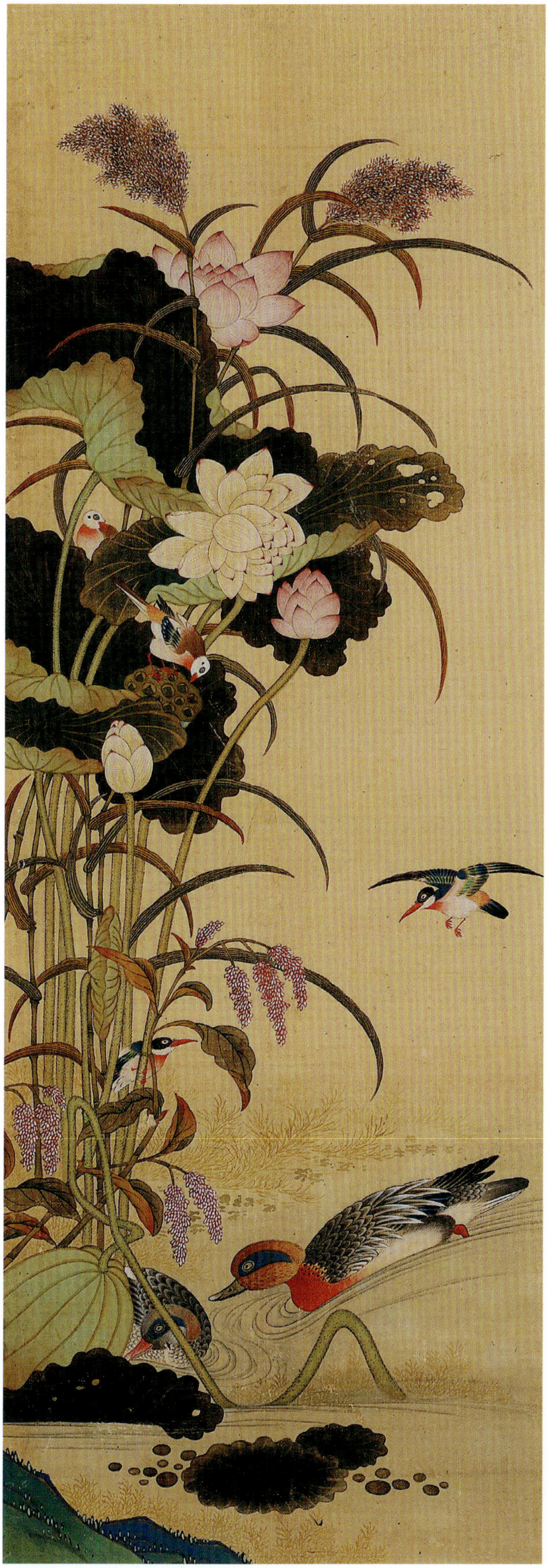
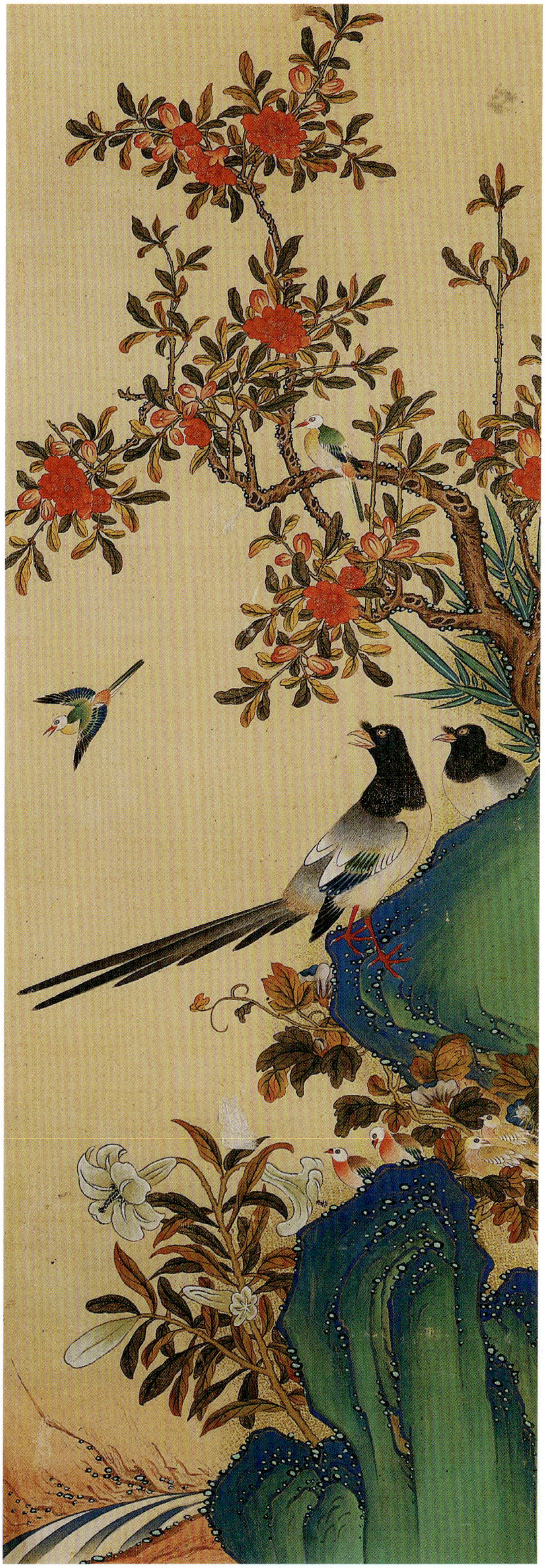

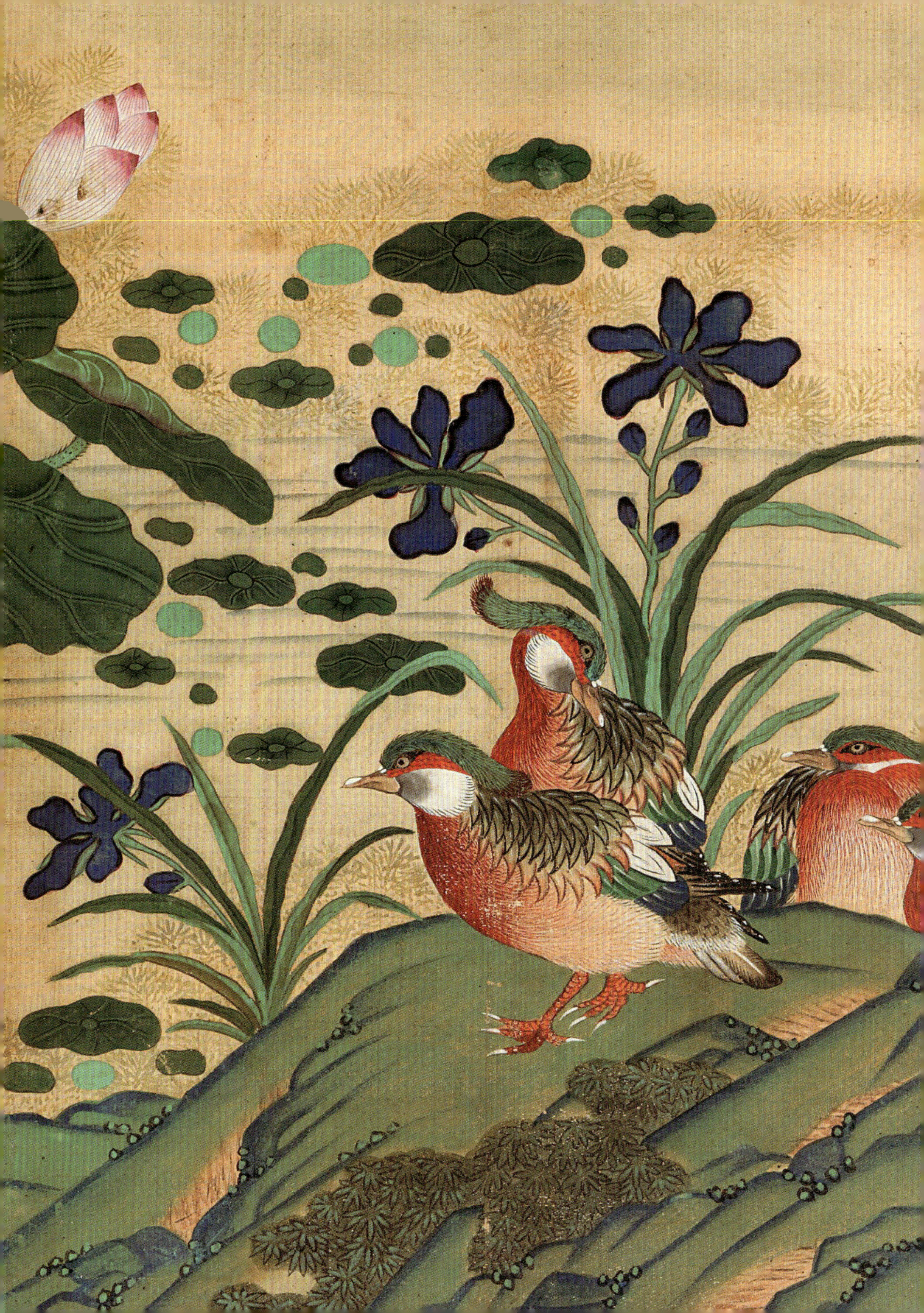

Lotus and Water Birds *Yeonhwa Sugeumdo*

19th century / four-fold screen / ink and color on silk / 75.4 × 177 cm / National Palace Museum of Korea

Lotus and Water Birds (*Yeonhwa Sugeumdo*), a short screen whose height only reaches approximately seventy centimeters, depicts a family of mandarin ducks, mallards, and other unnamed birds as they glide over an idyllic pond while lotus flowers splendidly bloom in the background. More than simply a riverside scene on a summer day, the combination of these three elements—lotus flowers, mandarin ducks, and mallards—undoubtedly shows the meaning of the painting: conjugal happiness and the bearing of many sons. Since its flowers and fruits mature at the same time, lotus was always related to the vitality of life in Joseon.

Given that the Chinese word for lotus, *héhuā* (荷花), sounds similar to another Chinese word for harmony and unity, *héhé* (和合), the flower also became a symbol of connubial bliss and the bearing of many offspring. The images of mandarin and mallard ducks carried similar meanings, for both breeds are known to socialize in pairs; some mandarin ducks have been known to remain loyal to partners that have died, sometimes even dying themselves.

For this reason, it was increasingly popular for Joseon-era painters to present an image of a lotus alongside a pair of mandarin ducks, as the two symbols of conjugal harmony and prosperity were thought to complement one another perfectly. In light of such iconography, this screen would have been used to decorate the temporary residence of a bride-to-be or the room of a newly wedded couple.

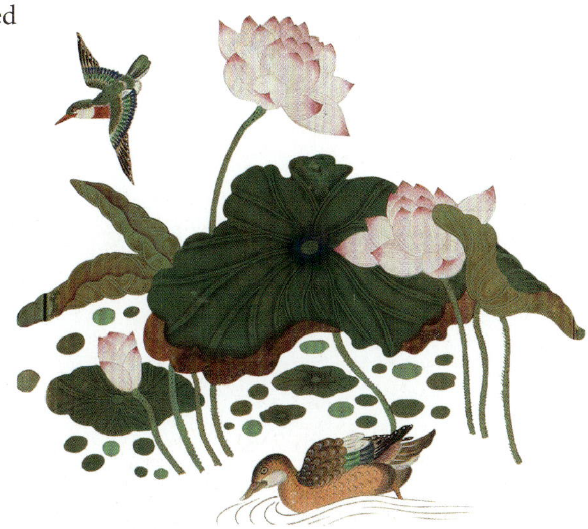

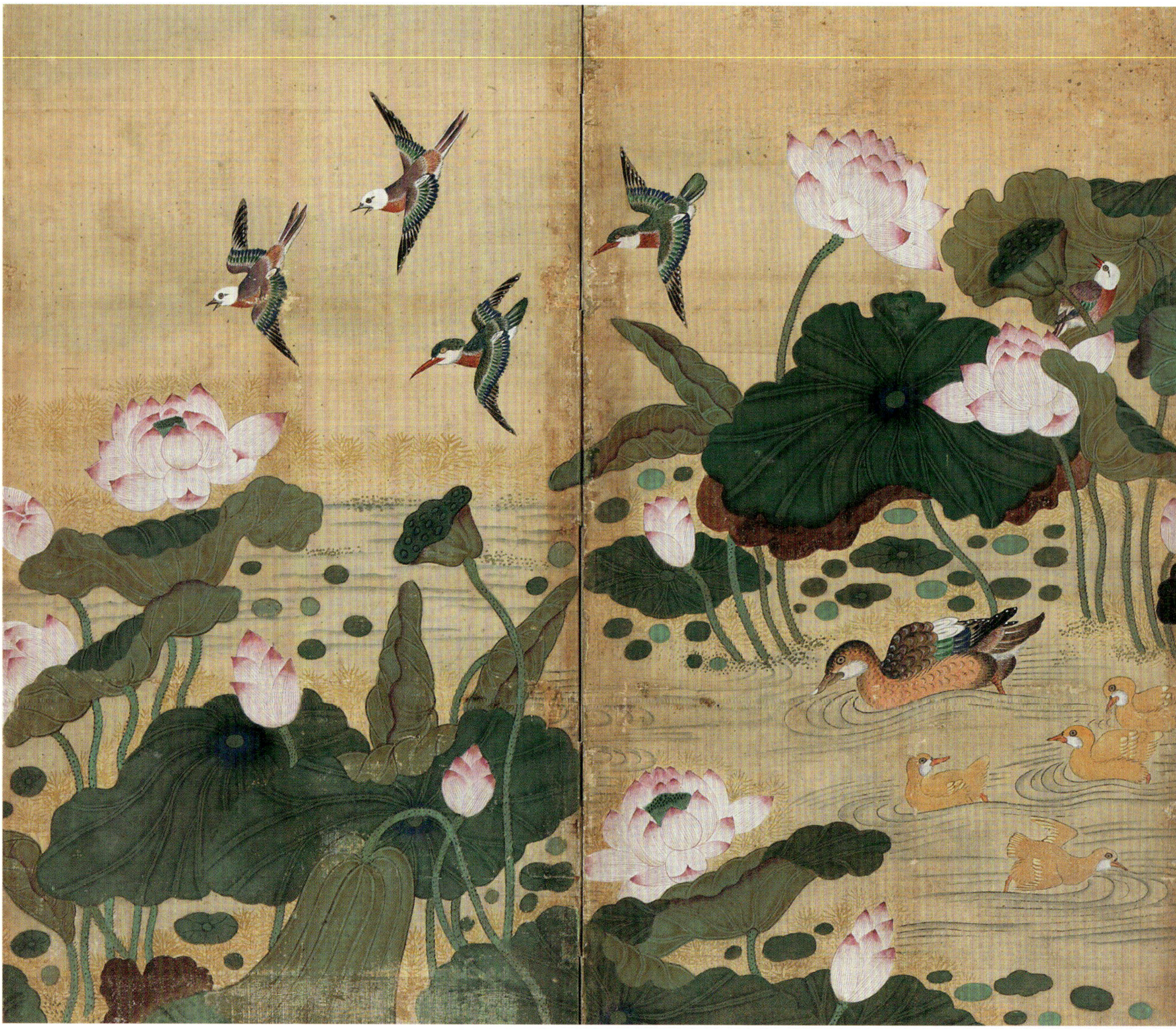

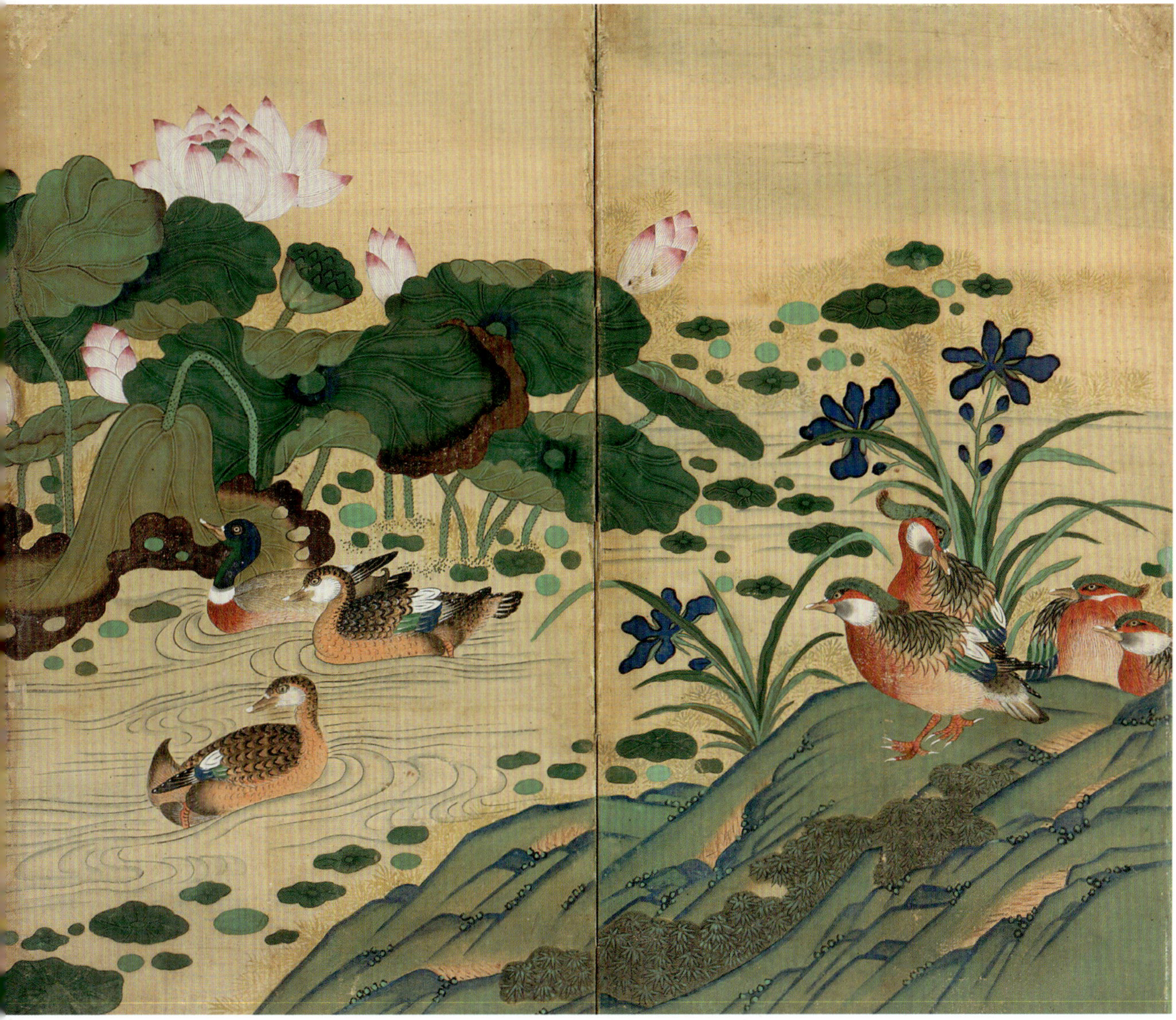

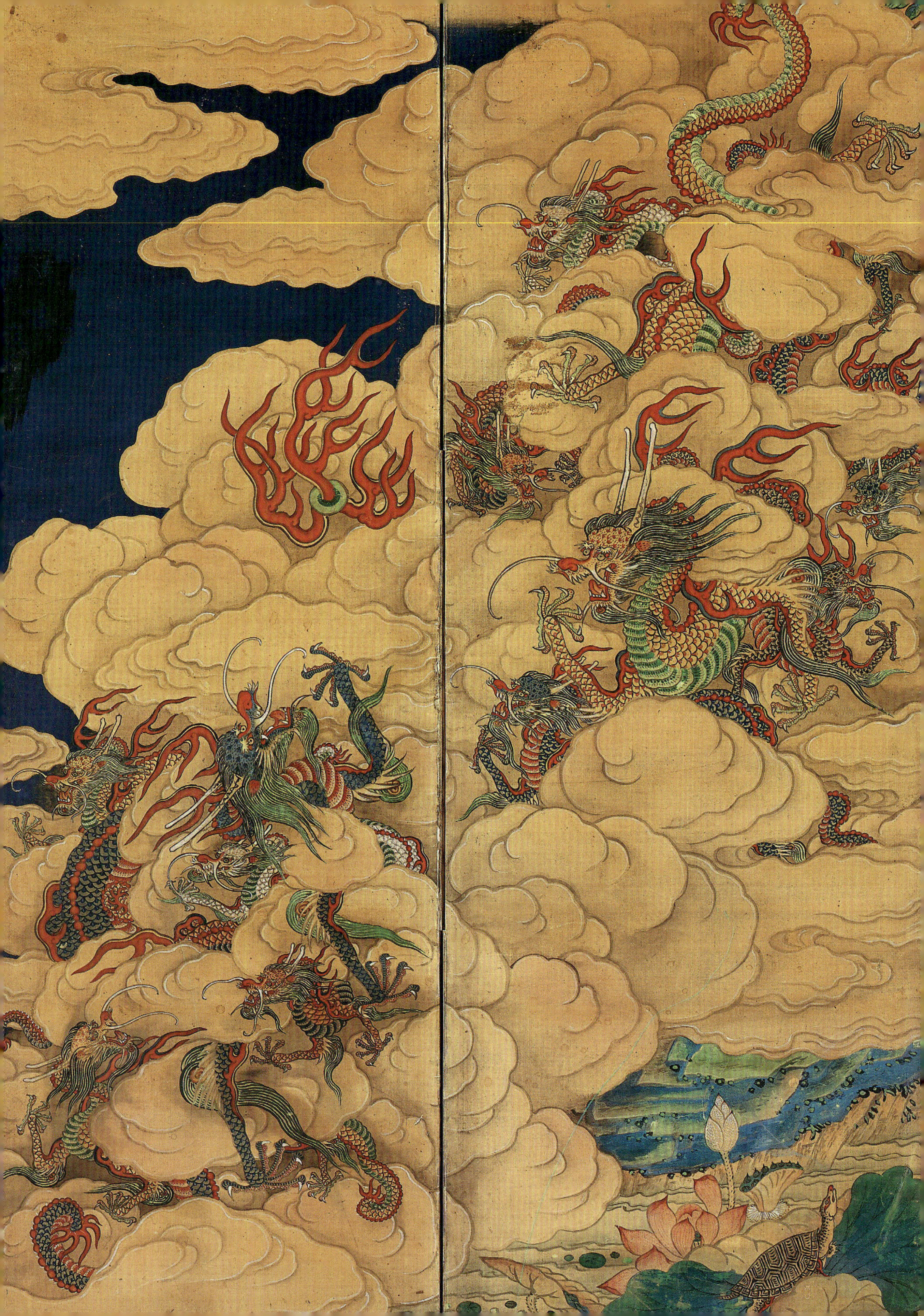

Harmony of Auspicious Animals

Seosu Jangsaengdo

Late 19th century / ten-fold screen / ink and color on silk / 113 × 320.3 cm / Leeum, Samsung Museum of Art

This ten-panel screen depicts a collection of animals that were considered highly auspicious in old Korea. Each species, including dragons, phoenixes, luan (鸞, mythical Chinese bird), qilin (麒麟, mythical Chinese creature), deer, tortoises, cranes, peacocks, and ducks, is drawn in a family group of two adults and nine offspring. Some of the pictorial elements, such as deer, crane, tortoises, fungus of immortality, and bamboo, show a close relationship to the paintings of ten symbols of longevity.

The composition of the screen, which is diagonally divided between the foreground on the right and the sky on the upper left, with the river in the middle, is also reminiscent of the ten symbols paintings. The screen also presents elements of conjugal harmony and the bearing of numerous sons, as seen in the depiction of the family of peacocks and ducks. Overall, this painting exemplifies the pictorial trends of the nineteenth-century Joseon court, where the portrayal of such auspicious animals allowed the artwork to serve as a symbol of good fortune to its viewers.

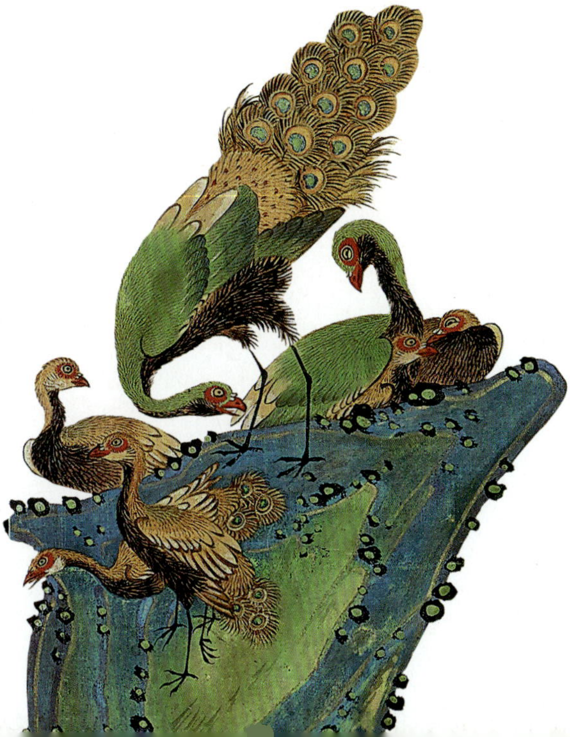

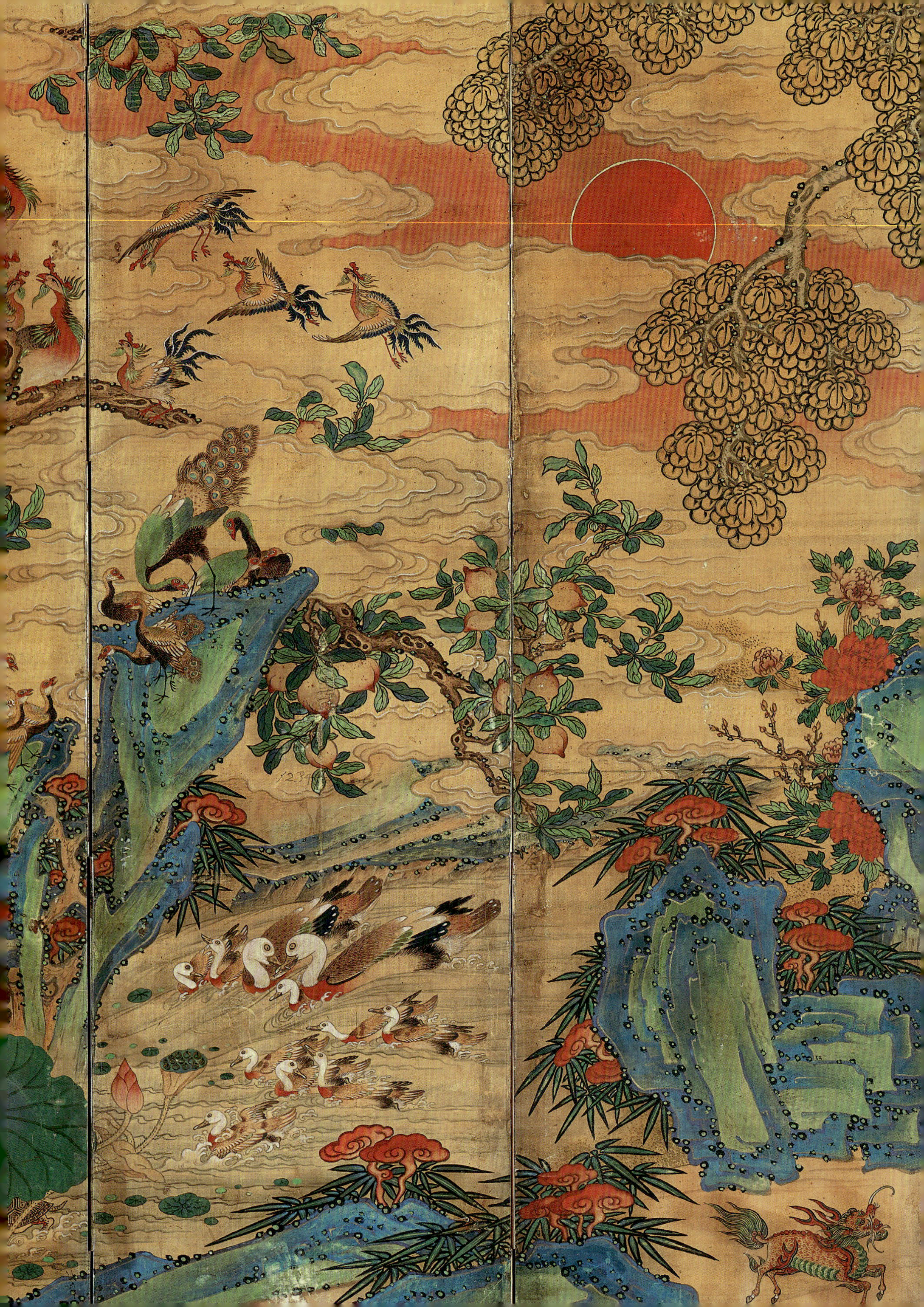

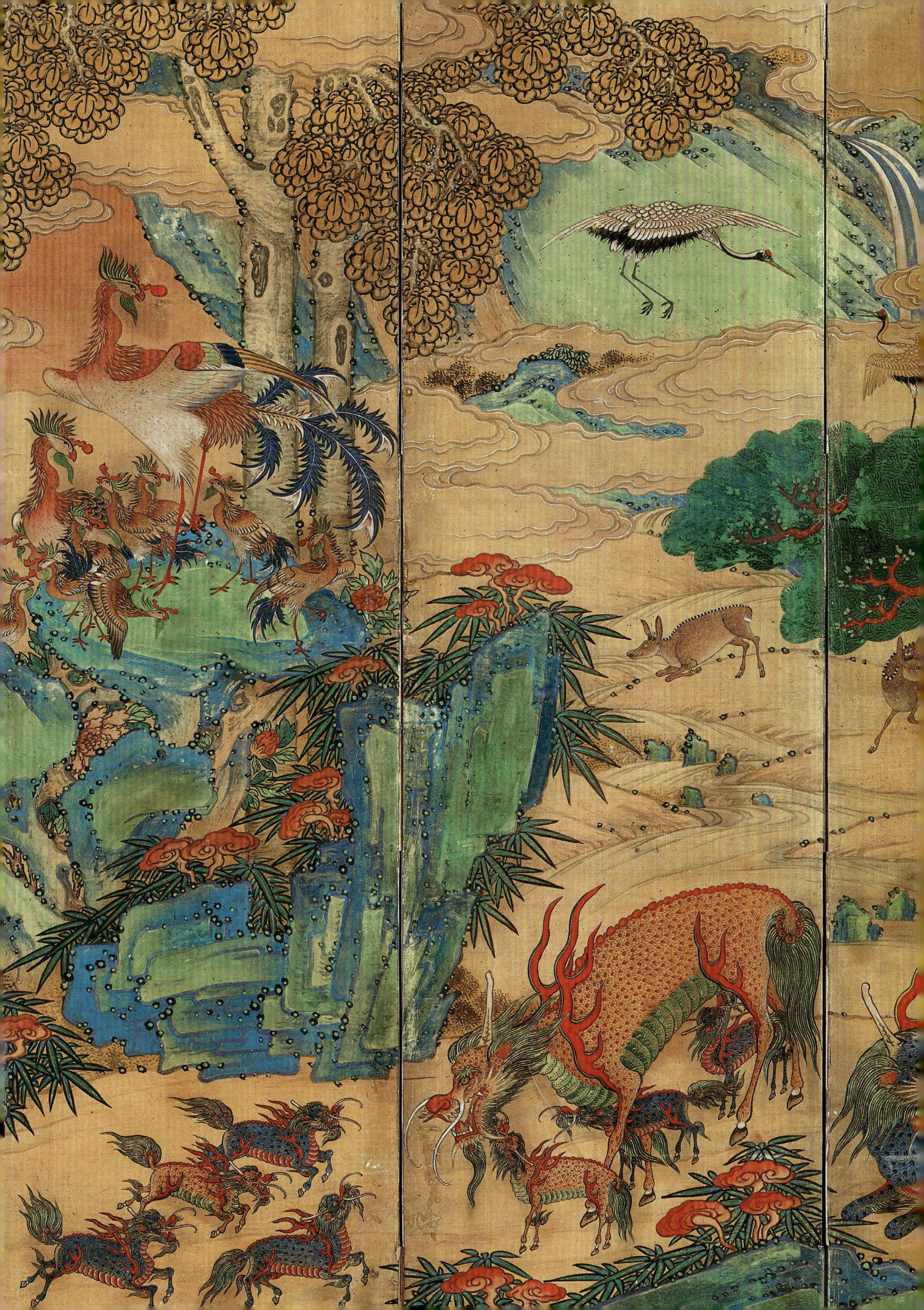

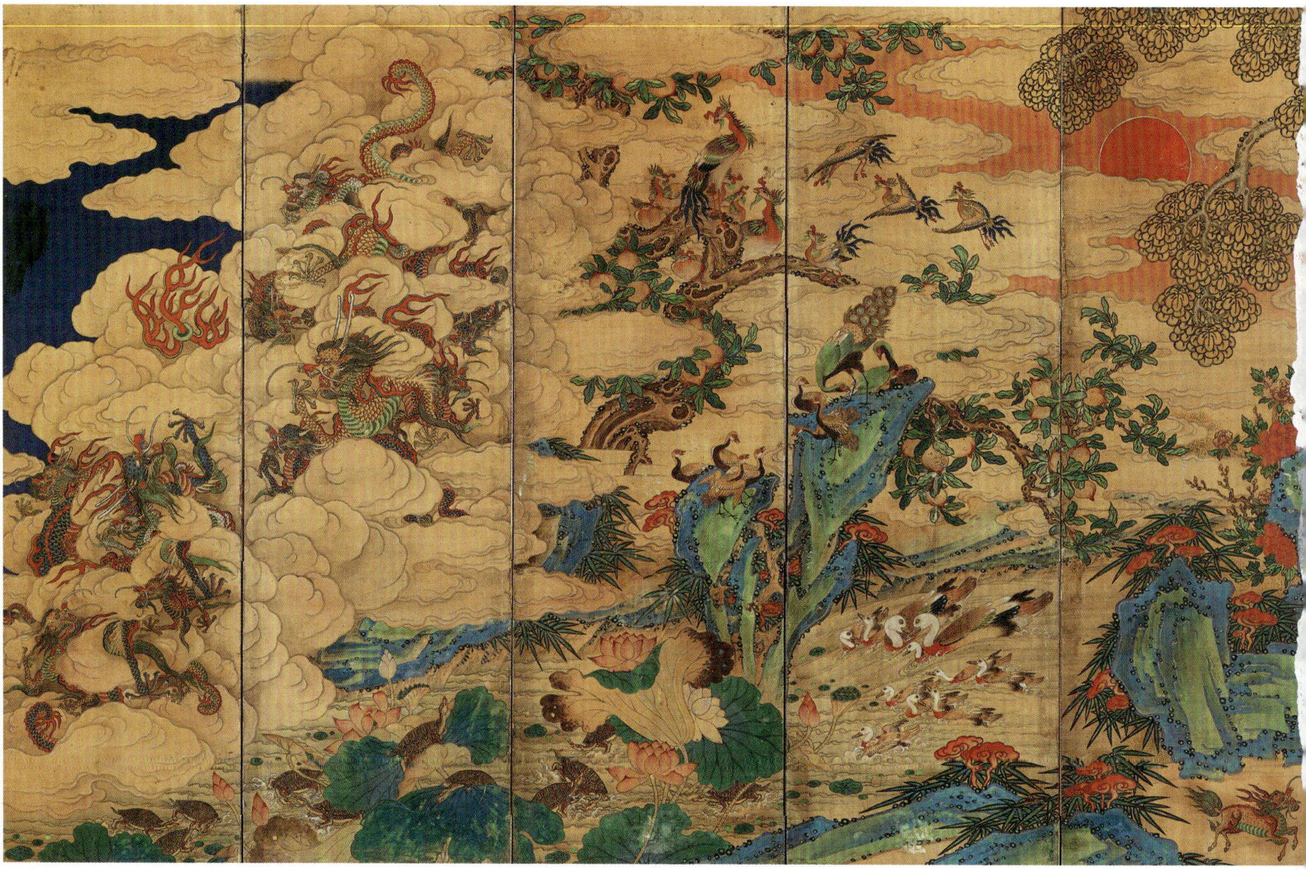

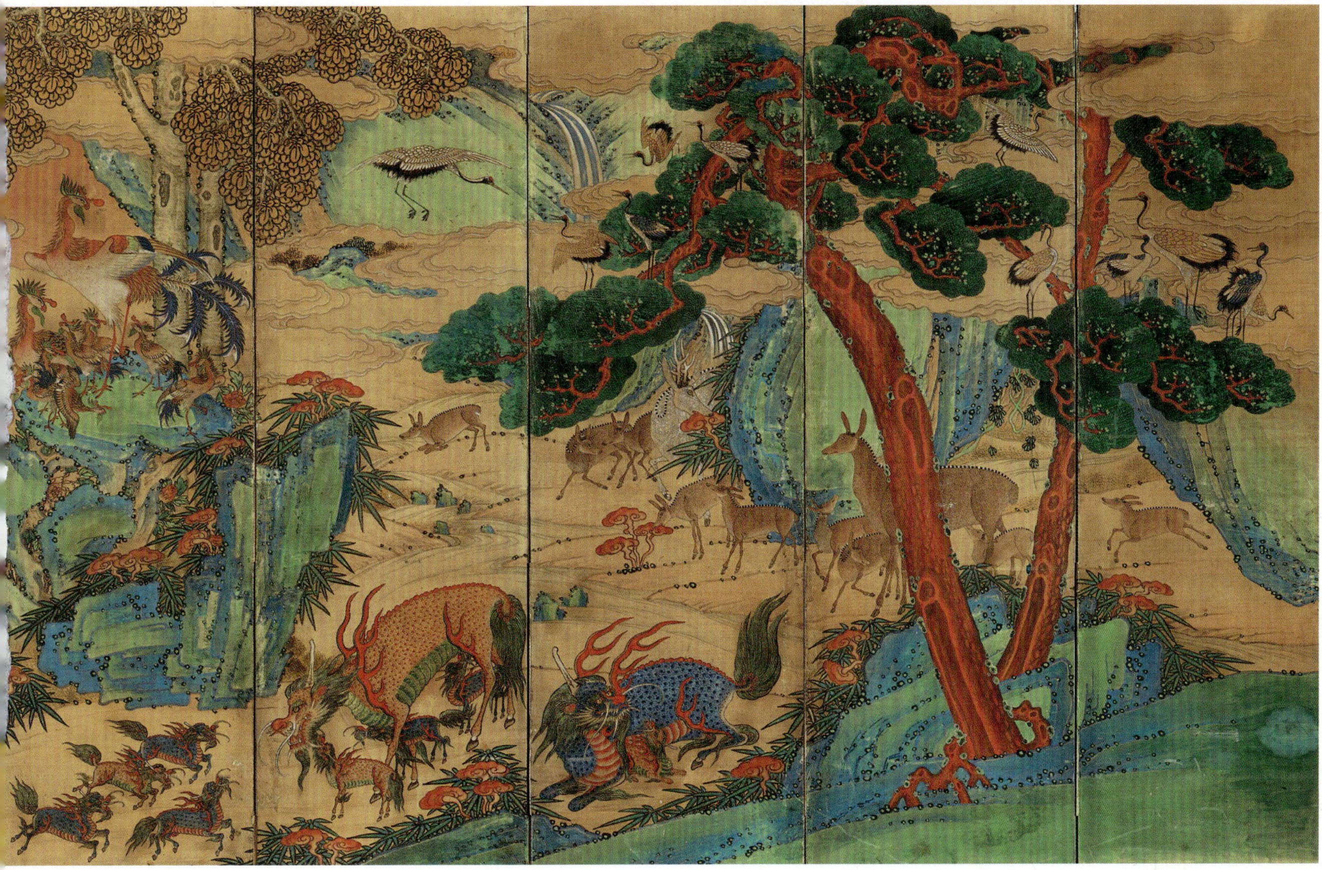

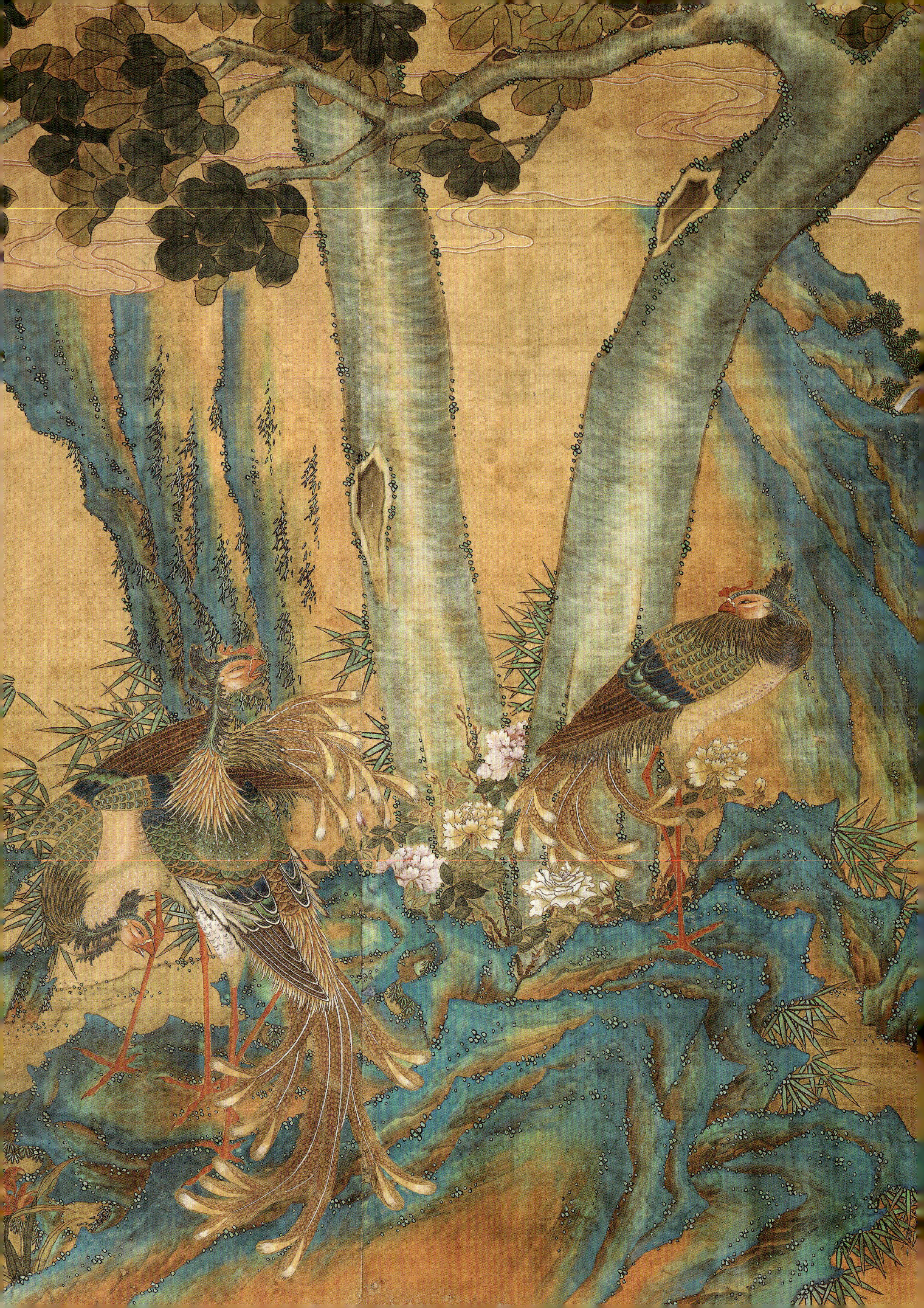

Phoenixes *Bonghwangdo*

By **Oh Ir-yeong** and **Yi Yong-woo** / 1920 / ink and color on silk / 197 × 579 cm / Daejojeon Hall in Changdeokgung

This wall painting of phoenixes (*bonghwangdo*) was created on the eastern wall of Daejojeon Hall, the queen's bedchamber at Changdeokgung Palace. In 1917, after a major fire occurred at the palace (then operating under Japanese rule), the Office of the Yi Dynasty initiated the project of restoring the palatial buildings of Daejojeon Hall, Huijeongdang Hall, and Gyeonghun-gak Hall. The new buildings were designed to incorporate Western architectural style of the 1920s and included large wall spaces near the ceilings.

Among other tasks, the project involved making plans for large mural paintings on the eastern and western walls of the three buildings. It was supervised and executed under Kim Gyu-jin (1868–1933), founder of the Institute of Painting and Calligraphy (Seohwa Yeonguhoe), an organization that served as a key authority on the art scene of its time.

Artists Oh Ir-yeong and Yi Yong-woo, who were then in their thirties and teens, respectively, also participated in this project, having chosen the subject matter of phoenixes and collaborated on this painting. In the court of Joseon, a dragon symbolized the king and a phoenix the queen. For this reason, the iconography of phoenixes was a suitable choice for the queen's chamber.

The painting is also reminiscent of a tale from *Classic of Poetry*. According to one of the book's legends, a phoenix will rest on no other tree than a Chinese parasol tree and will only feed on bamboo fruits. As a means of reenacting this story, the picture portrays five pairs of phoenixes flying over the sea in search of a Chinese parasol tree. The simultaneous presence of the rising sun, a phoenix, and a Chinese parasol tree, as seen in this painting, has long been a favored motif in auspicious paintings, as the trio of images was meant to signify that a phoenix is crying under the morning sunlight.

The background is filled with auspicious signs of eternity and happiness, from the clouds and waterfalls to the bamboo shoots, rocks, peonies, and fungus of immortality. A phoenix is typically rendered with the head of rooster and a large, multicolored tail. The phoenixes illustrated in this painting boast their exquisite figures through graceful yet confident flaps of their wings. Characterized by the use of meticulous details, strong color contrasts, and the aforementioned themes, this *bonghwangdo* is undoubtedly a masterpiece of phoenix painting produced in the late Joseon period.

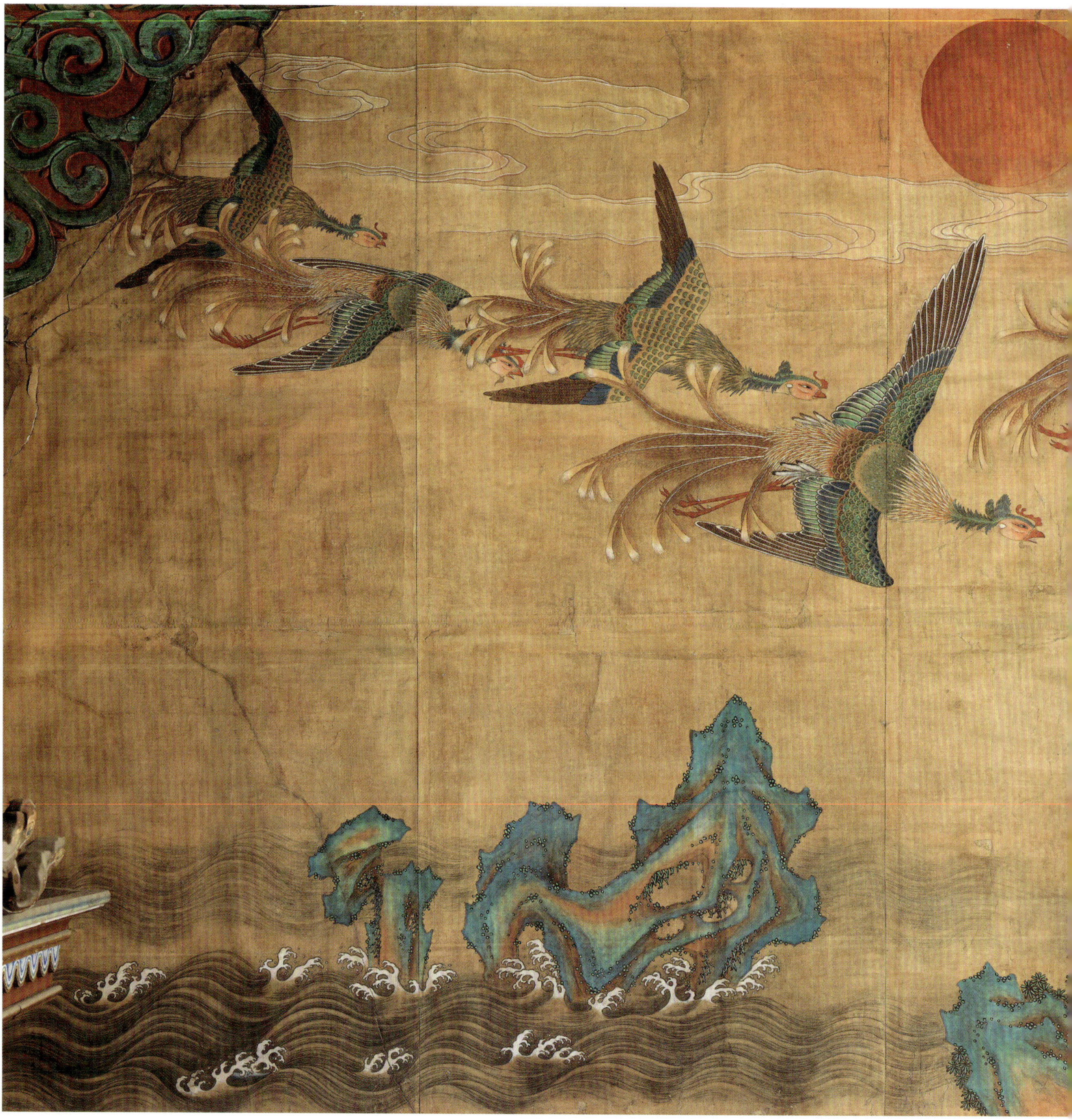

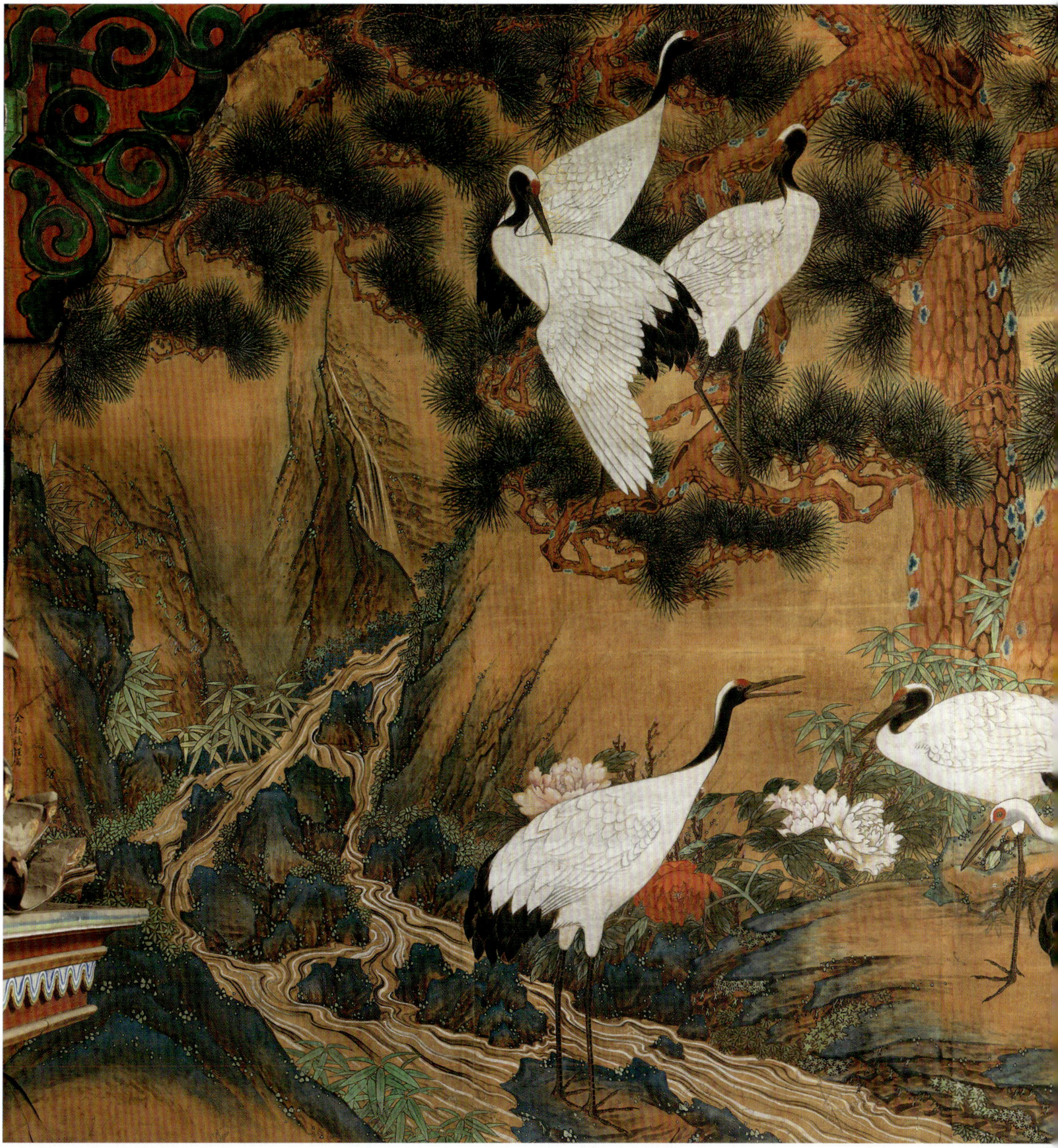

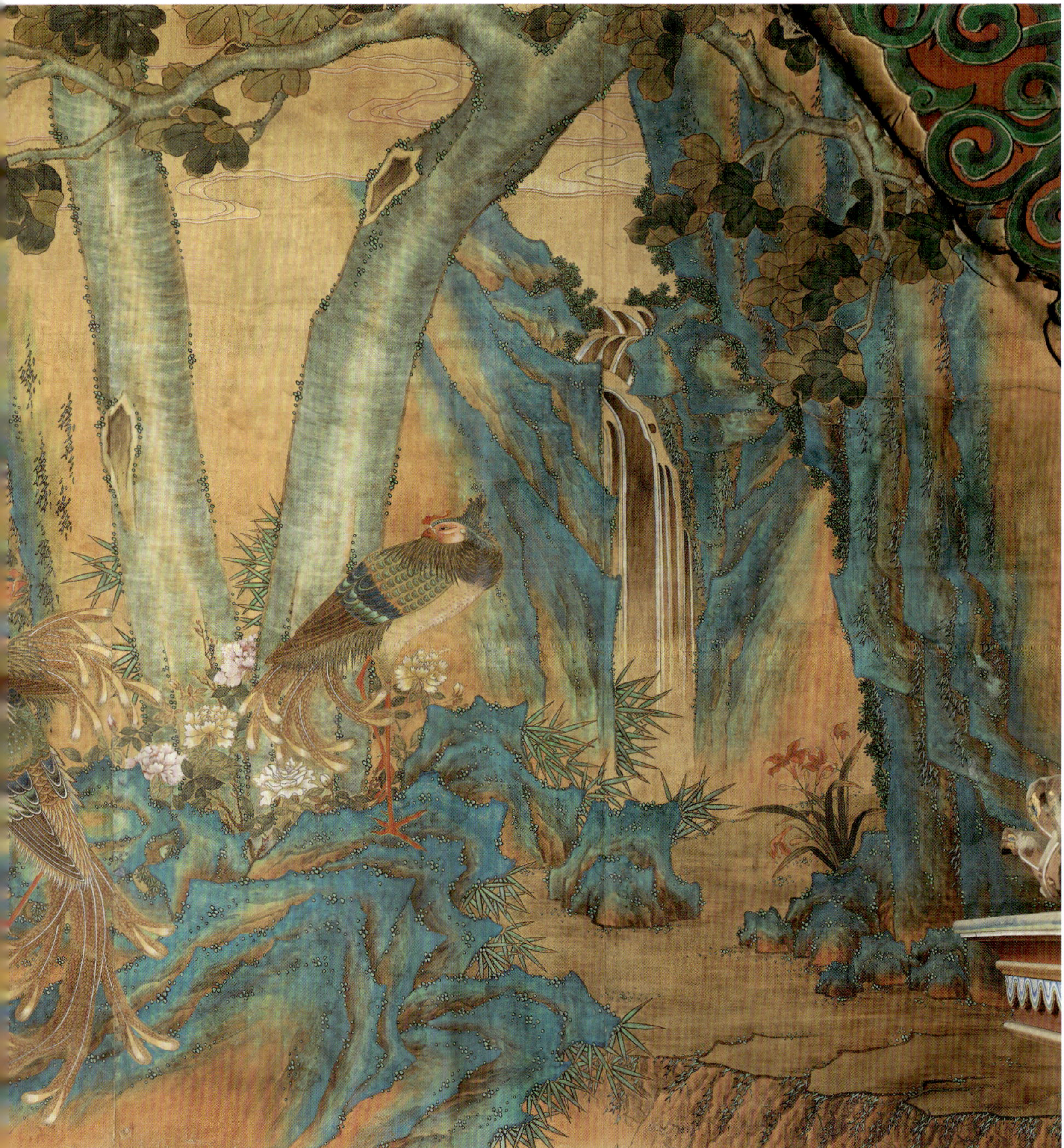

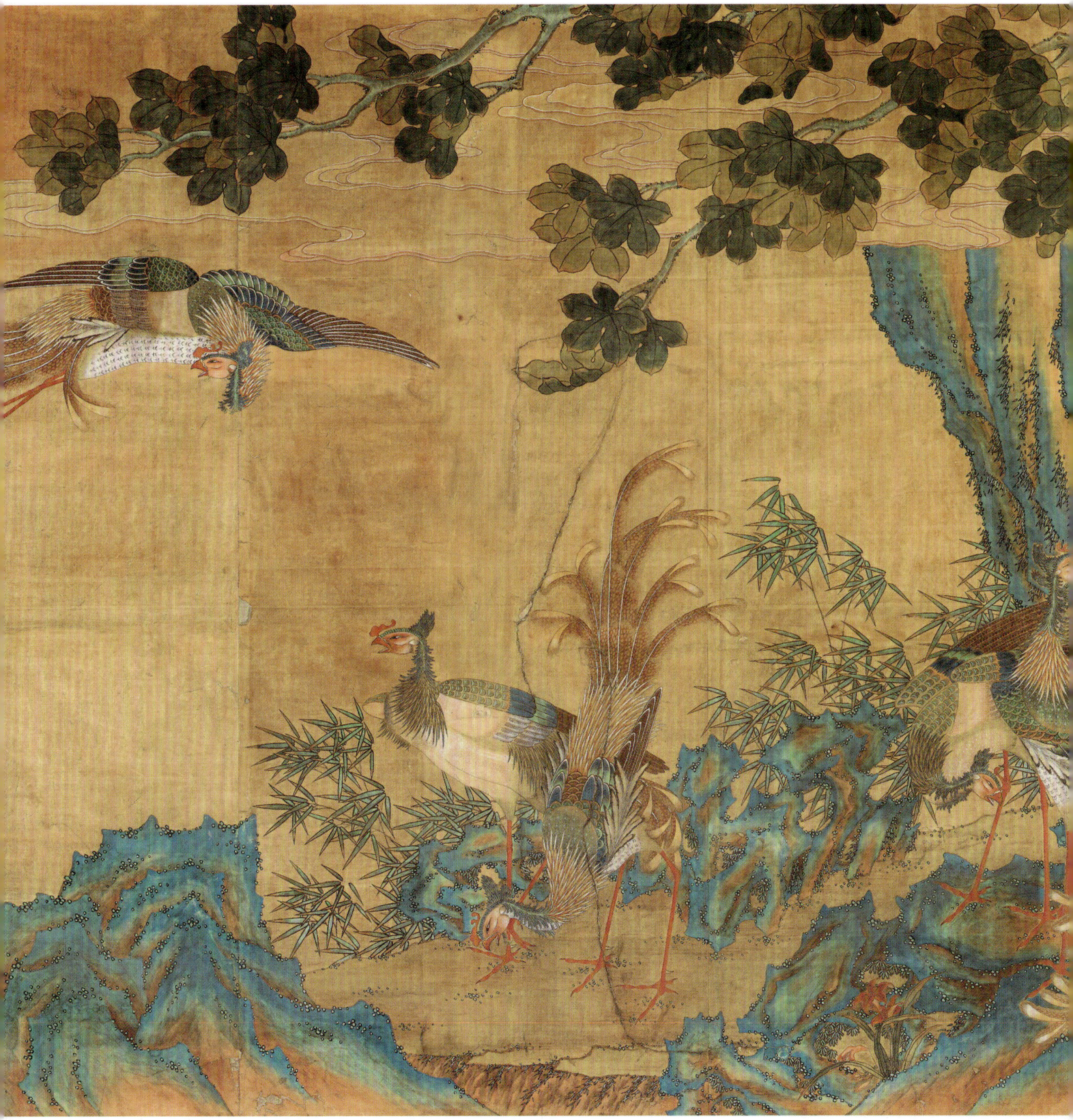

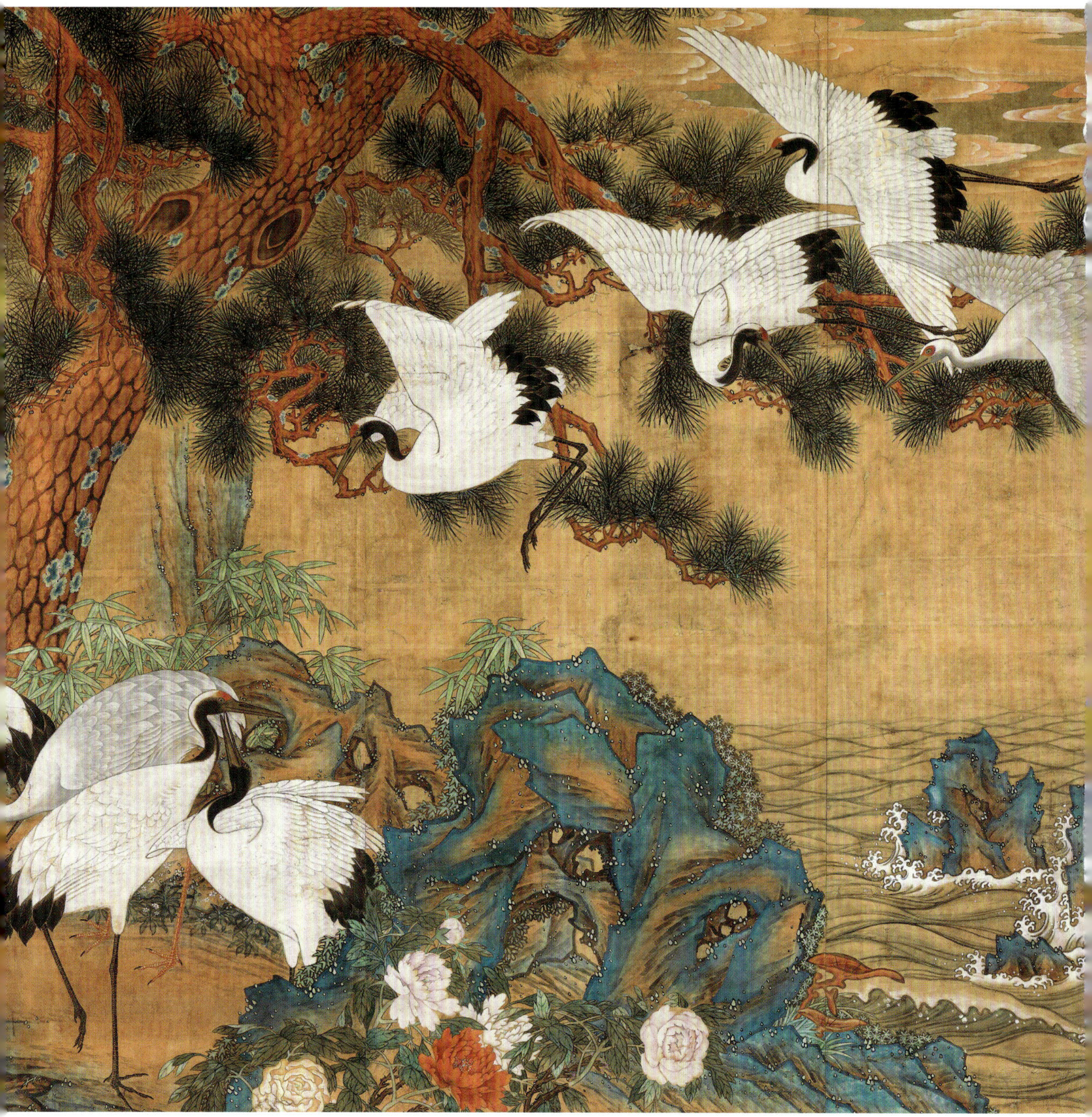

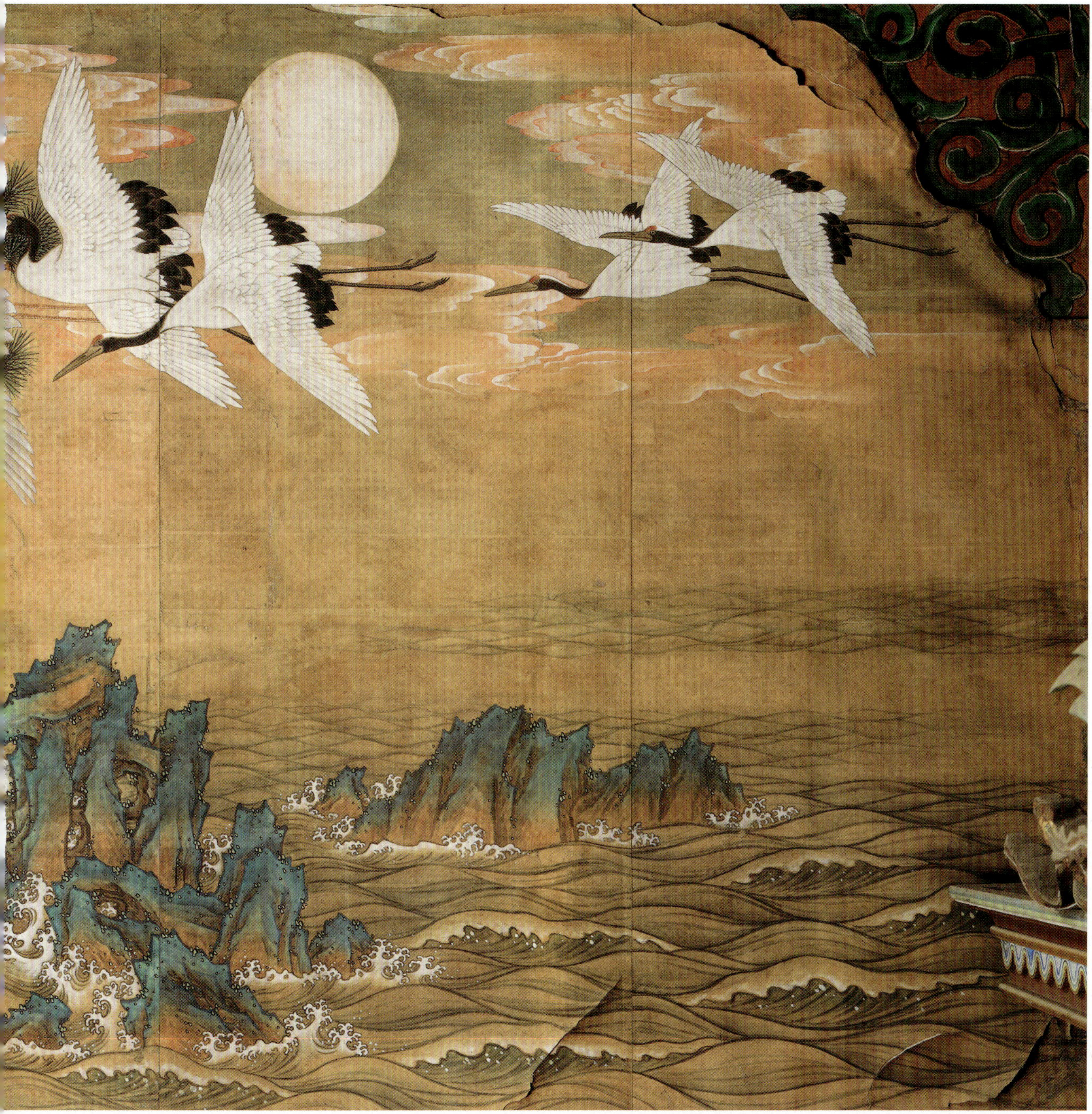

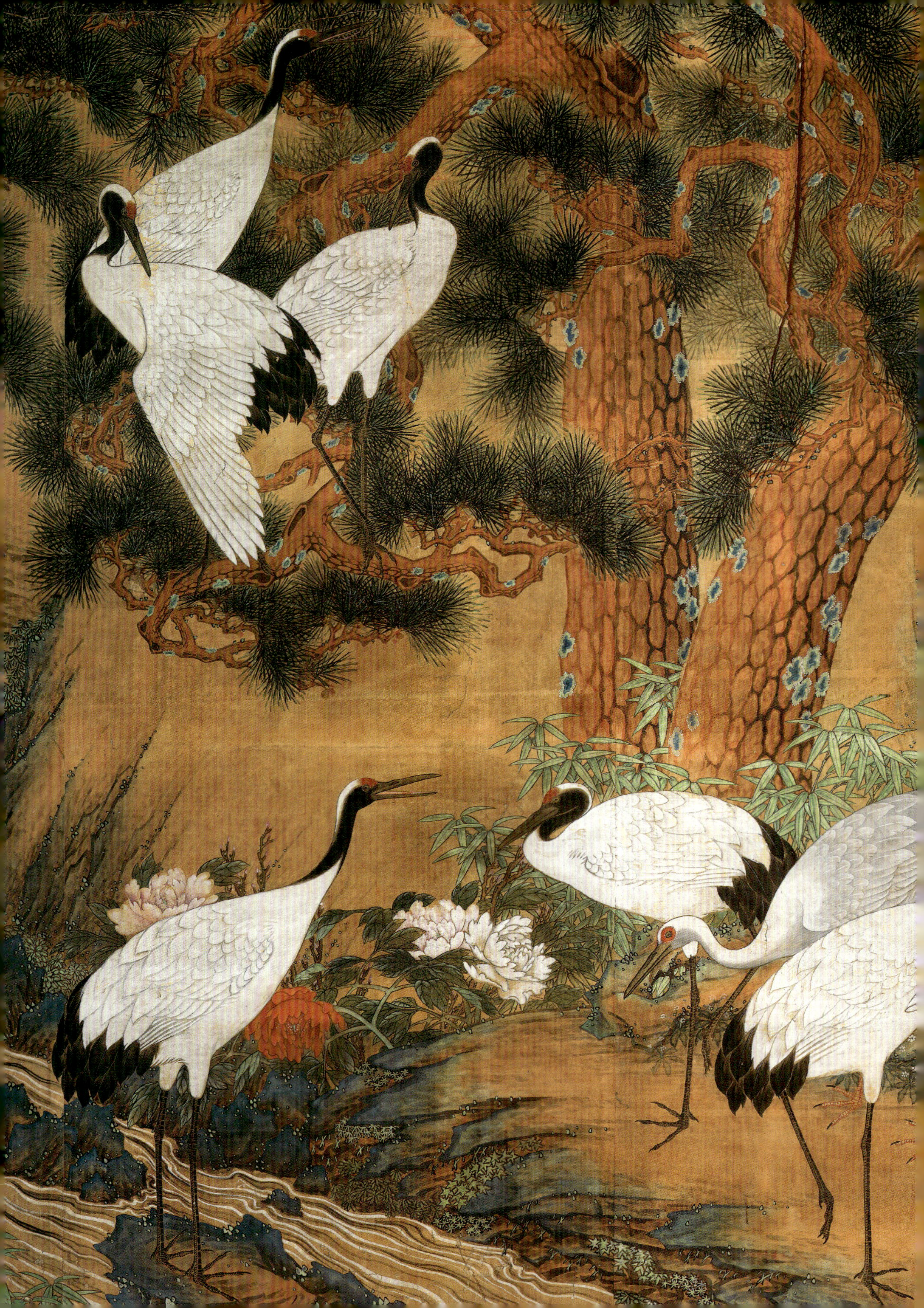

White Cranes *Baekhakdo*

By **Kim Eun-ho** / 1920 / ink and color on silk / 197 × 579 cm /
Daejojeon Hall in Changdeokgung

This mural painting on the western wall of Daejojeon Hall was done by Kim Eun-ho (1892–1979), who earned fame as the court painter commissioned to produce the portrait of Emperor Sunjong, the last king of Joseon. Displaying both traditional themes and style, the picture is considered one of Kim's finest pieces.

The mural portrays sixteen white cranes that are in the midst of flying over a white moon, heading toward the river valley where huge pine trees take rest. Thought to be the leader of all birds, in ancient documents, cranes were always referred to as birds that live for more than a thousand years. Along with pine trees and bamboo, cranes often symbolize longevity, and this wall painting is no exception. The birds boast their long, curvy necks, straight legs, and large feathers, all of which accentuate their flexible yet graceful movements.

Just as the compositions of the *Bonghwangdo* and *Baekhakdo* murals can be said to mirror one another, the choice of motifs shows an equal level of contrast: The red sun rises above the phoenixes on the eastern wall while the white moon floats above the roaming cranes on the western wall. Such a juxtaposition of pictorial elements on each wall expresses the painter's wish for a balance of yin and yang within the space of Daejojeon Hall and, ultimately, for the longevity of the king and queen in a peaceful dynasty.

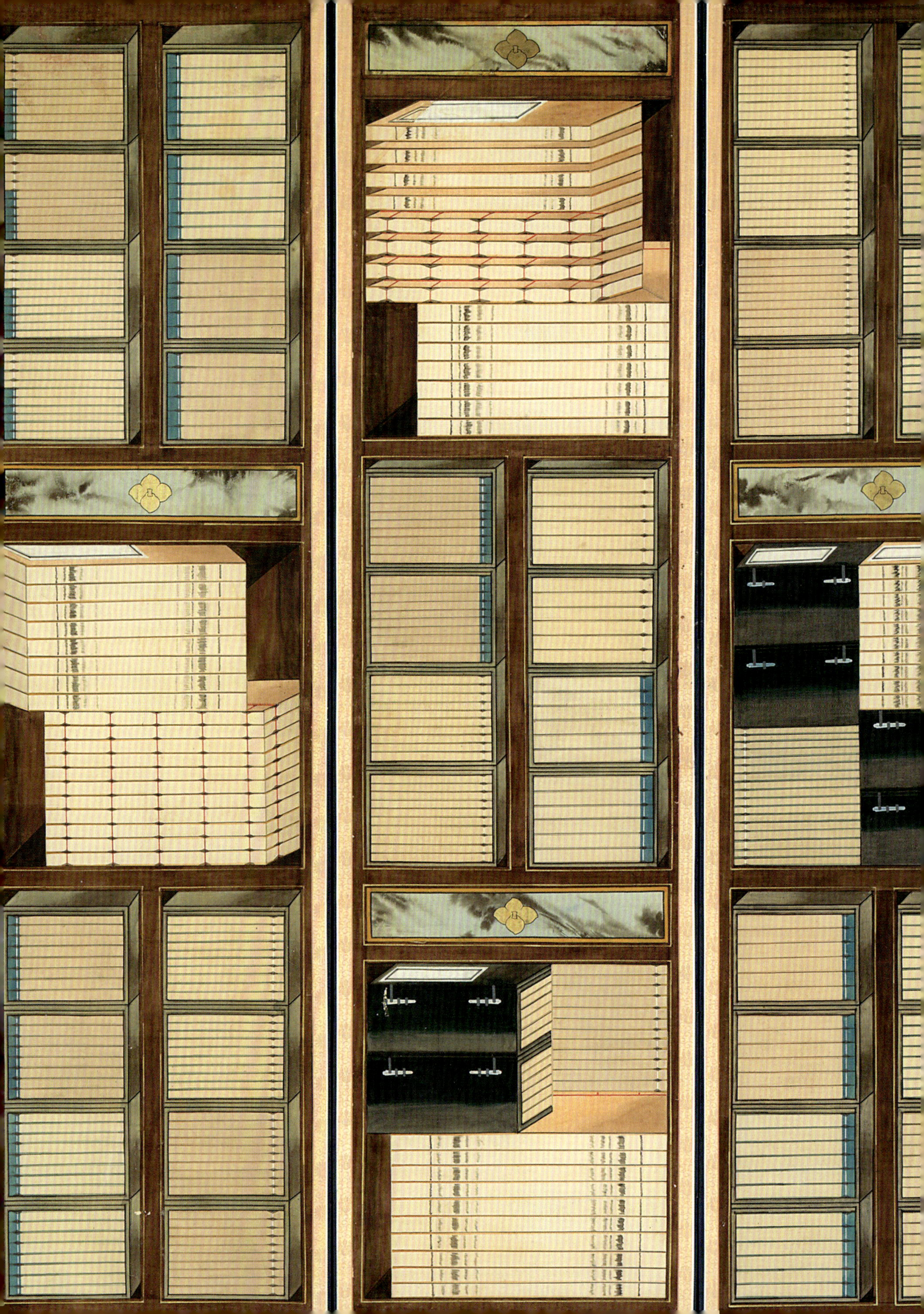

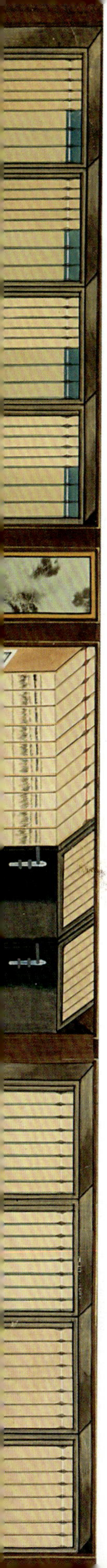

Scholar's Bookshelf | *Chaekgado*

19th century / ten-fold screen / ink and color on silk / each panel, 161.7 × 39.5 cm / National Palace Museum of Korea

Chaekgado are best known as pictures depicting bookshelves and associated objects, including books, ceramics, antiquities, scholastic paraphernalia, luxury goods, and flowers. The term *chaekgeori* is often used to refer to the same genre of painting—particularly for *minhwa* (folk paintings)—but for court paintings, the word *chaekgado* is typically used.

When first introduced during the reign of King Jeongjo, *chaekgado* simply included shelves full of books, as seen in this example. Such bookshelf paintings were usually placed as backdrops in the rooms at the *pyeonjeon*, or the royal council hall, as well as at the palace of the crown prince so as to foster a scholarly atmosphere for the princes, for whom academic cultivation was essential. While the thematic and stylistic techniques of *chaekgado* had originally come from China, the painting genre became more popular in Joseon, having even become practiced among commoners.

Chaekgado utilize perspective in such a way that creates an optical illusion, giving the impression that the space is enlarged and extended. This device demonstrates the artist's knowledge of Western painting techniques, such as the use of perspective as well as chiaroscuro. The repetition of book stacks with more than one viewpoint brings rhythmic unity and abstract beauty to the overall composition.

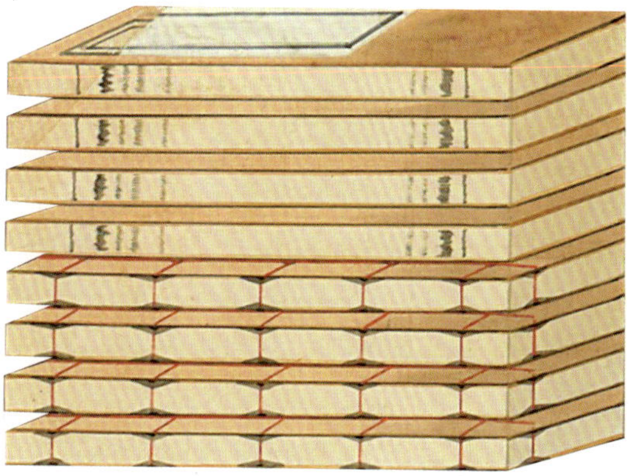

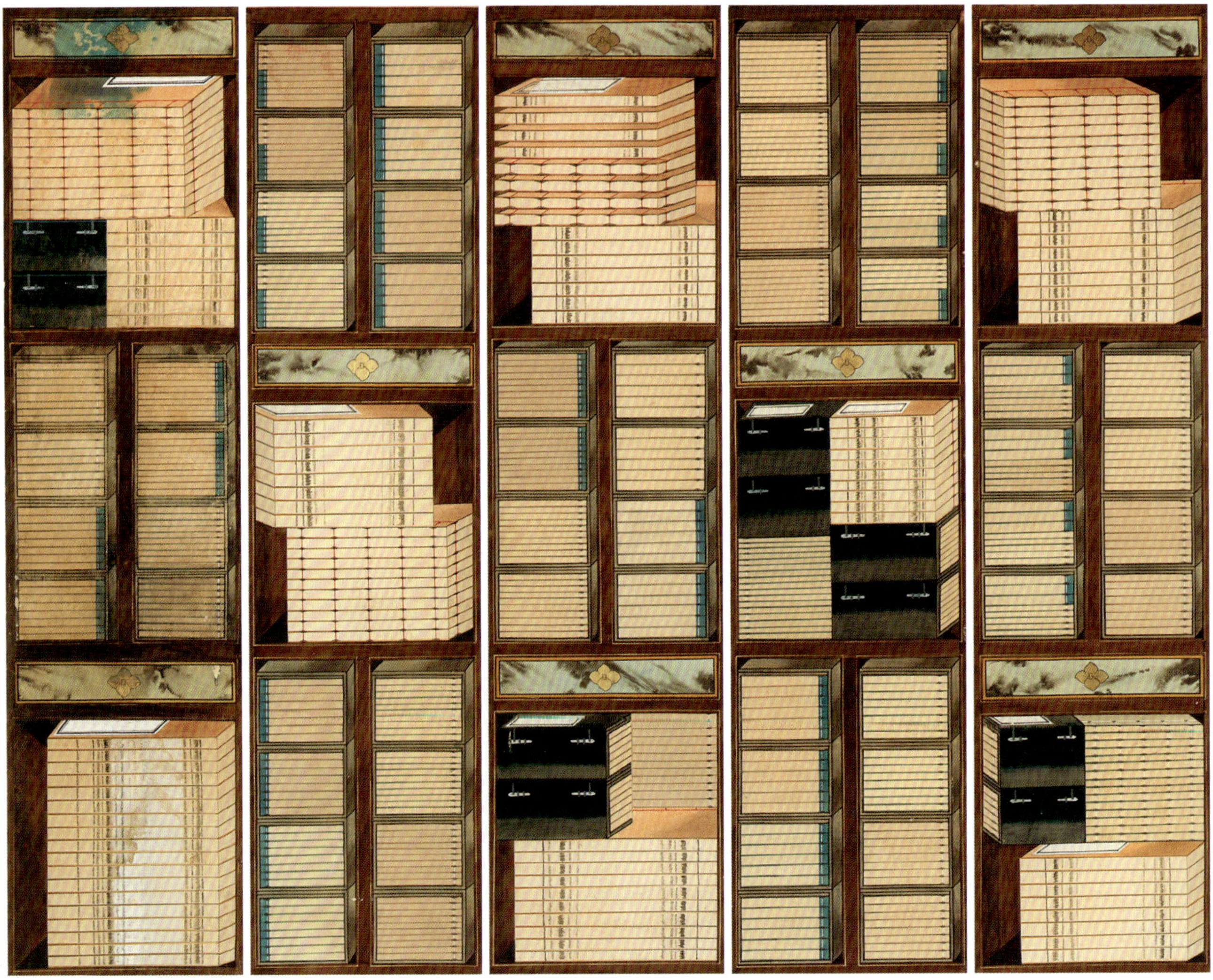

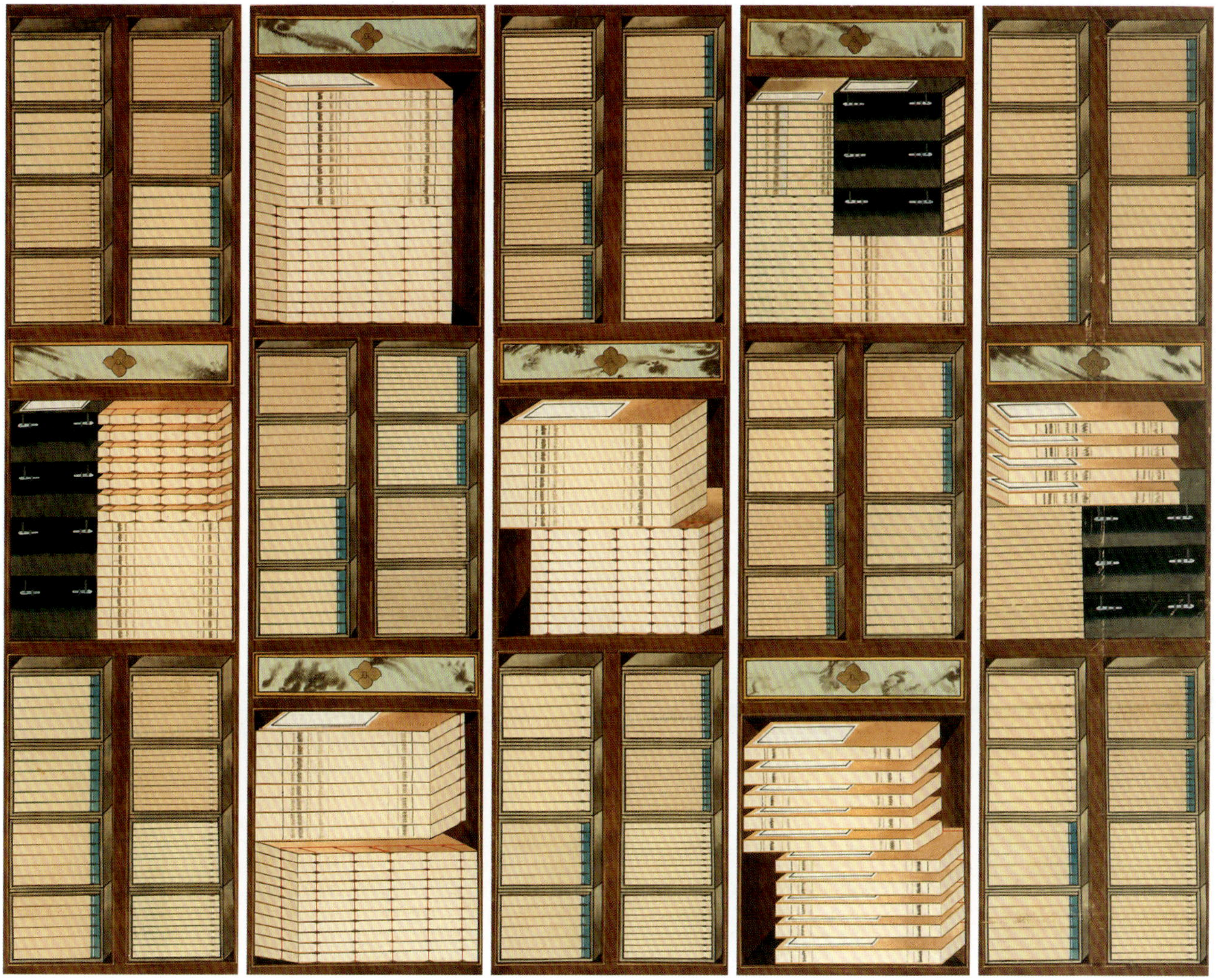

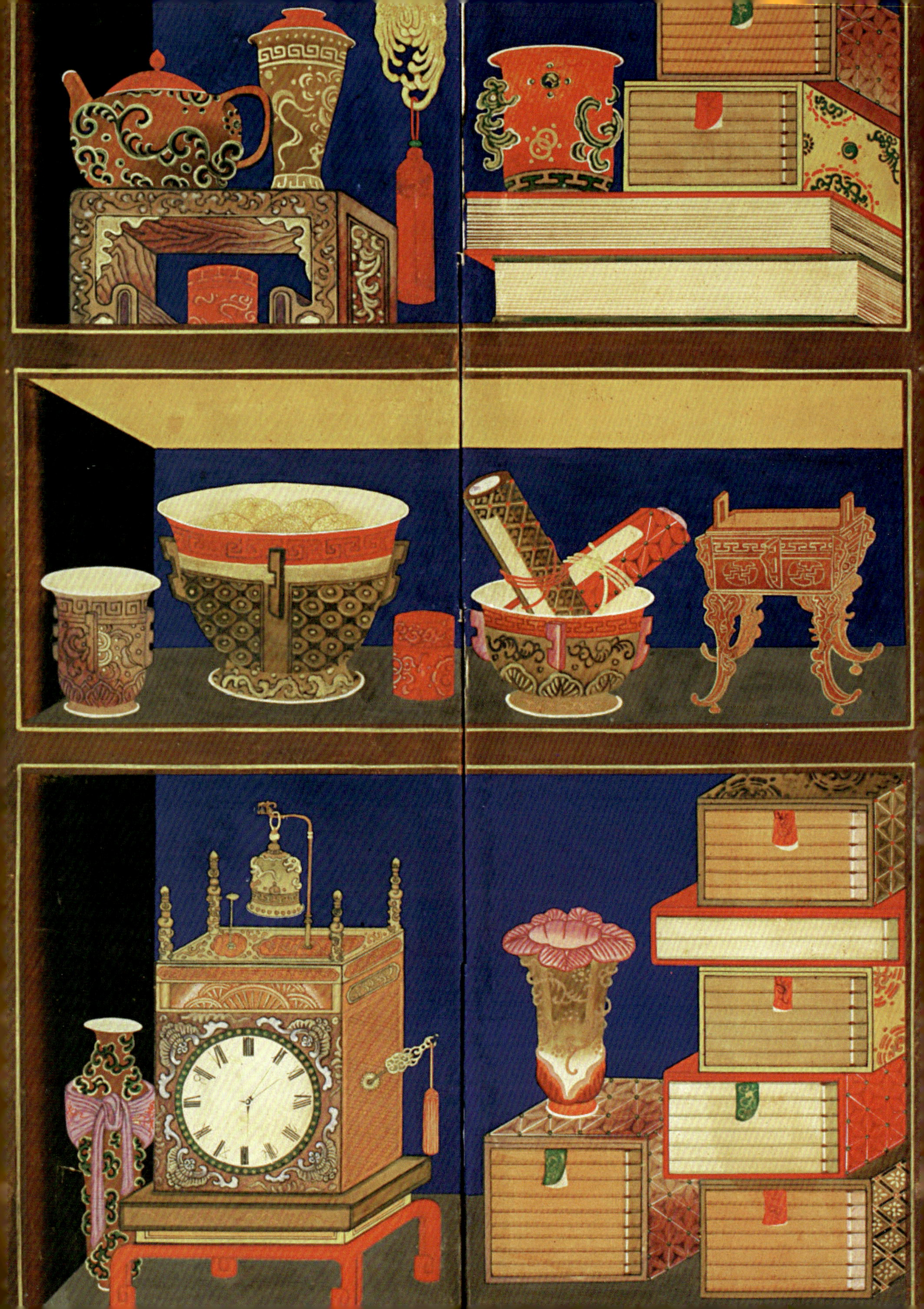

Scholar's Bookshelf II *Chaekgado*

Late 19th to early 20th century / ten-fold screen / ink and color on silk / each panel, 198.8 × 39.3 cm / National Museum of Korea

By the late eighteenth century, *chaekgado*, or painting of a scholar's bookshelf, became one of the major genres of Joseon court paintings, owing to the keen interest of King Jeongjo (r. 1777–1800). For those seeking the position of painter-in-waiting at Kyujanggak between the late eighteenth and early twentieth centuries, it was not uncommon for entrance exams to include books and scholarly instruments such as bookshelves as their painting subjects. Though many artists practiced at drawing such items, *chaekgado* was not the easiest genre to master, as it required painting skills newly adapted from the West, such as linear perspective and chiaroscuro.

Those who were thought to be notable *chaekgado* painters include Kim Hong-do (1745–ca. 1806), Shin Han-pyeong (1726–unknown), Jang Han-jong (1768–unknown), and Yi Yun-min during the reign of King Jeongjo, with Yi Hyeong-nok (1808–ca. 1874) having carried on the legacy of his father, Yi Yun-min. In the mid-nineteenth century, *chaekgado* became more stylized with antique embellishments, while the number of books portrayed decreased.

This *chaekgado* is characterized by the level of ornamentation and the bright blue wall behind the decorative objects. The cases that house each collection of books are embellished with different patterns and colors, while the decorations on each piece of porcelain are portrayed with great detail. The picture also includes an unusual number of vases and hand scrolls decorated with wrapping cloth, a popular custom originally derived from Qing China. In Chinese culture, vases wrapped in cloth symbolize peace and happiness because the Chinese character for vase, 瓶 (*ping*), is a homophone of 平 (*ping*), meaning peace, and the word for wrapping cloth, 袱 (*fu*), is a homophone of happiness, 福 (*fu*). Through these auspicious emblems, the picture emphasizes both peace and happiness.

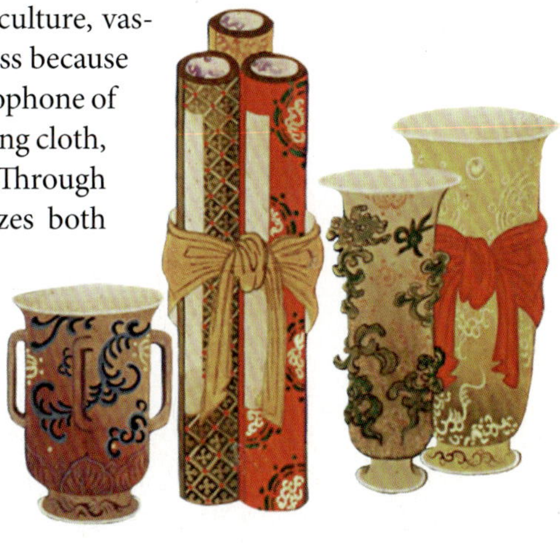

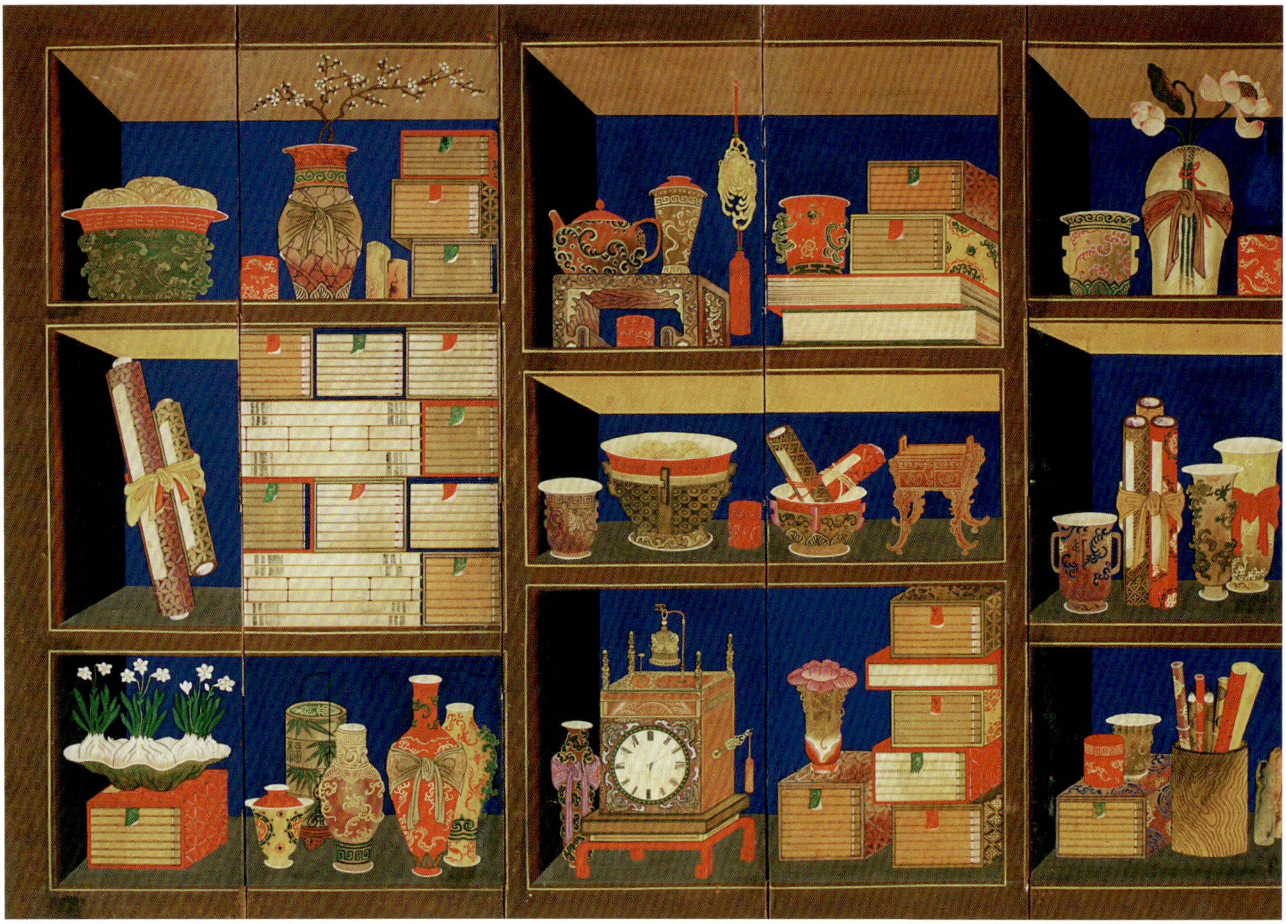

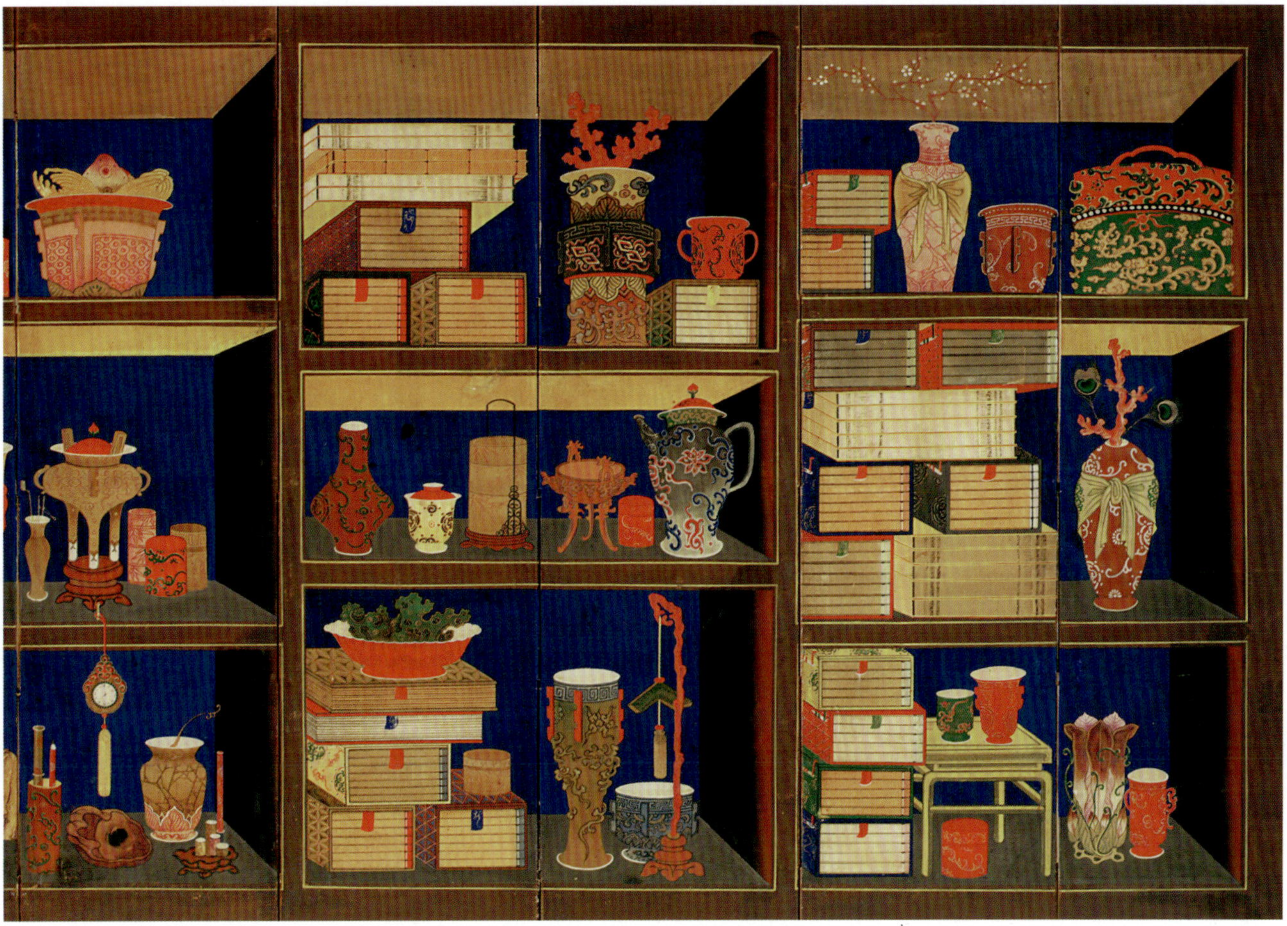

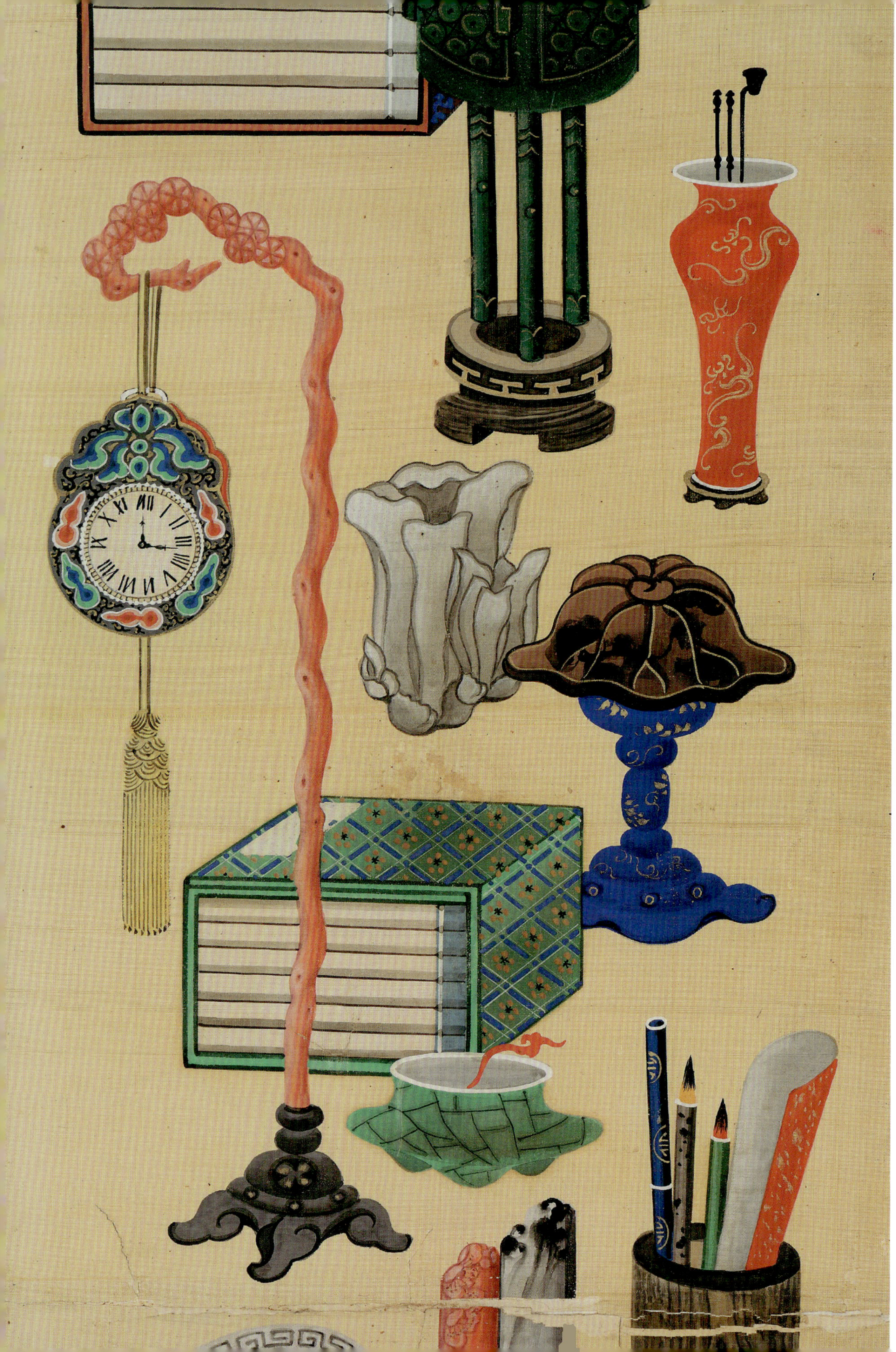

Books and Scholarly Instruments *Munbangdo*

By **Yi Taek-gyun** / late 19th century / ten-fold screen / ink and color on silk / 199 × 423.3 cm / Tongdosa Museum

Some *chaekgado* paintings did not incorporate images of bookshelves. Instead, there were those that depicted books and art objects without shelves, a subgenre called *munbangdo*, which were more popular among the commoners.

Although the individual objects in this painting are portrayed in a stereoscopic manner, they appear to be floating in midair due to the lack of perspective and the amount of unused space in the background. Almost everything painted—*ruyi* (a ceremonial scepter in Chinese Buddhism), the narcissus flower, the peaches, the pomegranate, the Buddha's hand citron, the carp sculpture, the peacock feathers, the coral branch, and the stone chime—is an auspicious symbol for the desire to bear numerous sons and also signifies luck and fame.

Objects in *chaekgado* or *munbangdo* tend to reflect the patron's preferences and interests, which corresponded to the time period. For example, the watch in the seventh panel demonstrates people's interest in Western technology. In other paintings created for the members of royal court, the variety of objects tended to be rather limited, reflecting the patron's highly conservative taste. Over time, the quantity and variety of objects displayed in *munbangdo* increased and took on a more decorative and wishful character.

In addition, the identity of the artist of this piece, Yi Taek-gyun (1808–ca. 1874), can be found on the ninth screen, where the seal is laid sideways, revealing the painter's signature. It should be noted that Yi Hyeong-nok renamed himself as Yi Taek-gyun in 1871.

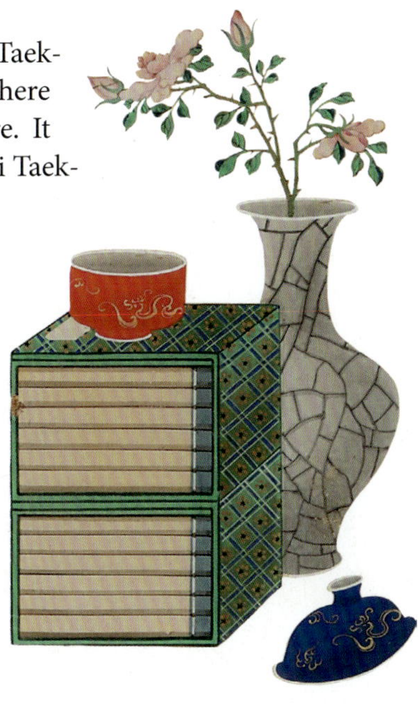

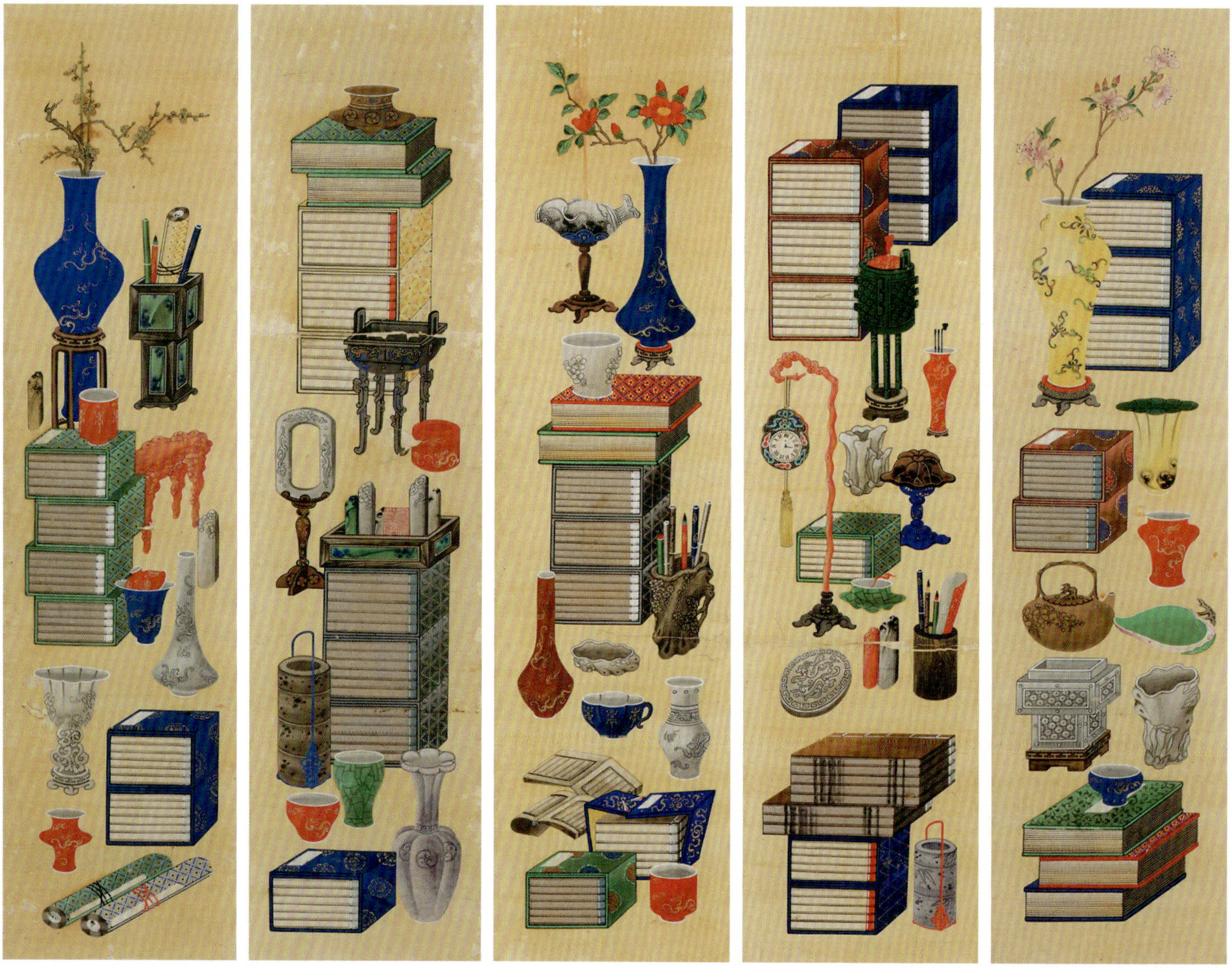

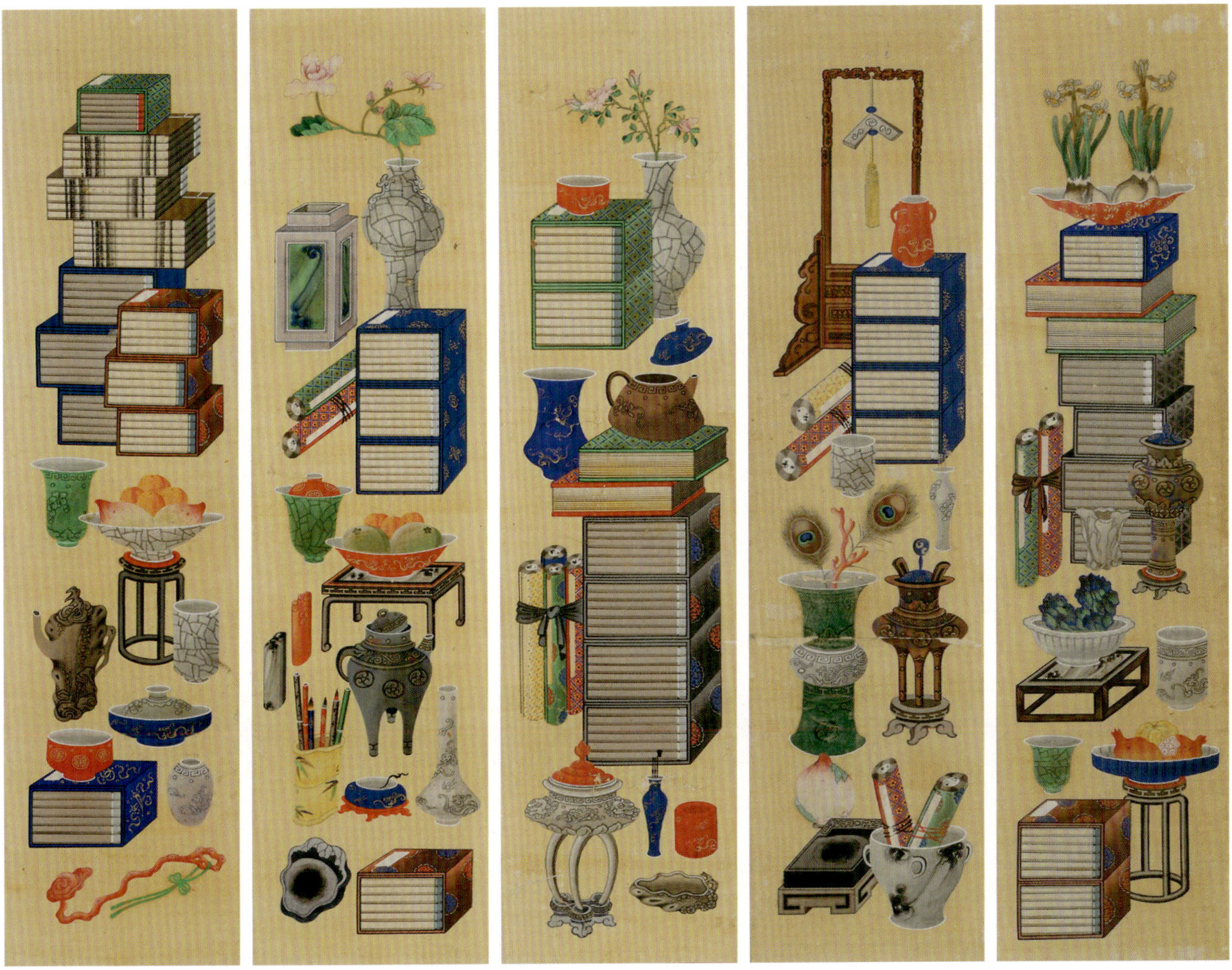

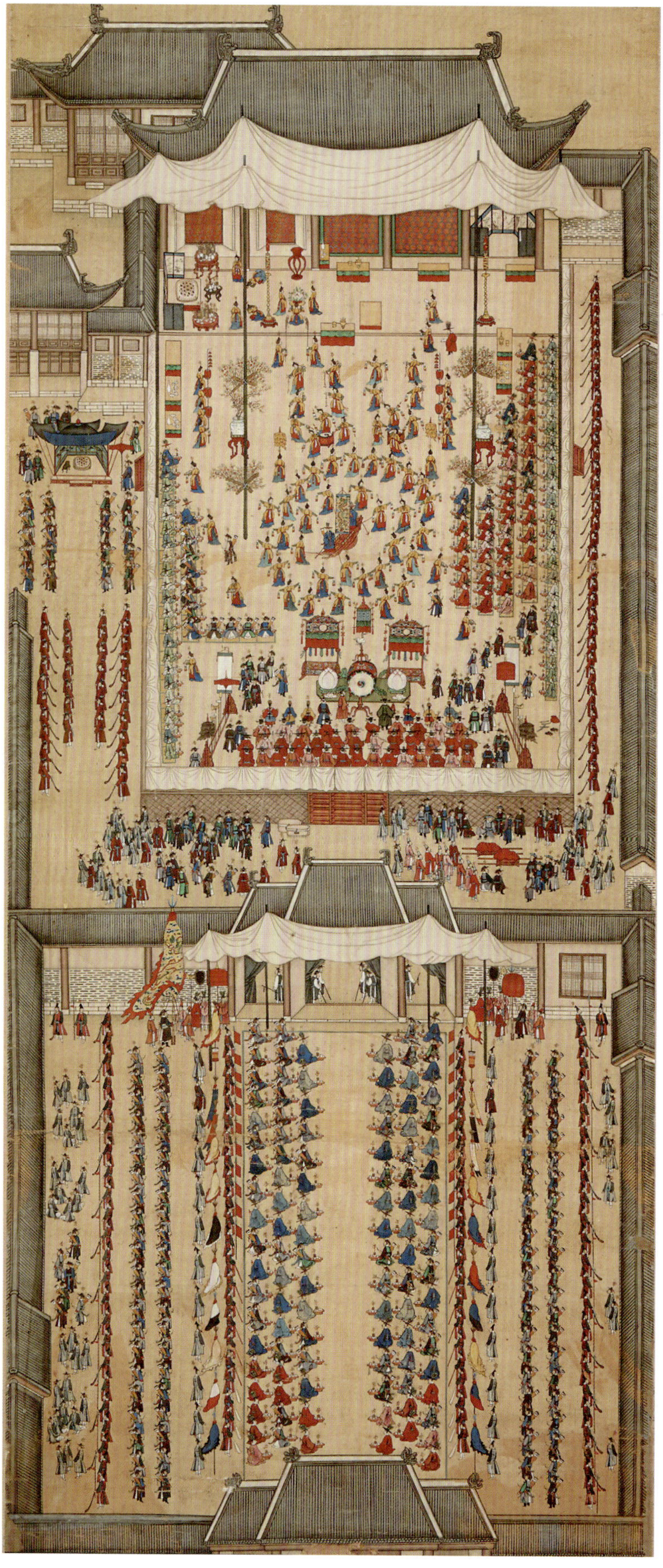

The Birthday Banquet for Lady Hyegyeong at Bongsudang *Bongsudang Jinchando*

Originally from *Screen Depicting King Jeongjo's Visit to Hwaseong* (*Hwaseong Haenghaeng Dobyeng*) / by **Kim Deuk-sin** et al. / 1795–1796 / ink and color on silk / 156.2 × 65 cm / Dongguk University Museum

In 1795, King Jeongjo, the twenty-second king of the Joseon Dynasty, visited the walled city of Hwaseong to pay his respects at Hyeollyung-won—the tomb of his father, Crown Prince Sado (1735–1762), who had unfortunately died at an early age. It was the first time in history of the Joseon Dynasty that a king paid a visit with his birth mother, Lady Hyegyeong (1735–1815), and held an ancestral worship at the tomb. By traveling to Hwaseong, Jeongjo commemorated the sixtieth year of birth of both Prince Sado and Lady Hyegyeong.

After the journey, some of the highlights of the visit were documented in the form of an eight-fold screen depicting the events of the king's visit. Thirteen copies were created, with the intention of having them presented to the king and distributed among the officials who had overseen the visit.

This picture, the first of the eight panels, depicts the sixtieth birthday banquet held for Lady Hyegyeong at Bongsudang Hall during the king and lady's six-day stay in Hwaseong Haenggung Palace. A closer look at the painting reveals the festive mood of the party in the midst of a series of solemn ceremonial events.

A temporary wooden stage had been built in the front courtyard of Bongsudang with white cotton drapes sheltering the stage on three sides. Although not depicted on the screen, according to the royal documents of *uigwe*, Lady Hyegyeong and her female entourage sat behind the red bamboo blind. Outside, on the left corner of the blind, a leopard-fur floor cushion symbolizes the presence of king, who was never depicted in paintings. The male royal family members invited to the event sit in rows on each side of the stage.

The various court dances are presented in a highly active manner, including *hyangbalmu* (small brass cymbal dance), *abakmu* (ivory clapper dance), *ssangmugo* (double drum dance), and *seonyurak* (boat dance). Outside the door, high-ranking officers who have accompanied the king from the capital sit in a row behind their own individual tables with food.

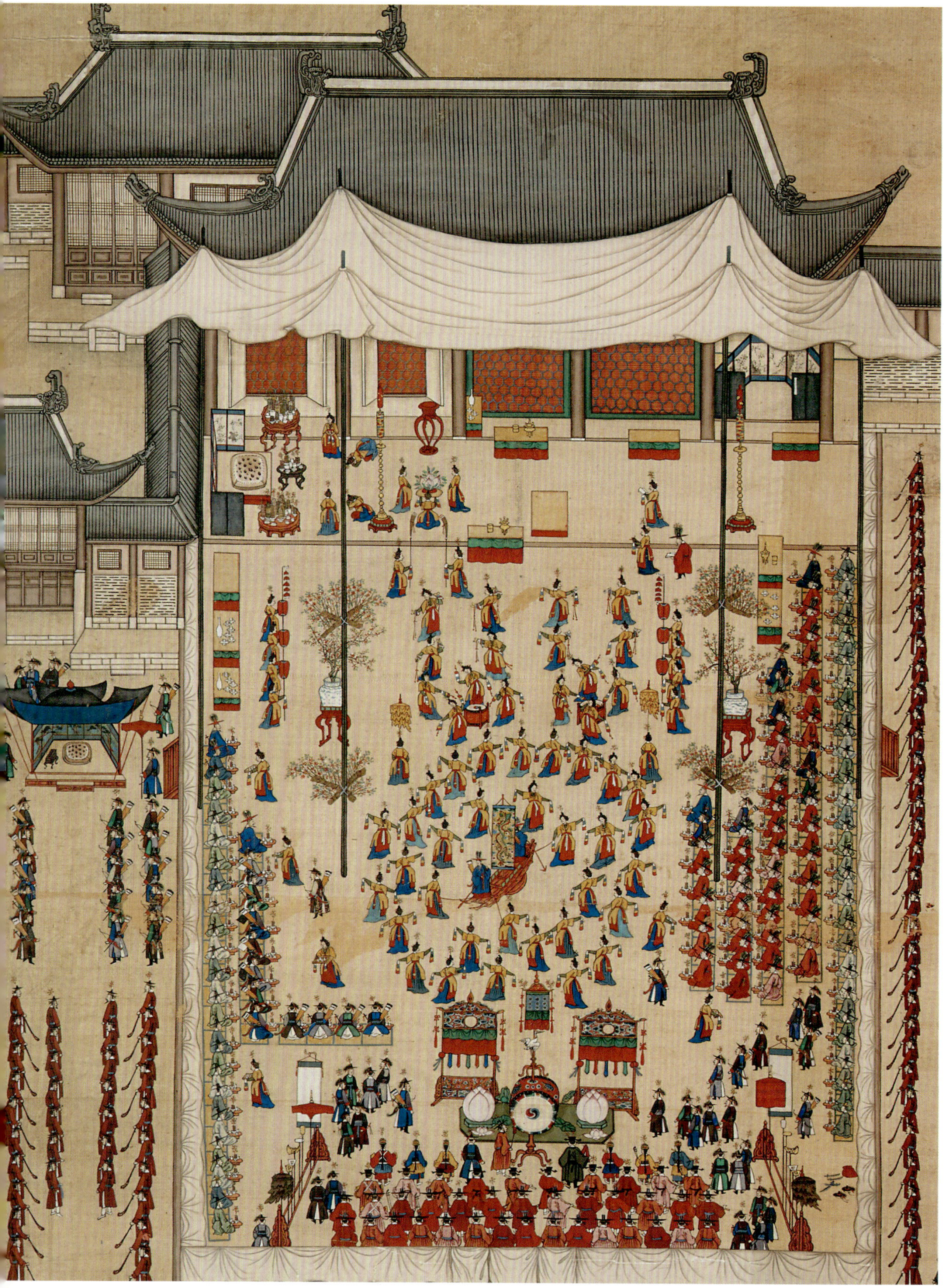

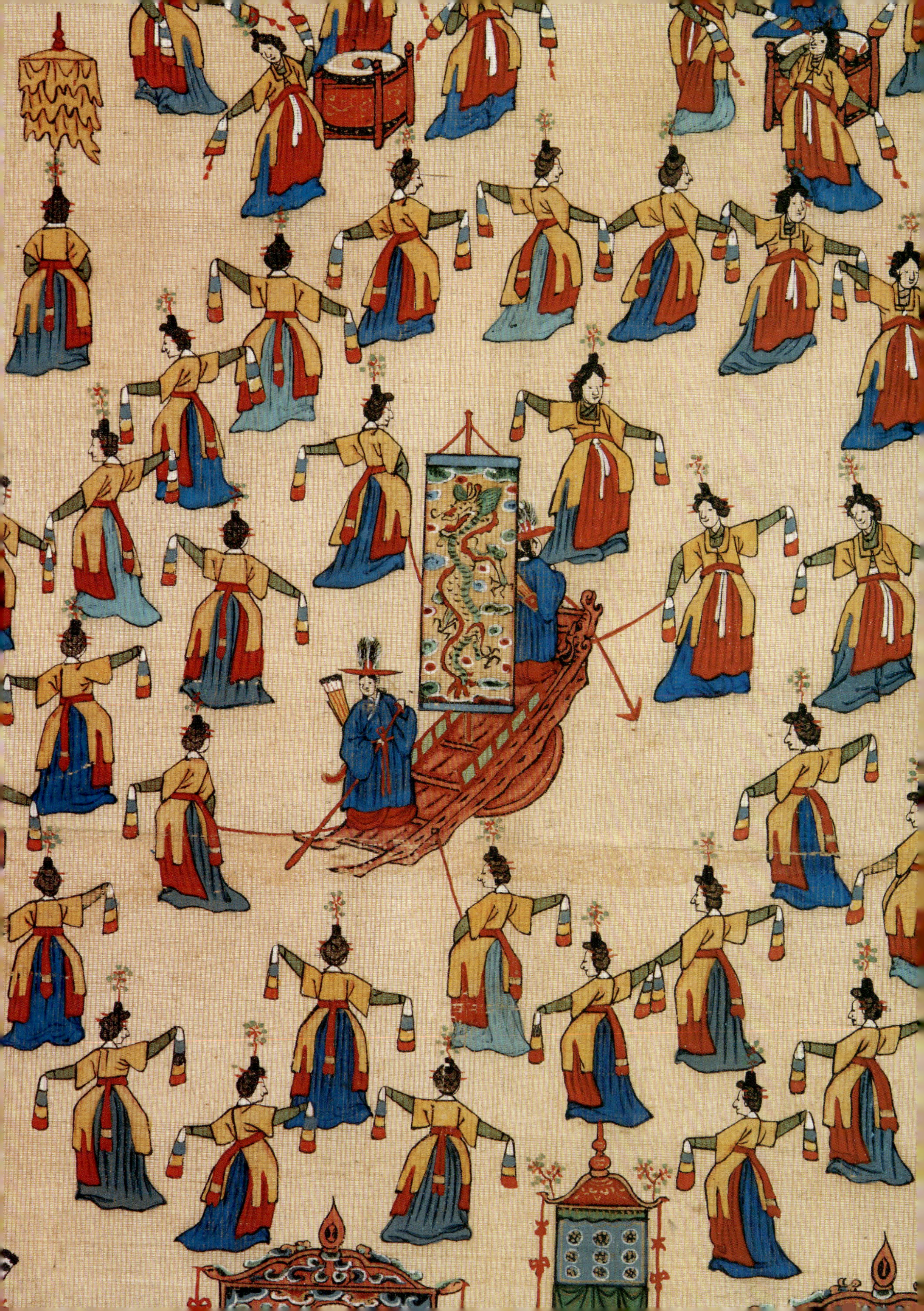

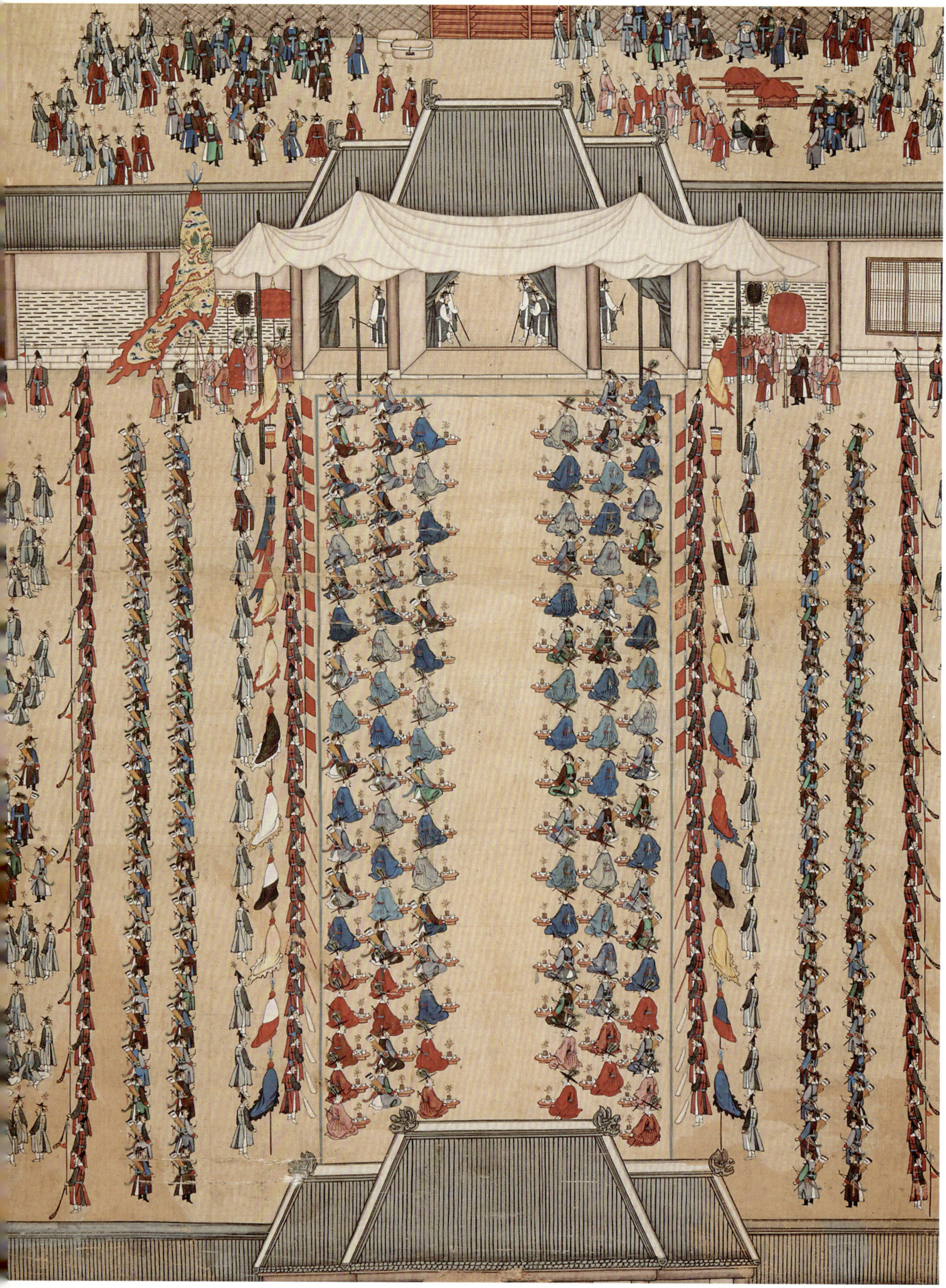

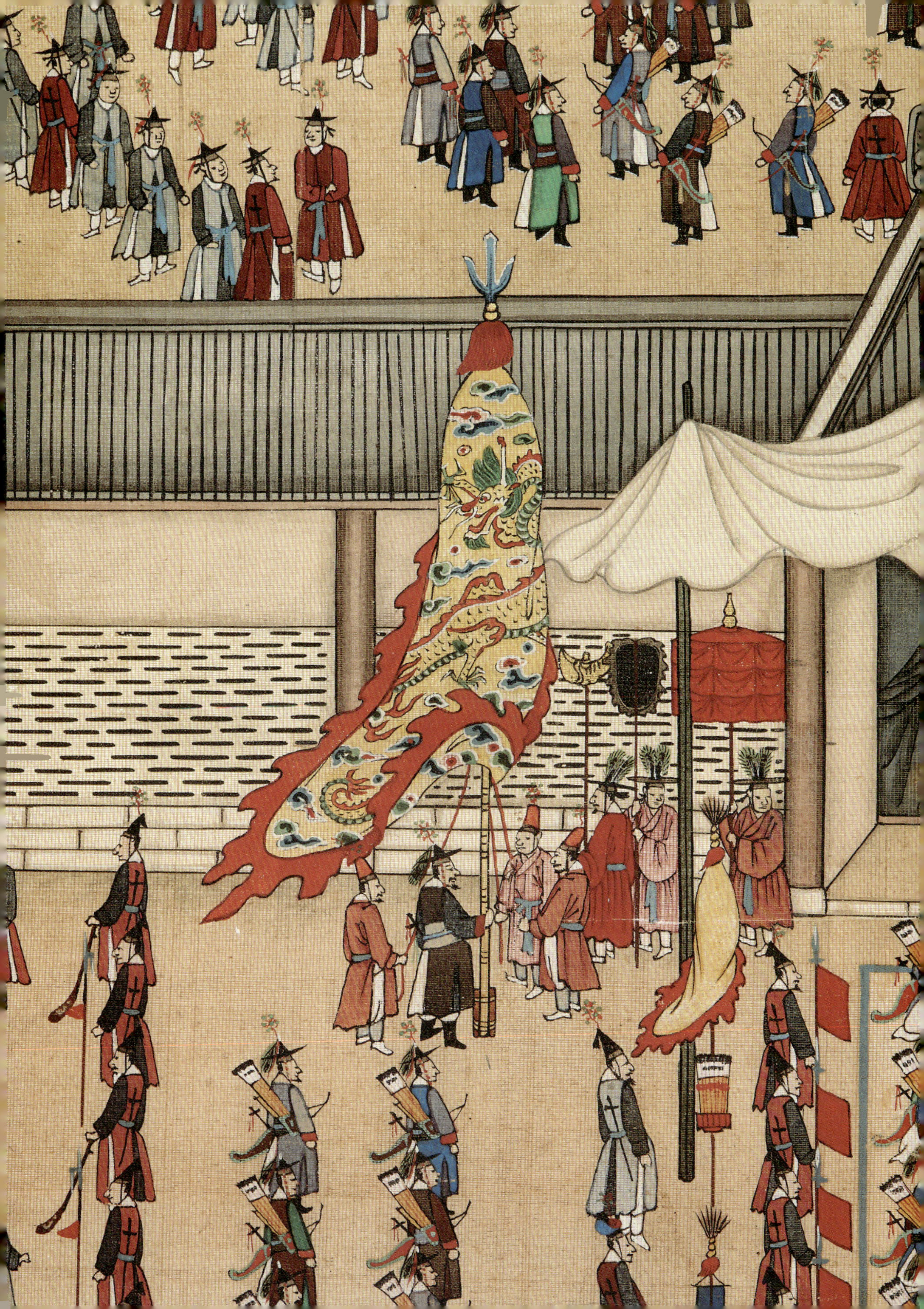

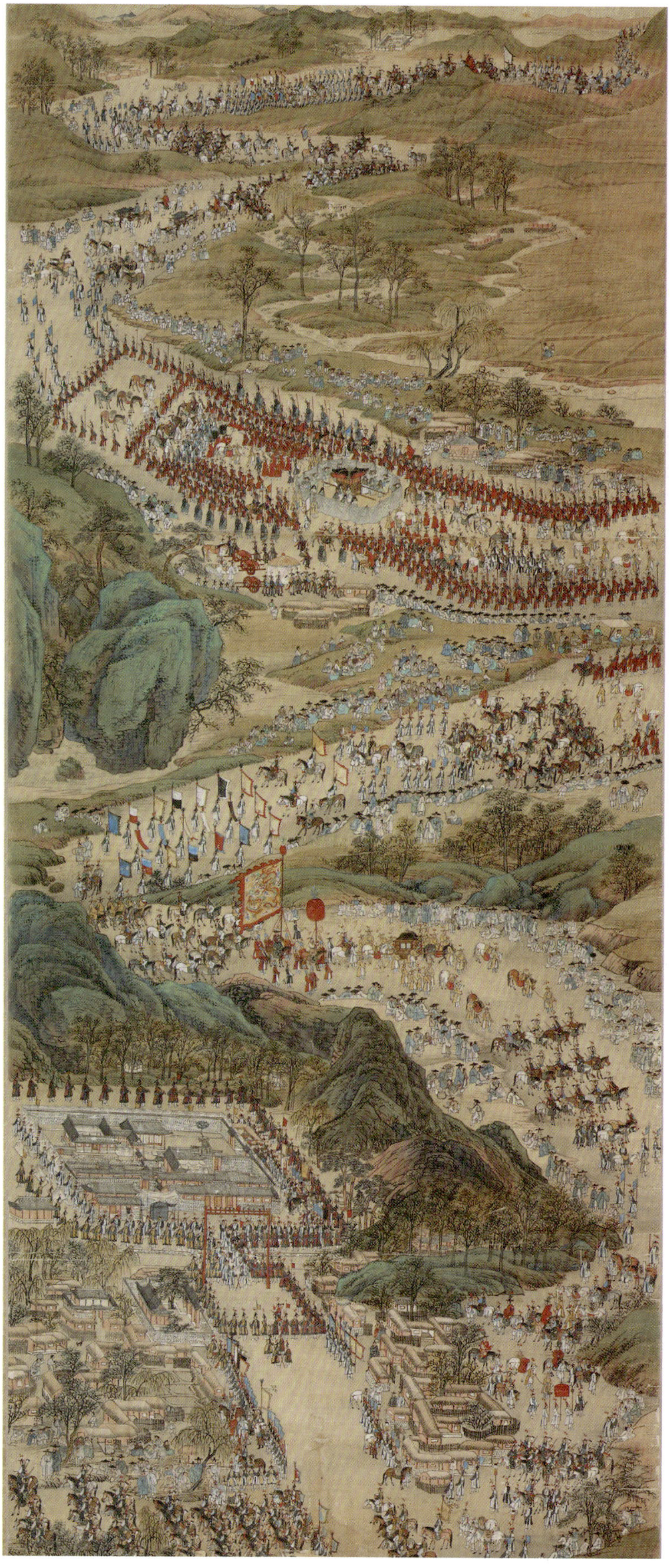

Royal Procession Back to Hanyang

Hwaneo Haengnyeoldo

Originally from *Screen Depicting King Jeongjo's Visit to Hwaseong* (*Hwaseong Haenghaeng Dobyeng*) / by **Kim Deuk-sin** et al. / 1795–1796 / ink and color on silk / 156.5 × 65.3 cm / Leeum, Samsung Museum of Art

Due to its excellent quality, this commemorative scene of King Jeongjo's procession back to Hanyang, or present-day Seoul, is considered a true masterpiece of Joseon court documentary paintings. Its exquisite quality clearly speaks to its usage; it is assumed to have come from a folding screen that was created for the viewing of the king himself.

Although the picture now remains as a free-standing hanging scroll, it was created as part of an eight-fold screen that also included the previous scroll, *Bongsudang Jinchando* (p. 115). Originally the seventh of eight panels, the painting records the royal procession of King Jeongjo and his mother, Lady Hyegyeong, marching into Siheung Palace, where they spent a night on their way back to Hanyang.

By employing layers of zigzagged roads, the painters managed to include thousands of people who were present for the royal procession—participants and bystanders alike. The large palanquin housing Lady Hyegyeong and the white horse behind it ridden by the king are undoubtedly most highly embellished; it is as if no single element was to be missed or simplified in this documentary scroll.

A closer examination reveals that the pursuit of such detailed documentation was not limited to the royal figures. Almost every participant wears a flower adornment on his or her headdress, though different groups of civil and military officers are distinguished according to their garments and accessories. Equally intriguing is the amusing depiction of the crowd who gathered to watch the procession. Individualized with natural poses and gestures, some on the lower ground throw curious looks at the procession, while others have come out to sell snacks.

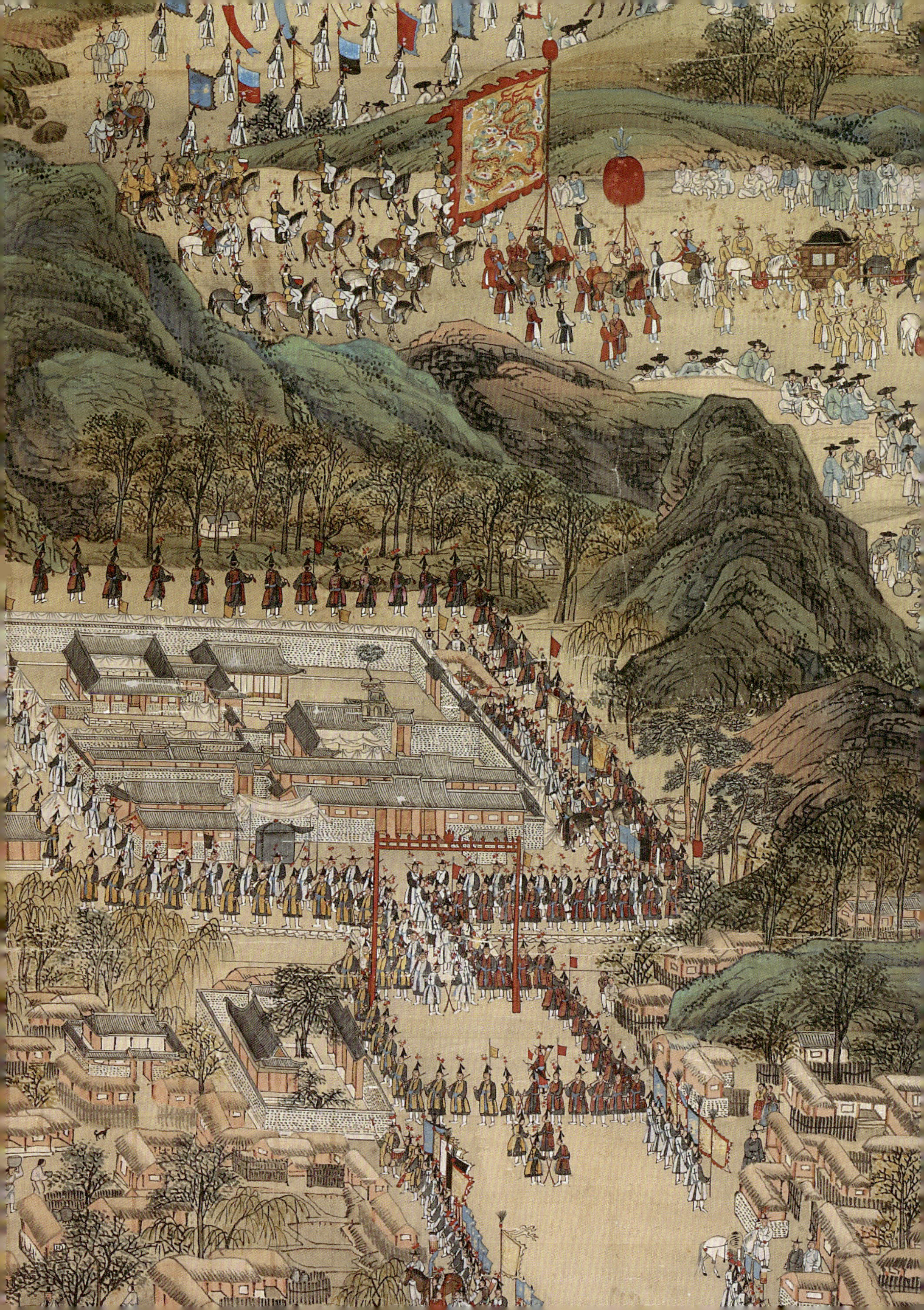

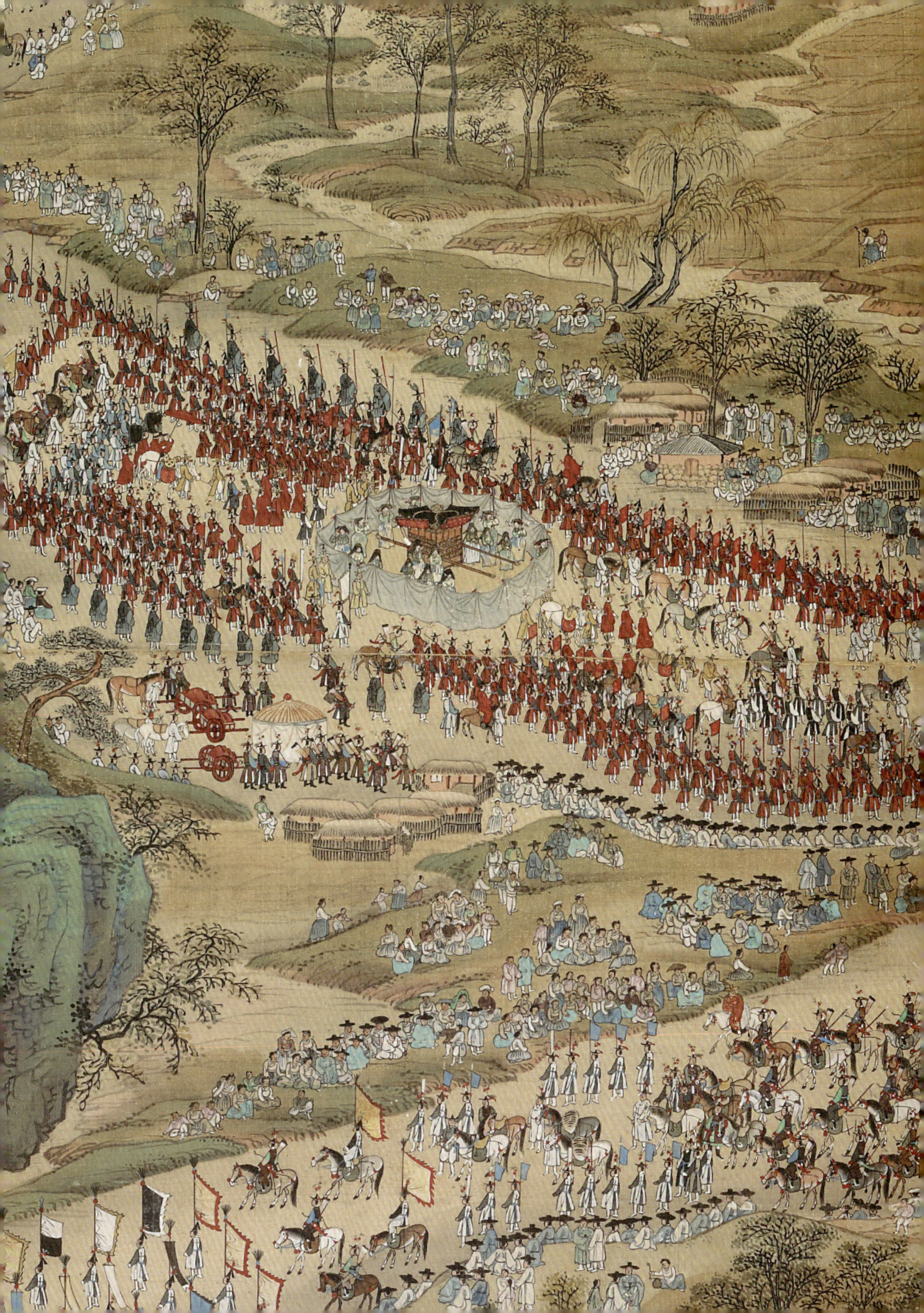

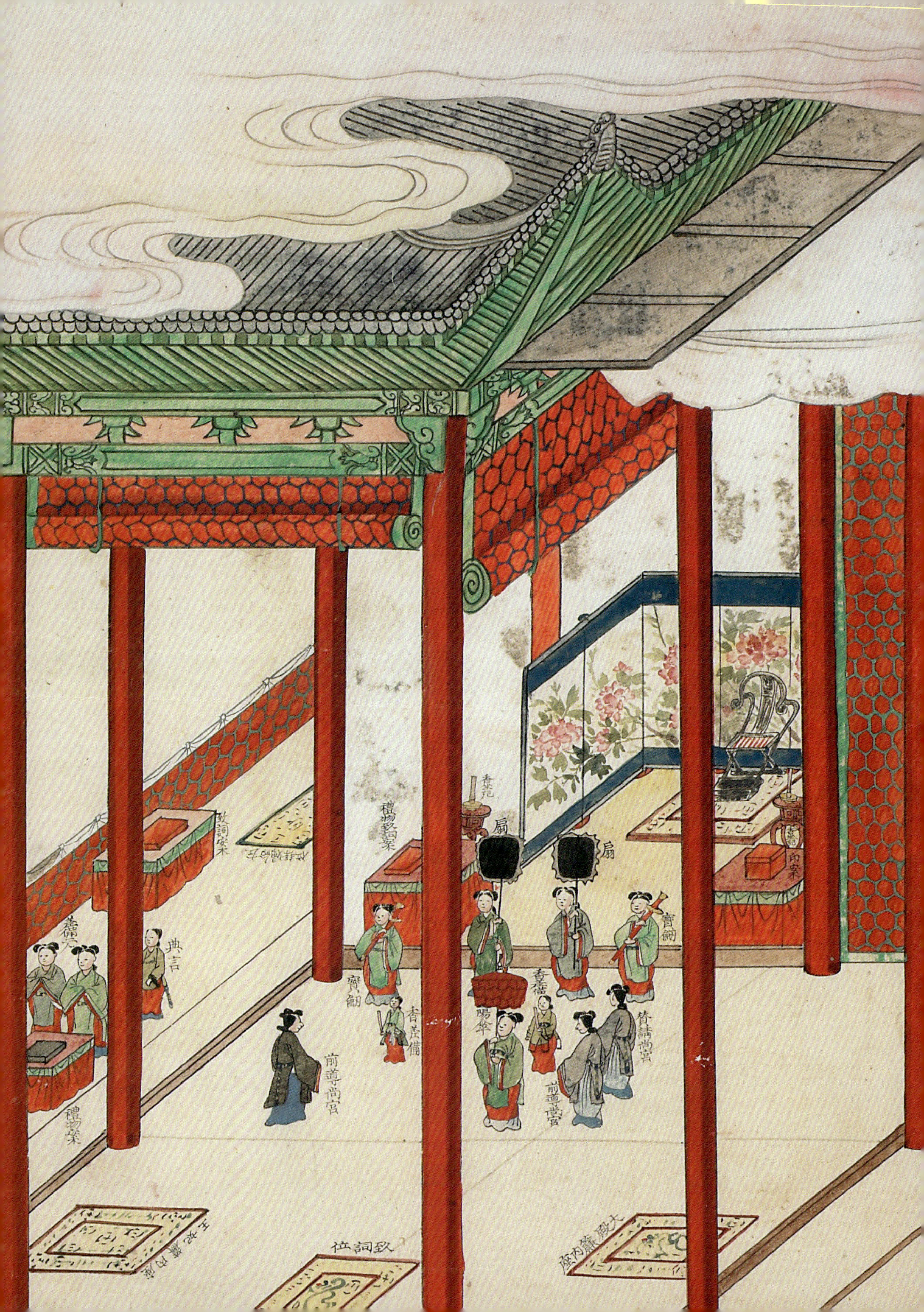
禮物致詞案
扇
扇
寶劒
典言
寶劒
香差備
陽傘
贊請尚宮
前導尚宮
前導尚宮
禮物案
致詞位

Court Banquet & Ceremony of Presenting the Cloth *Jinpyorido & Jinchando*

From *Uigwe for the Sixtieth Anniversary of Lady Hyegyeong's Coming-of-age Ceremony* (*Gisa Jinpyori Jinchan Uigwe*) / 1809 / ink and color on paper / 47.2 × 33.5 cm / The British Library

This *uigwe* (book of court rites) documents the entire event of the sixtieth anniversary of Lady Hyegyeong's *gwanrye*, or coming-of-age ceremony, in 1809. This is the only existing *uigwe* that commemorates the celebration of such an event for the royal family.

The first scene documents a ceremony in which precious cloth (*jinpyori*) is offered as a gift to Lady Hyegyeong, held on January 22 that year, and the second depicts a mid-sized court banquet (*jinchan*) held five days later, offered to promote the longevity of the birth mother of King Jeongjo. Both events were held at Gyeongchunjeon Hall at Changgyeonggung Palace, where Lady Hyegyeong resided.

After the ceremony, only three copies of *uigwe* were created: Two were offered to King Sunjo and Lady Hyegyeong, while this *uigwe* entry was stored at the Outer Kyujanggak Library at Ganghwado Island. In 1866, this copy was taken to France by the invading French armies. Both written and illustrated by hand, this *uigwe* is made in accordance with the style of other *uigwe* books that were made for the king's viewing.

On the *jinpyorido* (pp. 128–129), a silver chair and peony screens can be seen through the red columns. In the foreground, multiple mats are drawn; these indicate the areas where the king and queen bowed and offered the cloth to the lady. The second painting, *jinchando* (pp. 130–131) has a similar arrangement as the first one, though it includes lavish tables of food and a large group of musicians sitting in the lower right corner of the image.

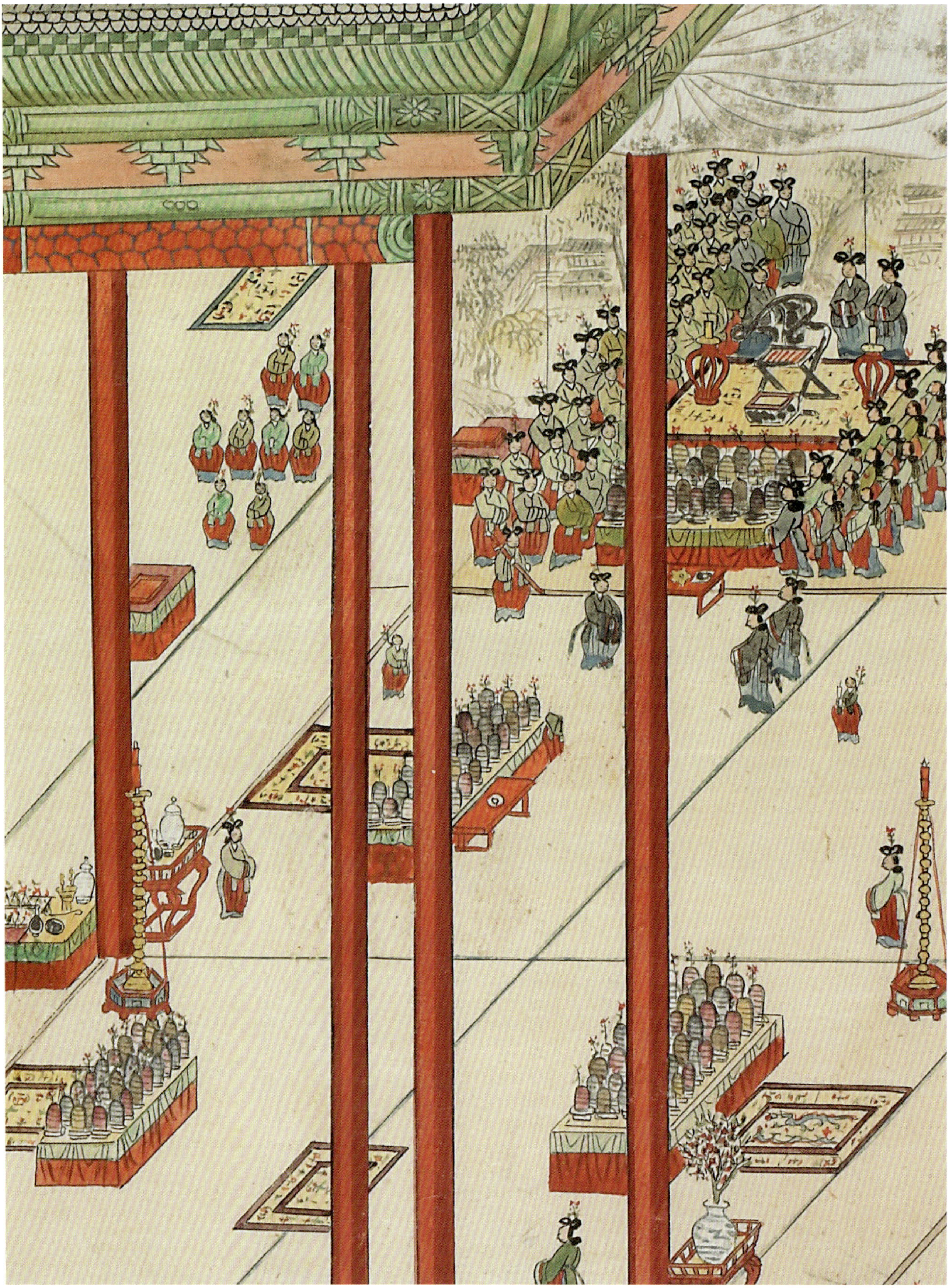

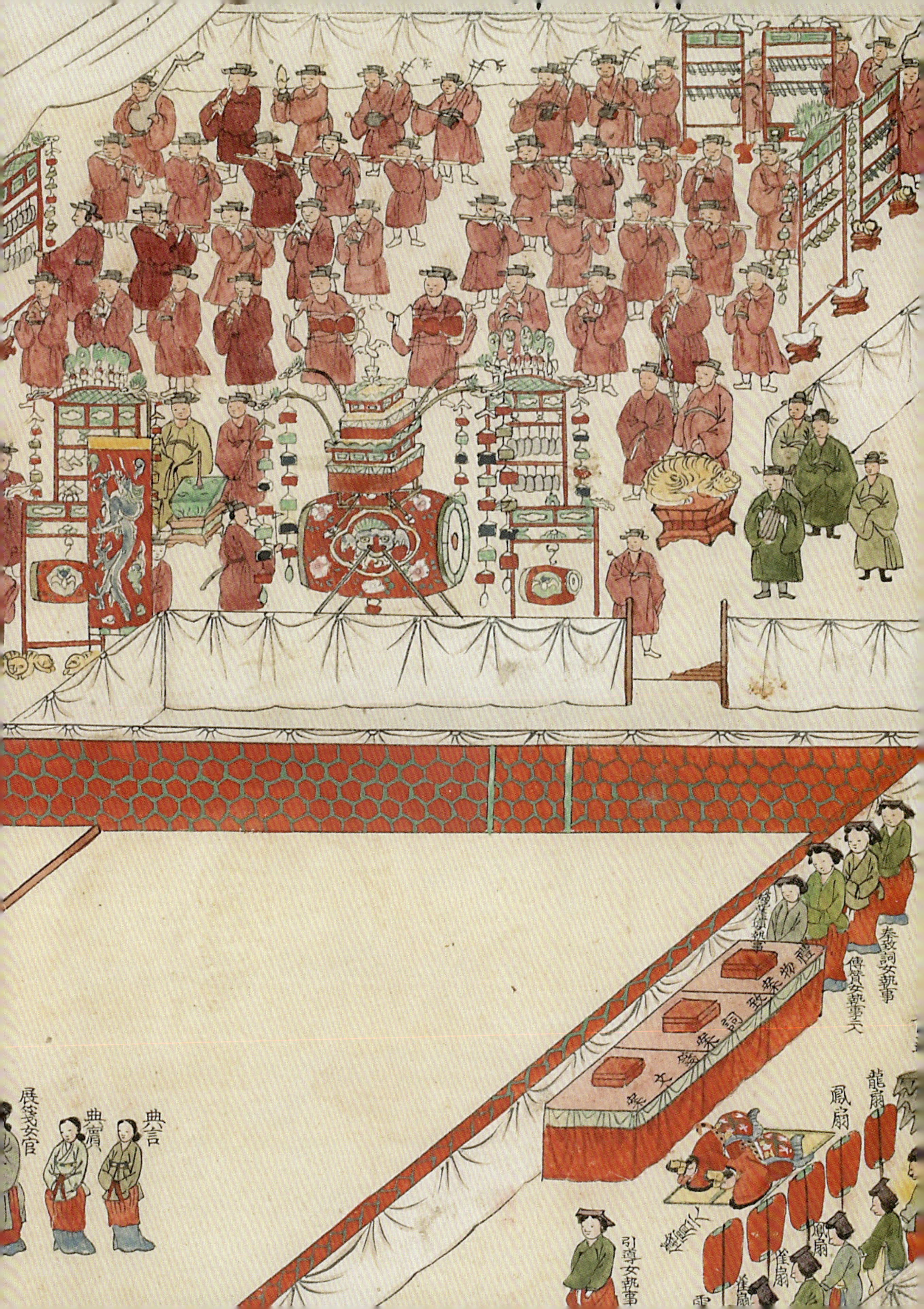
奏致詞女執事
禮物案
致詞案
箋文案
龍扇
鳳扇
鳳扇
雀扇
雀扇
典言
典賓
展箋女官
引導女執事

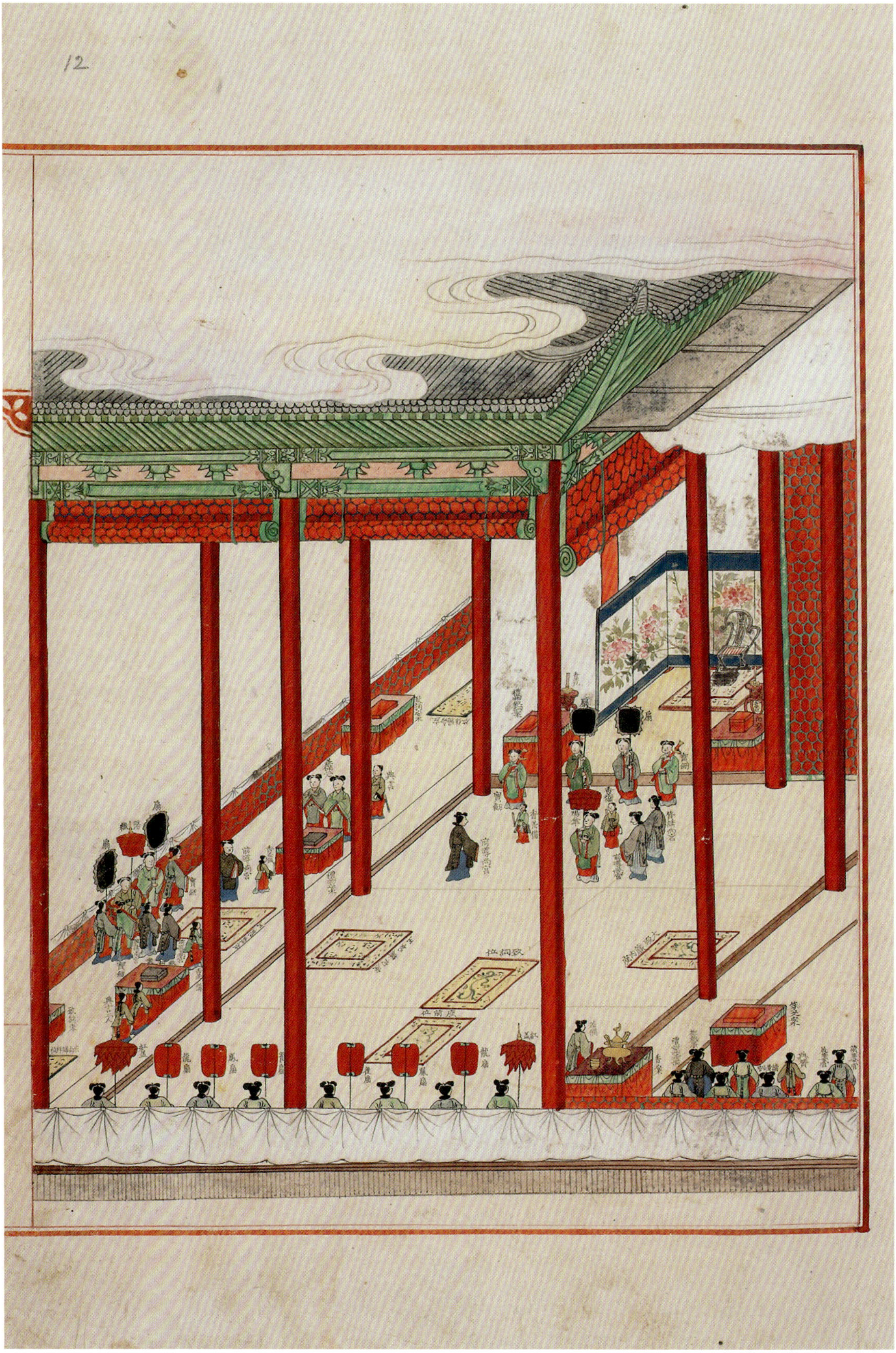

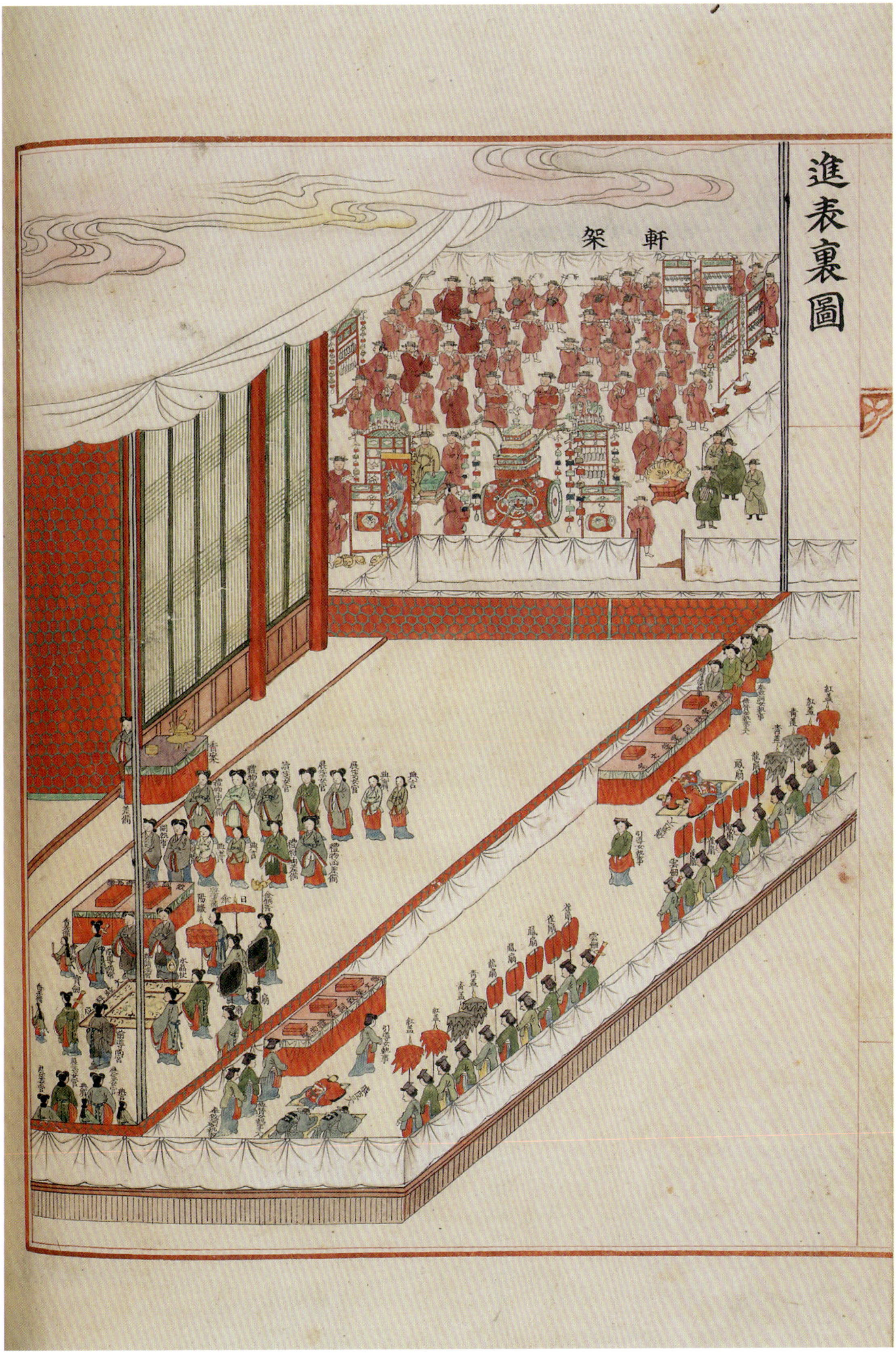
進表裏圖
軒架

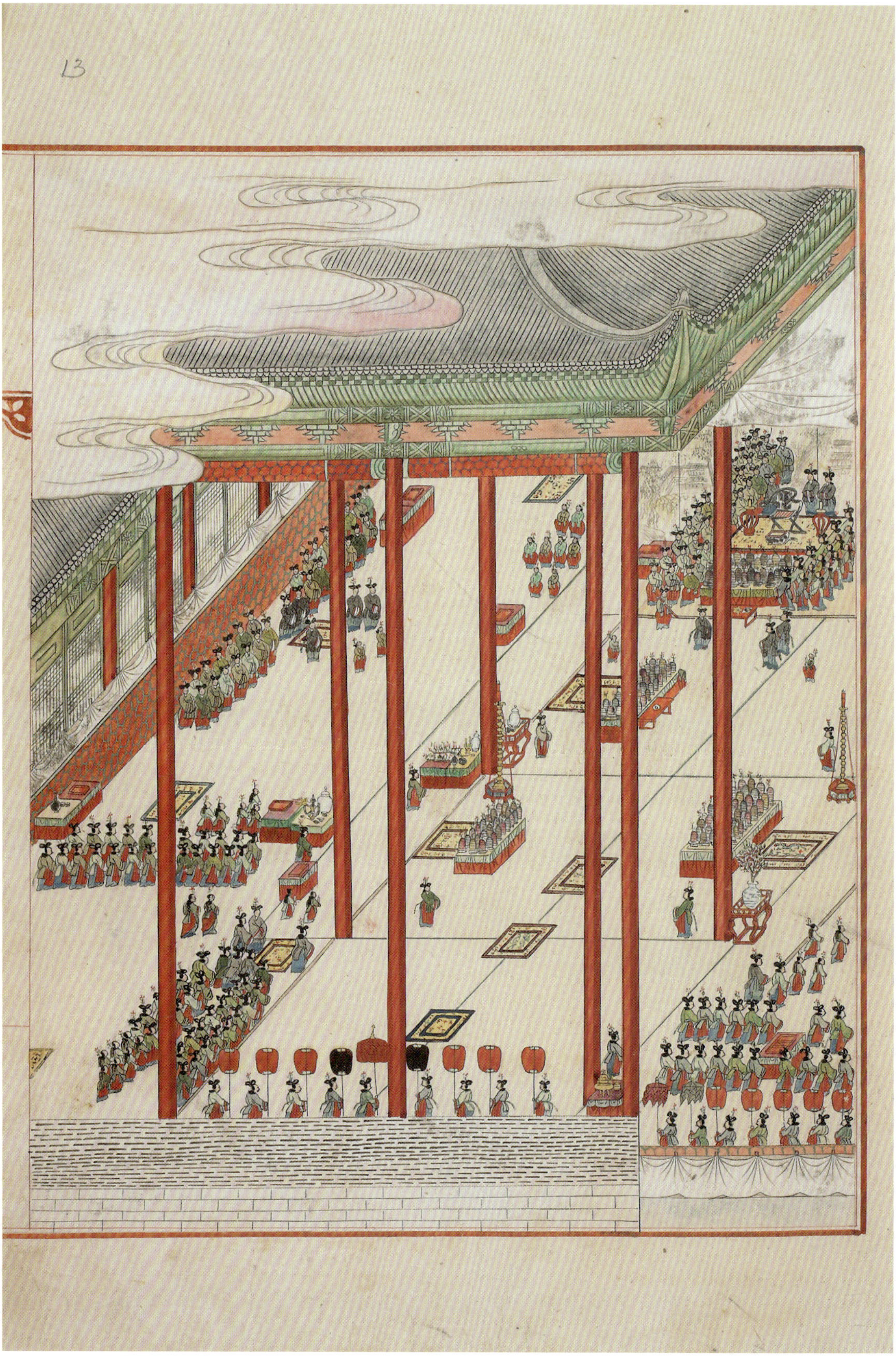
13

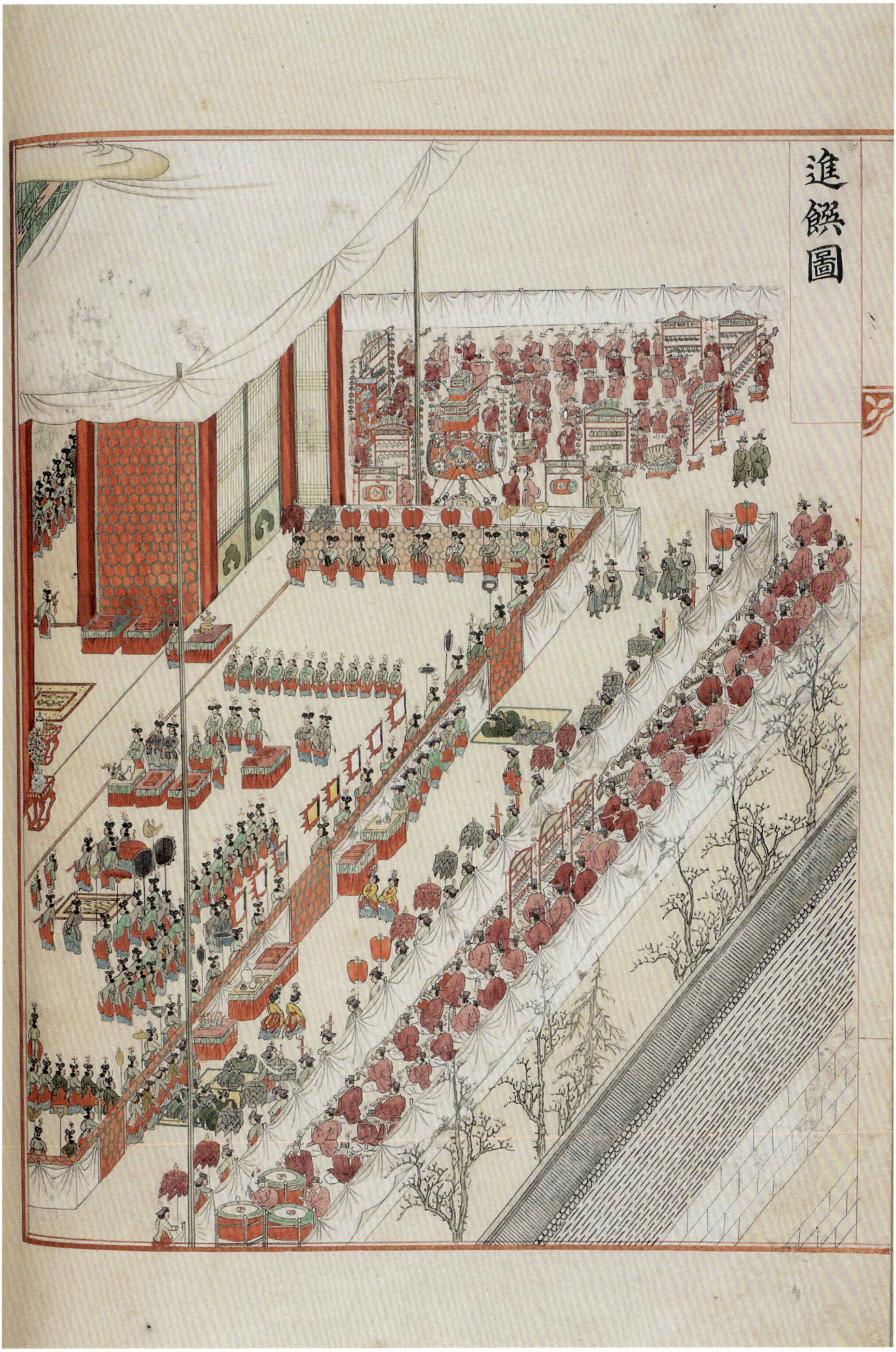
進饌圖

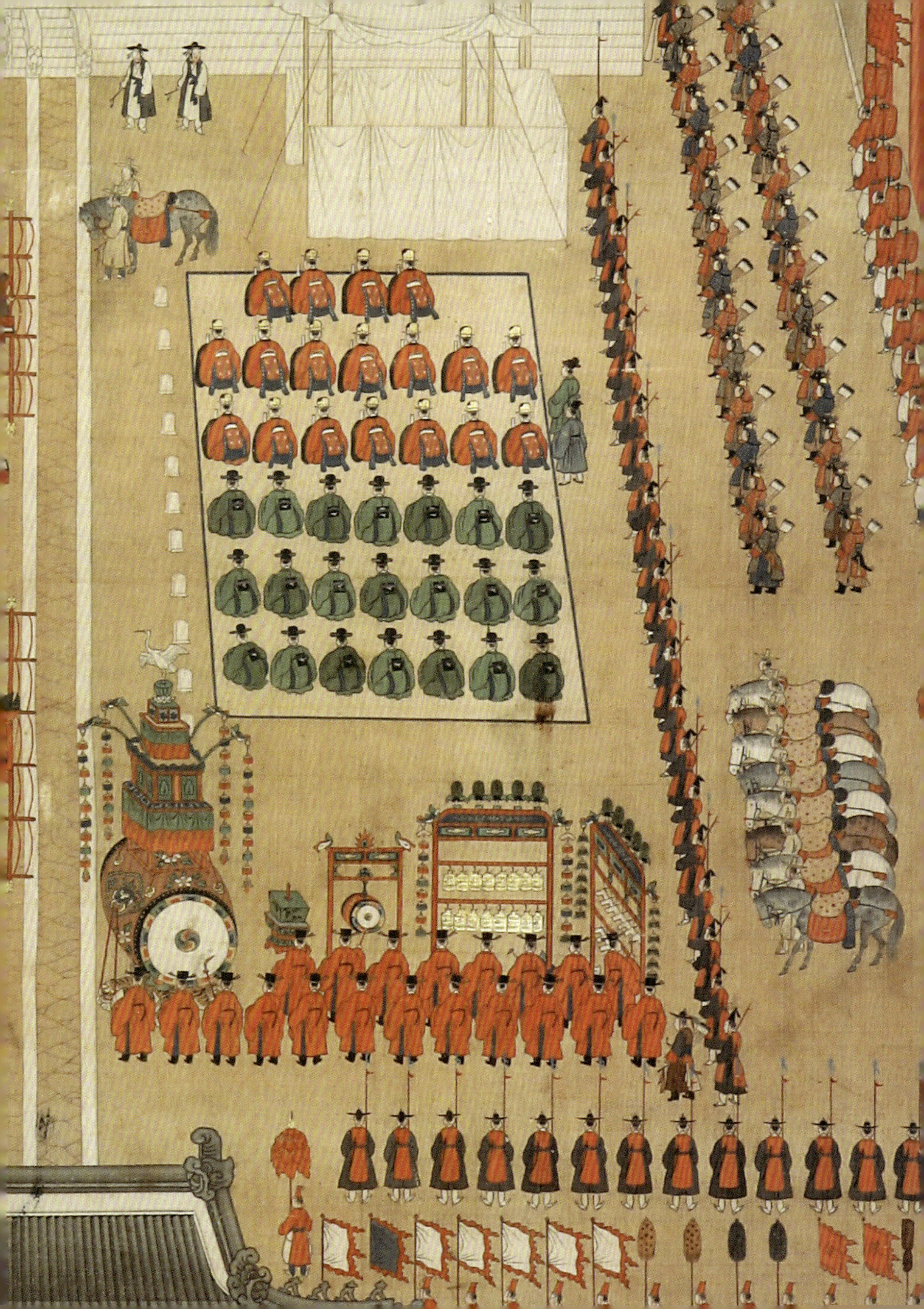

Grand Congratulatory Ceremony at Injeongjeon Hall & Day Banquet at Tongmyeongjeon Hall

Injeongjeon Jinhado & Tongmyeongjeon Jinchando

From the screen of *Court Banquets Celebrating the Fifty-Ninth Birthday of Grand Queen Dowager Sunwon* (*Musin Jinchan Dobyeong*) / by **Yi Han-cheol** et al. / 1848 / eight-fold screen / ink and color on silk / each panel, 136.1 × 47.6 cm / National Museum of Korea

In nineteenth-century Joseon, commemorative banquets for female members of the royal household were often held when these women had lived a long life. The full eight-panel screen, titled *Court Banquets Celebrating the Fifty-Ninth Birthday of Grand Queen Dowager Sunwon* (*Musin Jinchan Dobyeong*), depicts the 1848 ceremonies that commemorated the fifty-ninth birthday of King Heonjong's grandmother, Grand Queen Dowager Sunwon (1789–1857), and the forty-first birthday of the king's mother, Queen Dowager Sinjeong (1808–1890).

Starting from the right, the first two panels (*Grand Congratulatory Ceremony at Injeongjeon Hall*, p. 137) of the screen depict the scene in which the congratulatory ceremony (*jinharye*) was held in Injeongjeon Hall at Changdeokgung Palace on March 16. Panels three and four (*Day Banquet at Tongmyeongjeon Hall*, p. 136) portray the scene of a mid-sized day banquet (*jinchan*) and panels five and six depict the scene of a night banquet (*yajinchan*) on the third day. The seventh panel portrays a reception banquet (*hoejak*) that King Heonjong (r. 1834–1849) presented to the officials who prepared and administered the banquets. Located at the far left, the last panel lists the names and titles of those who oversaw the ceremony. The three banquets were held in Tongmyeongjeon Hall at the same palace.

All four scenes employ a semi-linear perspective in which figures get smaller on the upper portion of the background, emphasizing the grand scale of the space and ceremony. The naturalistic depiction, especially in the architectural structure—roofs, columns, and stairs—is further reinforced by the use of the Western technique of chiaroscuro. For the latter three panels, the banquet spaces are divided into different sections using screens made of red silk and bamboo according to the participant's status and gender. The use of these divisive red walls has the effect of reinforcing the liveliness of banquet scenes. The format of this painting influenced the style of royal banquet screens in the years that followed, an impact that was felt until the early twentieth century.

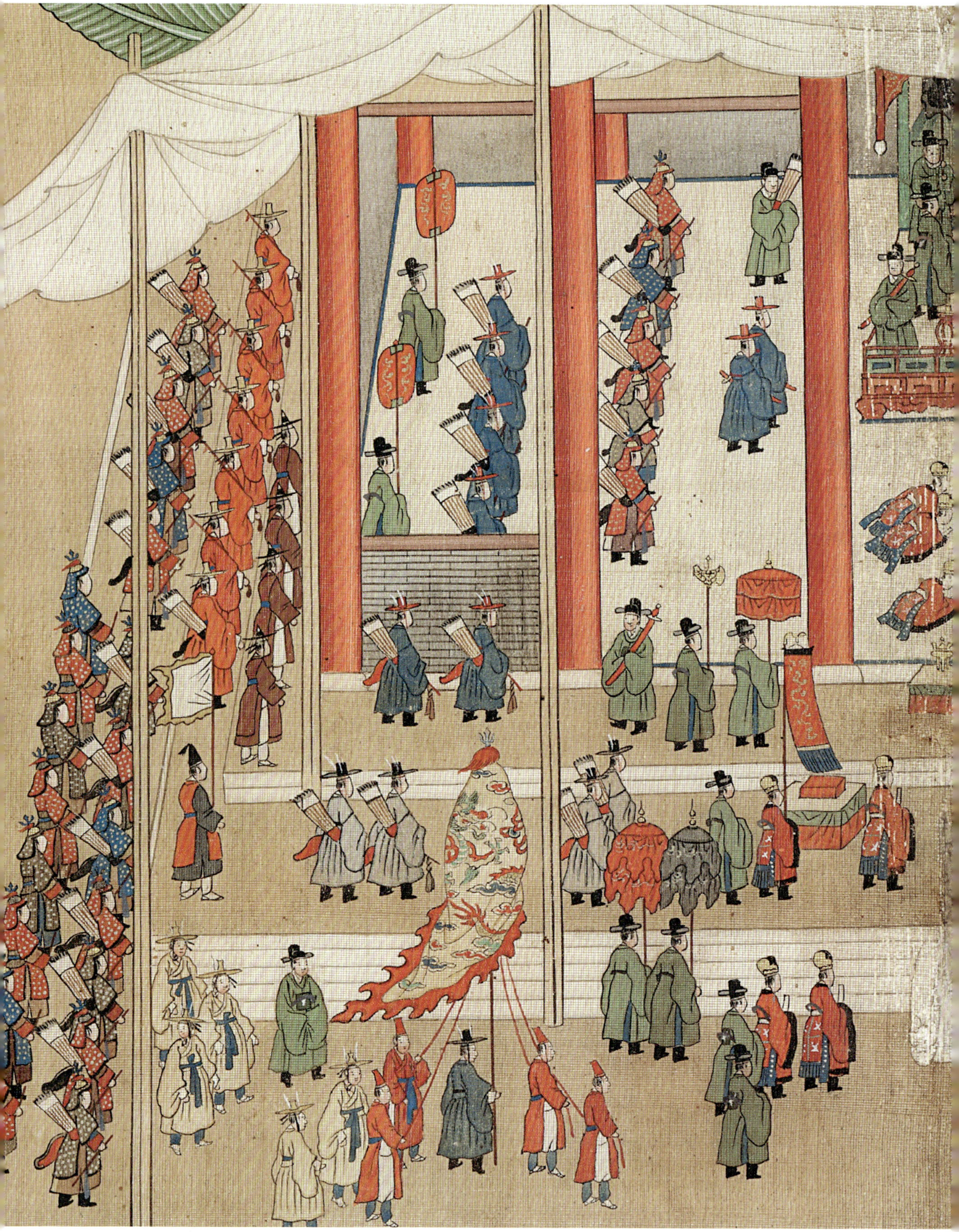

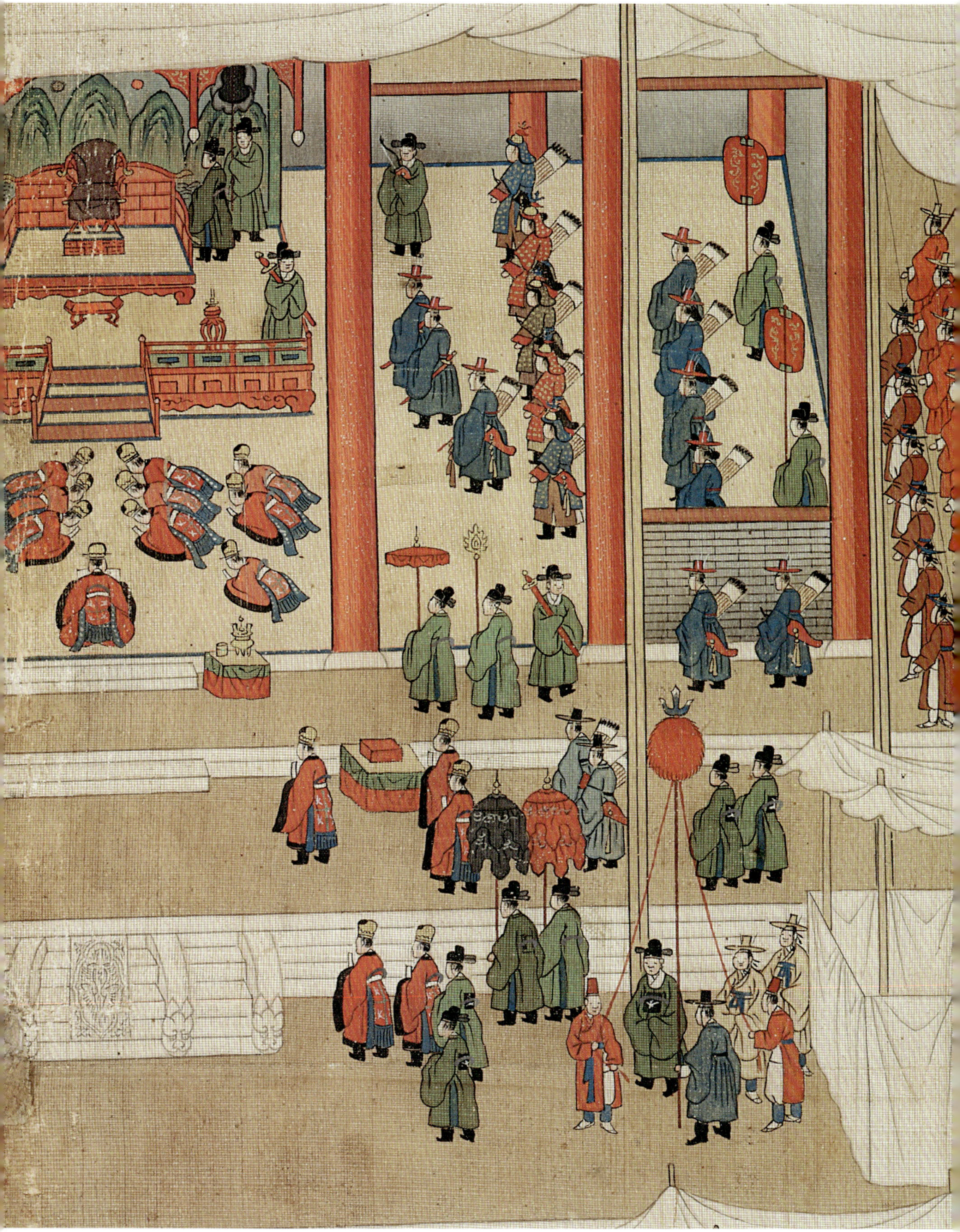

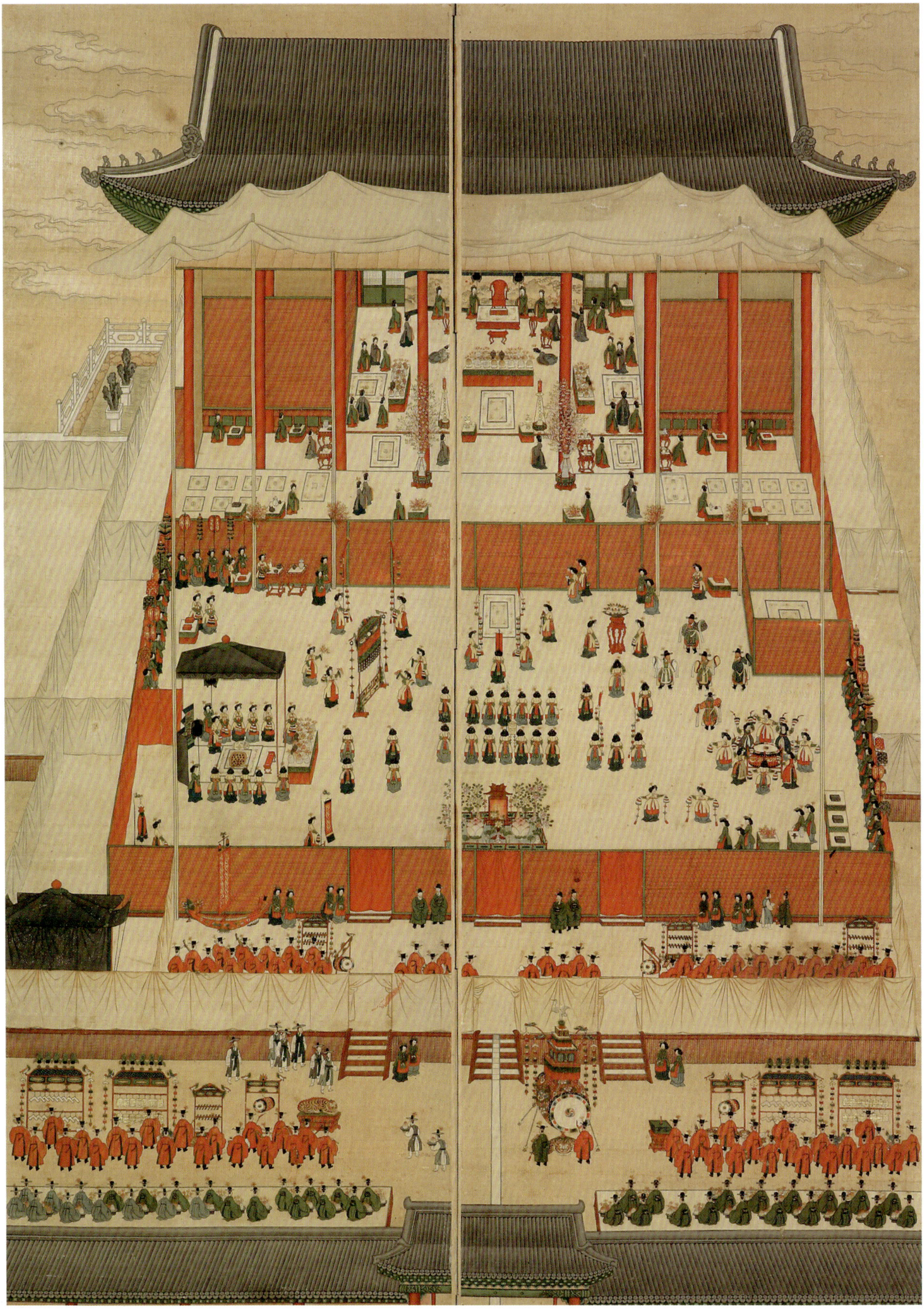

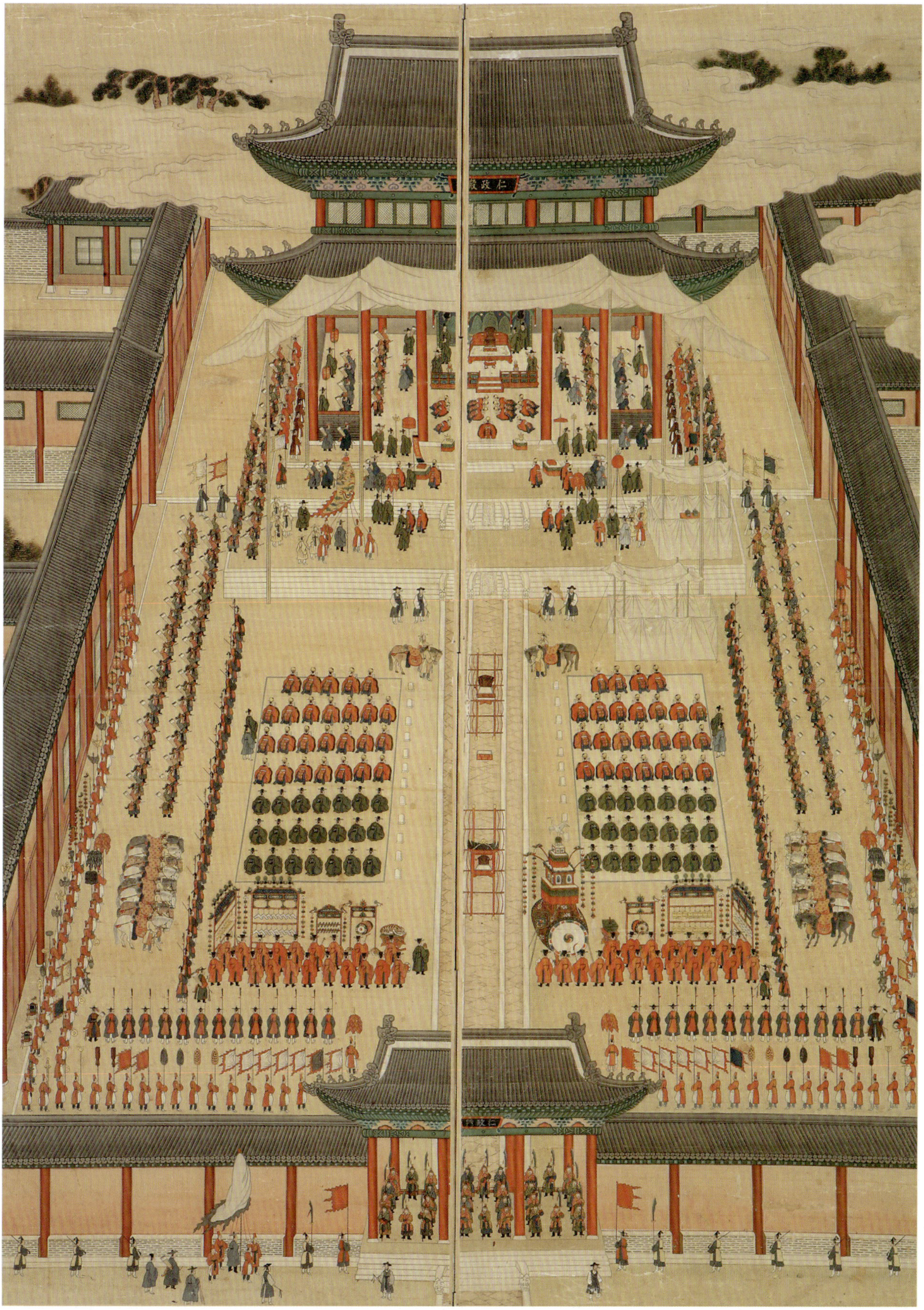
殿政仁
門政仁

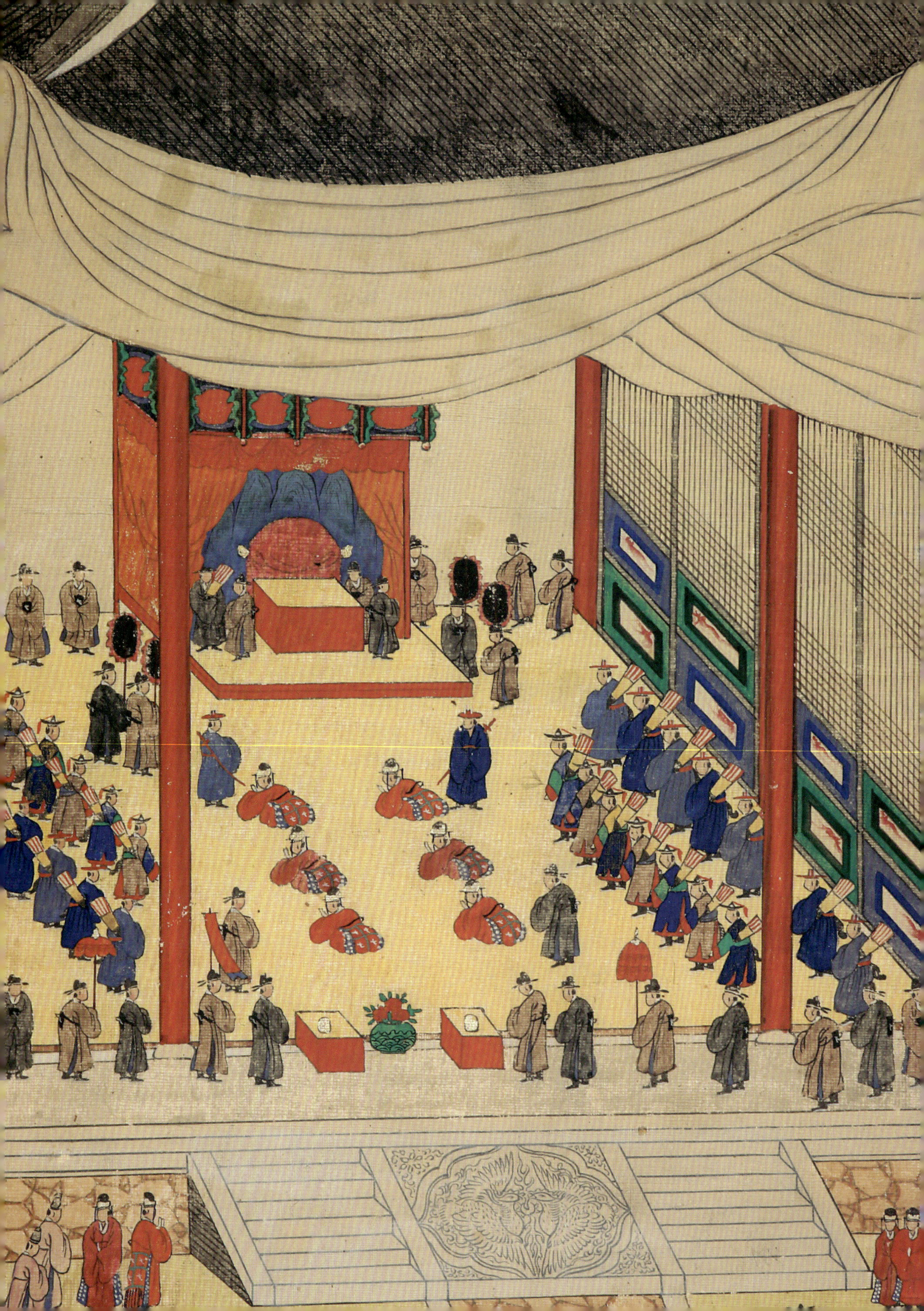

The Grand Congratulatory Ceremony for the Birth of Crown Prince Yi Cheok

Wangseja Tangang Jinha Dobyeong

1874 / ten-fold screen / ink and color on silk / each panel, 101.2 × 41.5 cm / National Museum of Korea

This documentary screen painting commemorates the birth of the second son of King Gojong and Queen Min (posthumously known as Empress Myeongseong) on February 8, 1874, who would later be known as Emperor Sunjong. Since Gojong's first son died during childbirth, the second born automatically became the eldest royal son (*wonja*), an event that warranted one of the biggest celebrations in court. This painting depicts the ceremony, which was held in Injeongjeon Hall of Changdeokgung Palace.

The second through ninth panels illustrate the banquet in detail: The royal throne (referring to the king), his guards, and civil and military officials in their appropriate robes— golden crown and ceremonial attire—have gathered for the special occasion. The panoramic composition and the use of perspective, which creates a sense of distance and scale, reinforce the significance of the event.

The architectural setting around the main audience hall is accurately illustrated, save for a few omissions; a layer of auspicious clouds covers the rest of the palatial complex beyond Injeongjeon Hall and the garden in the mountains on the right refers to the Rear Garden, or *huwon*. Such a painstaking rendering of the architecture indicates the influence of the techniques and visual aesthetics developed by the court painters of *Donggwoldo* (p. 15).

That the work was commissioned by the officials of the Royal Maternity Directorate, a temporary office established for the queen's childbirth, is indicated on the first and last panels. These panels enumerate the names and titles of related figures, such as an official from the Office of Royal Medicine or doctors who had been recruited to the court from outside the capital.

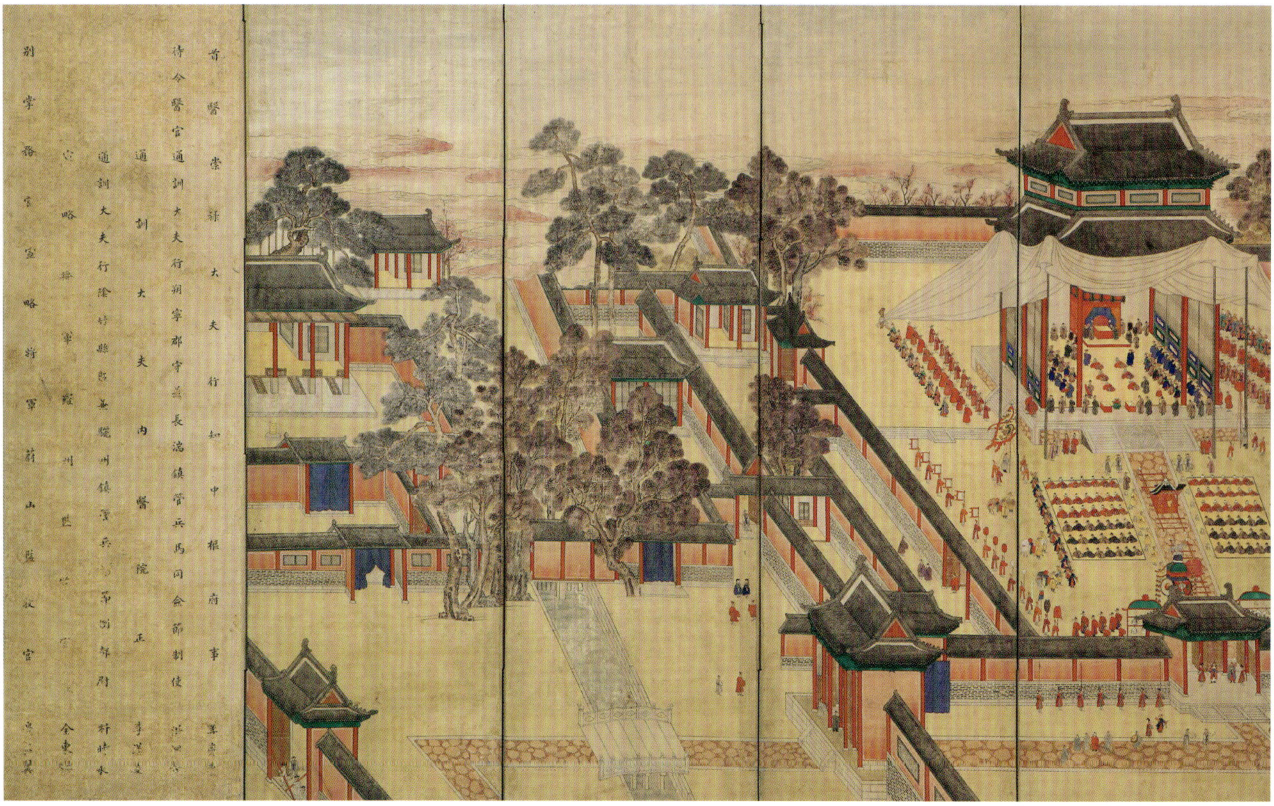

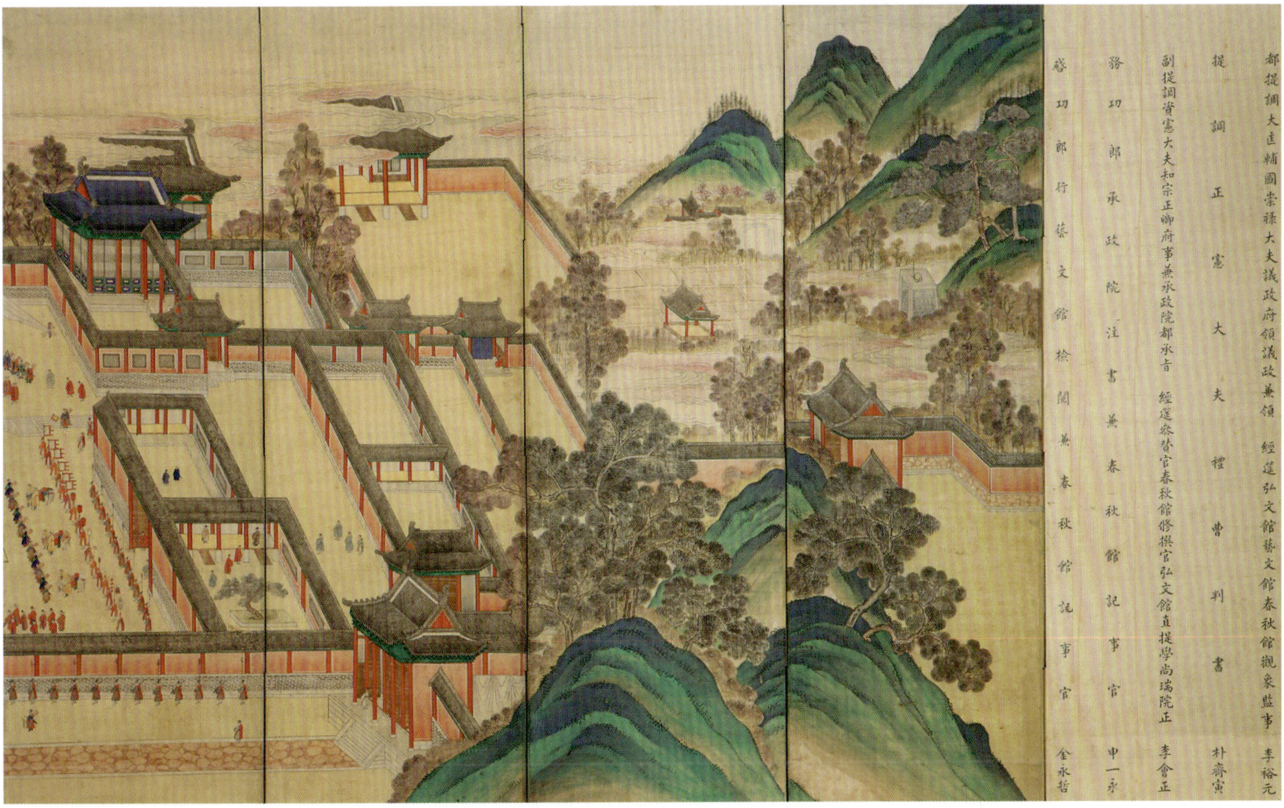
都提調大匡輔國崇祿大夫議政府領議政兼領 經筵弘文館藝文館春秋館觀象監事 李裕元
提調正憲大夫禮曹判書 朴齊寅
副提調資憲大夫知宗正卿府事兼承政院都承旨 經筵參贊官春秋館修撰官弘文館直提學尚瑞院正 李會正
務功郎承政院注書兼春秋館記事官 申一永
啓功郎行藝文館檢閱兼春秋館記事官 金永哲

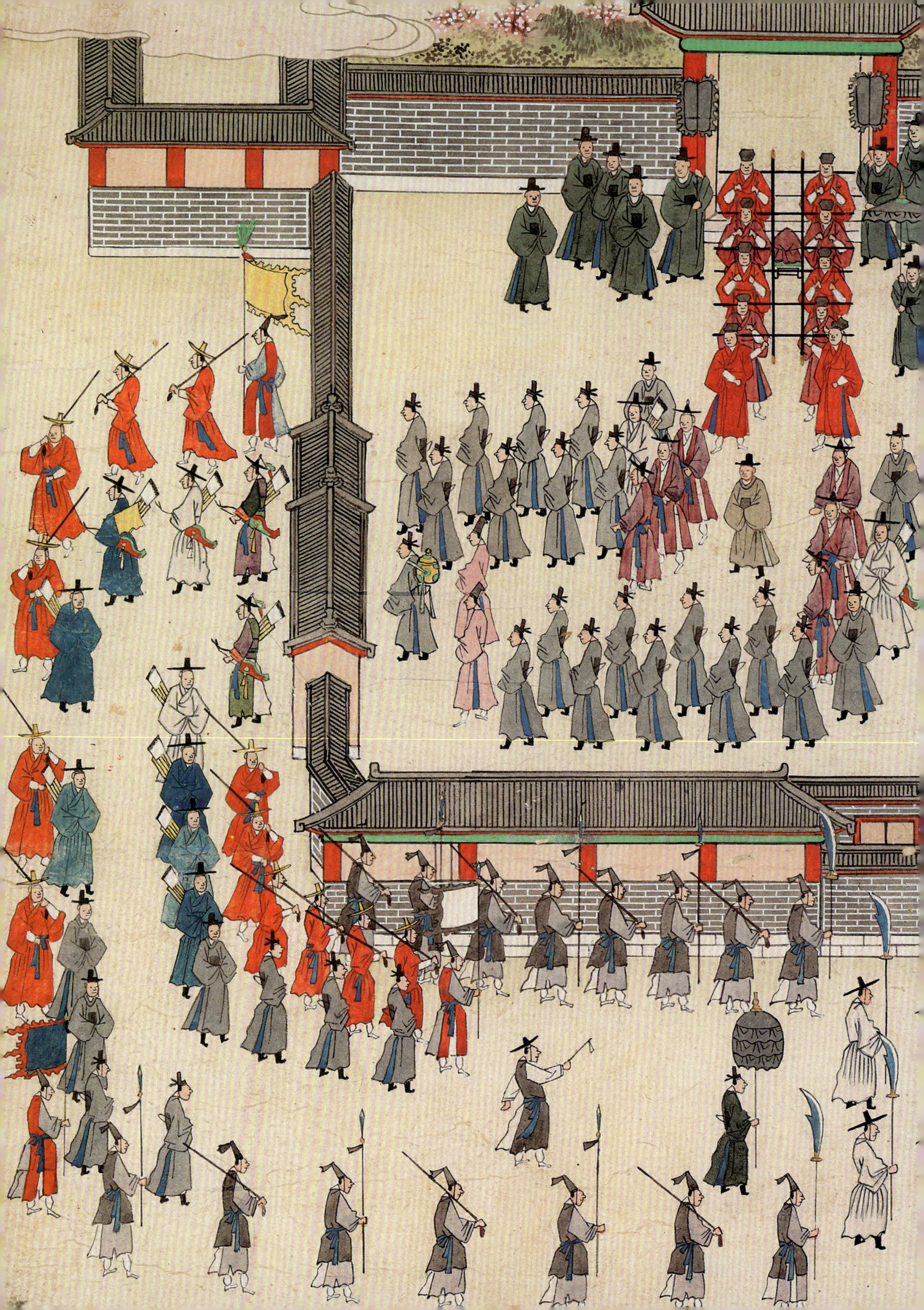

The Crown Prince's Procession Departing from the Palace *Chulgungdo*

First scene from *Crown Prince Yi Yeong's Entrance Ceremony to the Royal Confucian Academy* (*Wangseja Ipakdocheob*) / 1817 / painting album / ink and color on paper / 37.8 × 50 cm / National Research Institute of Cultural Heritage

This painting album contains six painted scenes of the entrance ceremony of nine-year-old Crown Prince Hyomyeong (1809–1830) in Seonggyungwan, Royal Confucian Academy, on March 11, 1817. As part of the admission ceremony, the prince visited Seonggyungwan, worshipped at Daeseongjeon Hall (the Hall of Confucius), and paid homage to his future professors at Myeongryundang Hall. The symbolic ceremony served as the official announcement that the prince was to be a student of Confucian principles.

The album consists of the paintings; their corresponding captions, which outline the process of the ceremony; a series of congratulatory poems written by the thirteen officers at the Office of Education of the Crown Prince, who administered the ceremony; and, lastly, an epilogue written by Nam Gong-cheol (1760–1840).

The first of the six painted scenes, *Chulgungdo*, portrays the procession of Prince Hyomyeong as he exits his residence, Junghuidang Hall, and heads toward Seonggyungwan. The crown prince's open palanquin, hoisted by eight carriers, has just passed through a door in the upper left corner toward the west. A guard who bears the seal of the crown prince is about to pass through another door on the left. In the lower right, various ceremonial flags and horses, decorated to represent the crown prince, lead the procession, escorted by a group of honor guards. The architectural depiction is done with enough detail that viewers can make out the bricks on wall, and the manner in which the pine trees were done by fine brushstrokes gives a sense of season.

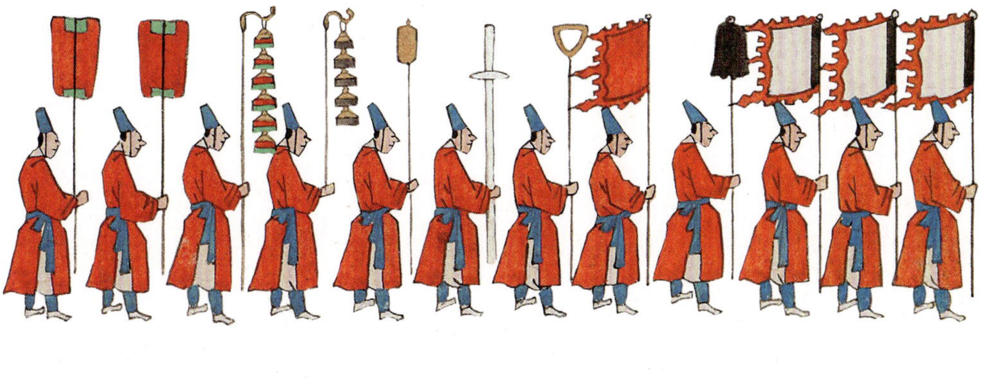

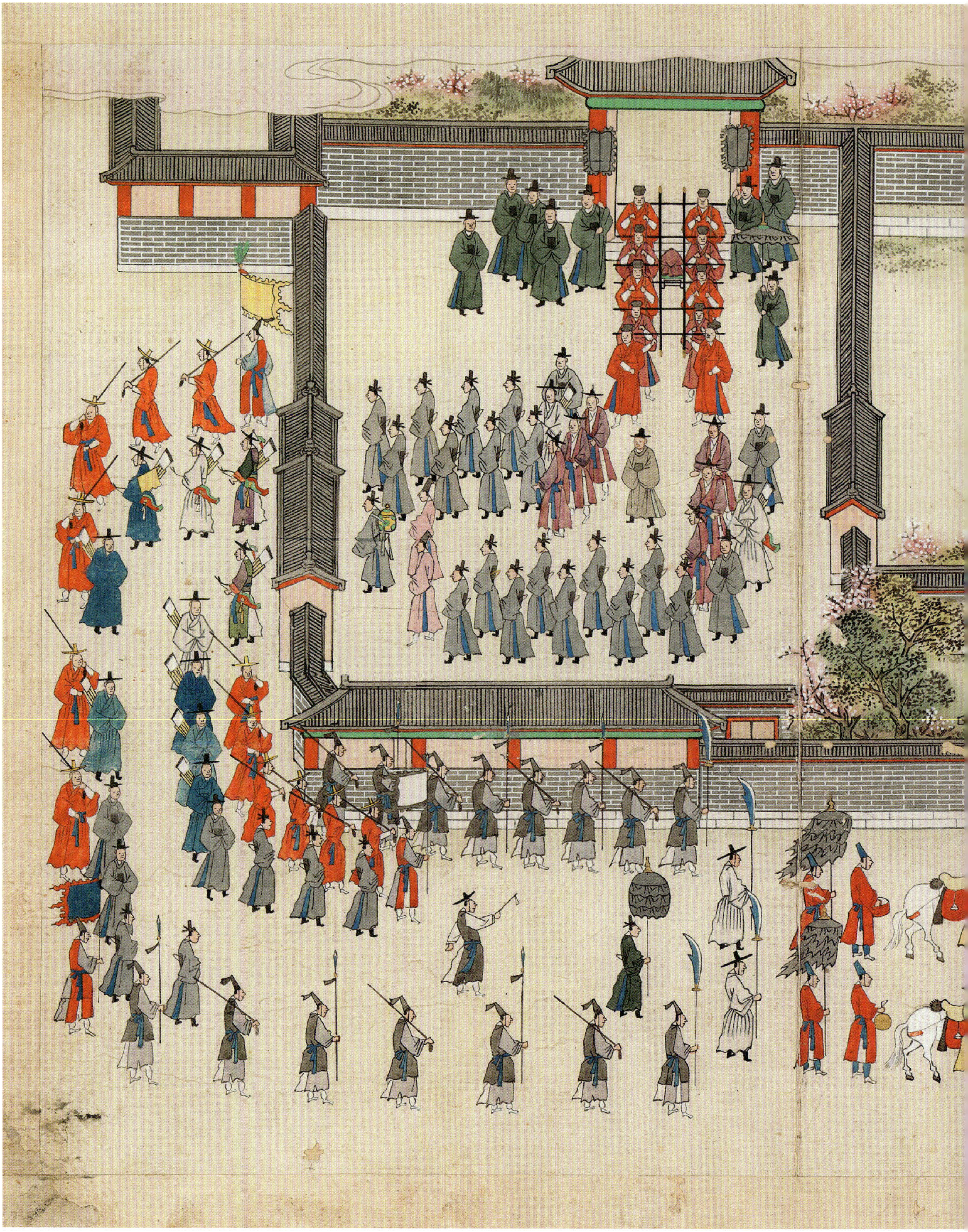

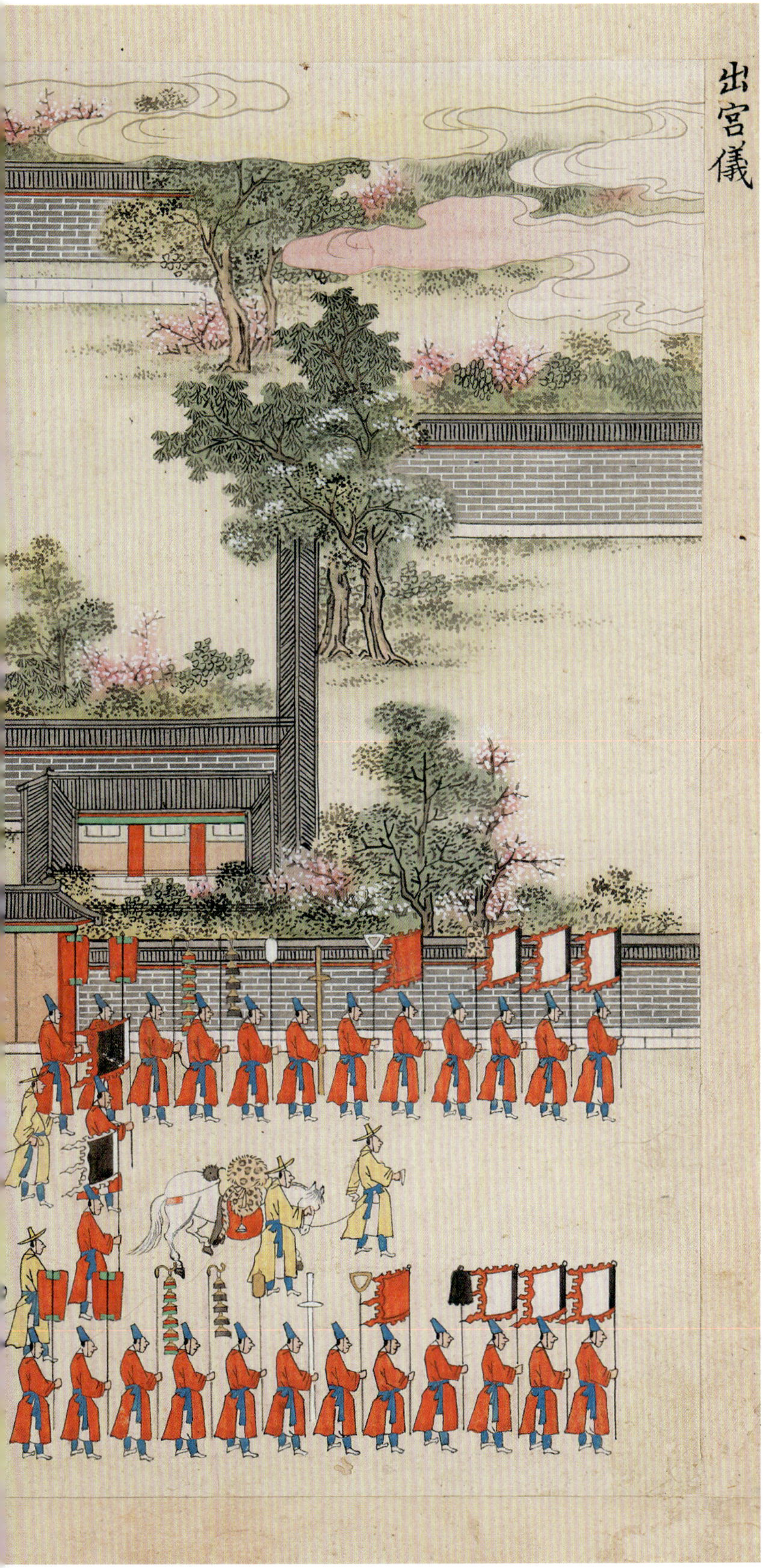
出宮儀

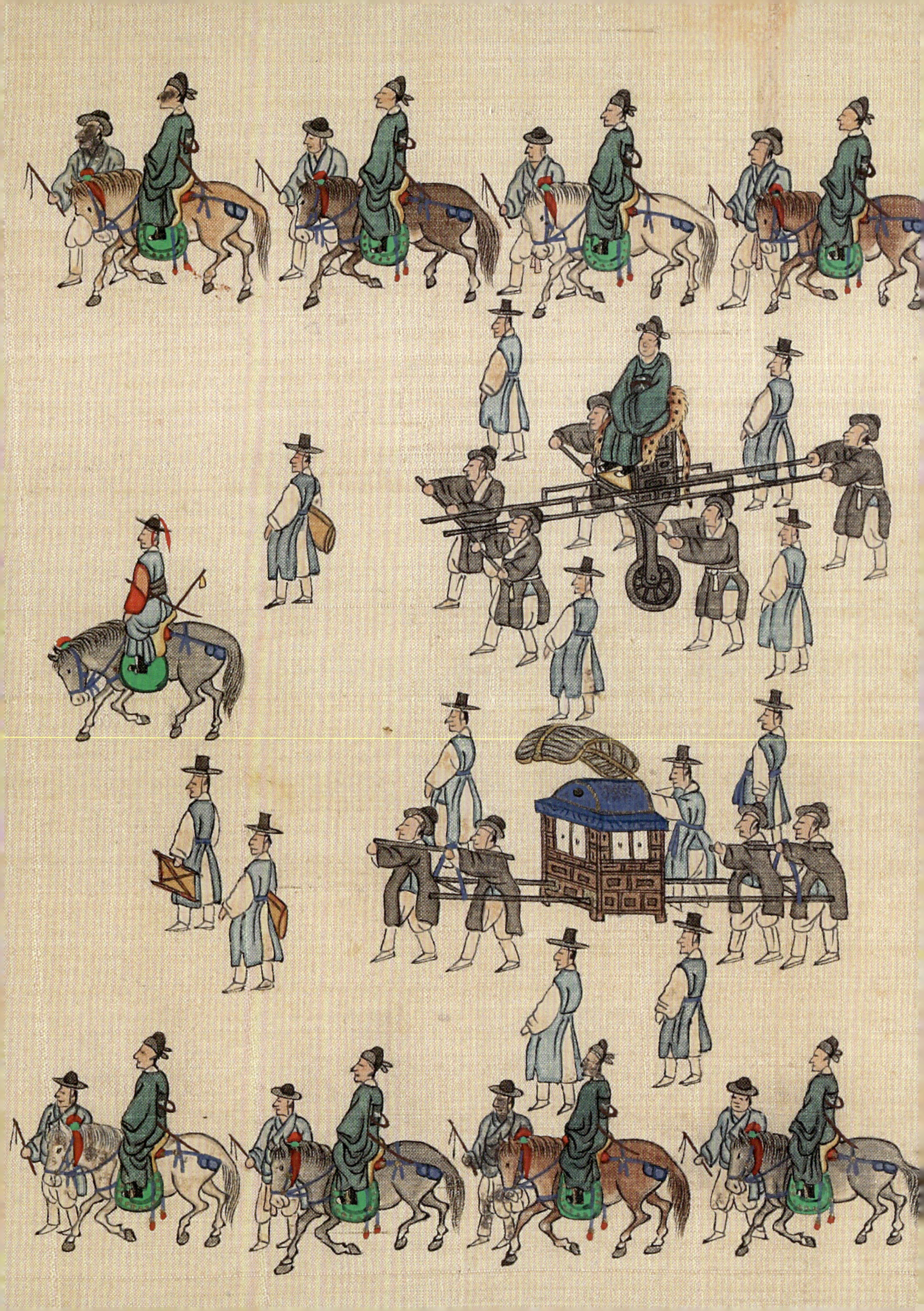

Rank-positioned Procession of a Royal Visit

Dongga Banchado

Late 19th century / ink and color on paper / 31 × 996 cm / Leeum, Samsung Museum of Art
(The images for this painiting in this book show only part of the whole work.)

A *banchado* is a royal documentary painting that records various ceremonies held in court in great detail. In order to serve this purpose, details such as the location of individuals in the procession, the costumes worn, and the accessories carried were all included as a means of distinguishing the social rank and trade of those present. In addition, the number and kind of the king's garments and accessories were also illustrated. Regarded by many as one of the most exquisite *banchado* to exist, *Rank-positioned Procession of a Royal Visit* (*Dongga Banchdo*) documents the procession of King Gojong, Queen Min, the crown prince (later Emperor Sunjong), and the prince regent Heungseon Daewongun, who is accompanied by his wife.

The figures and objects were created using simple black outlines that were subsequently filled with color. Next, the images were outlined once more with deeper colors to provide stability to the forms and offer a sense of depth. This extra step, along with the skilled brushstrokes and attention to detail, indicates that the picture was created to be viewed by the king. The picture also holds the rare distinction of portraying King Gojong's entire family in striking detail. In the painting, the king and queen are present with their son riding on palanquins (pp. 150–151), while Heungseon and his wife ride on a mono-wheeled chair and a palanquin (p. 146), respectively, which are notably less ornamental than those of the royal family.

The destination of this procession, however, remains unclear. The date of production can be narrowed down to between 1883, the point at which the *taegeukgi*, or Korean flag, held by one of the mounted soldiers (pp. 148–149), was nationally announced as the official flag of Joseon, and 1895, when Queen Min died.

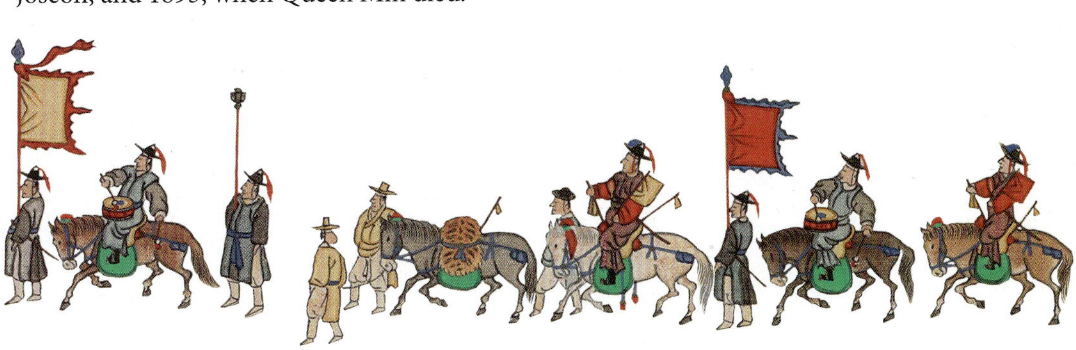

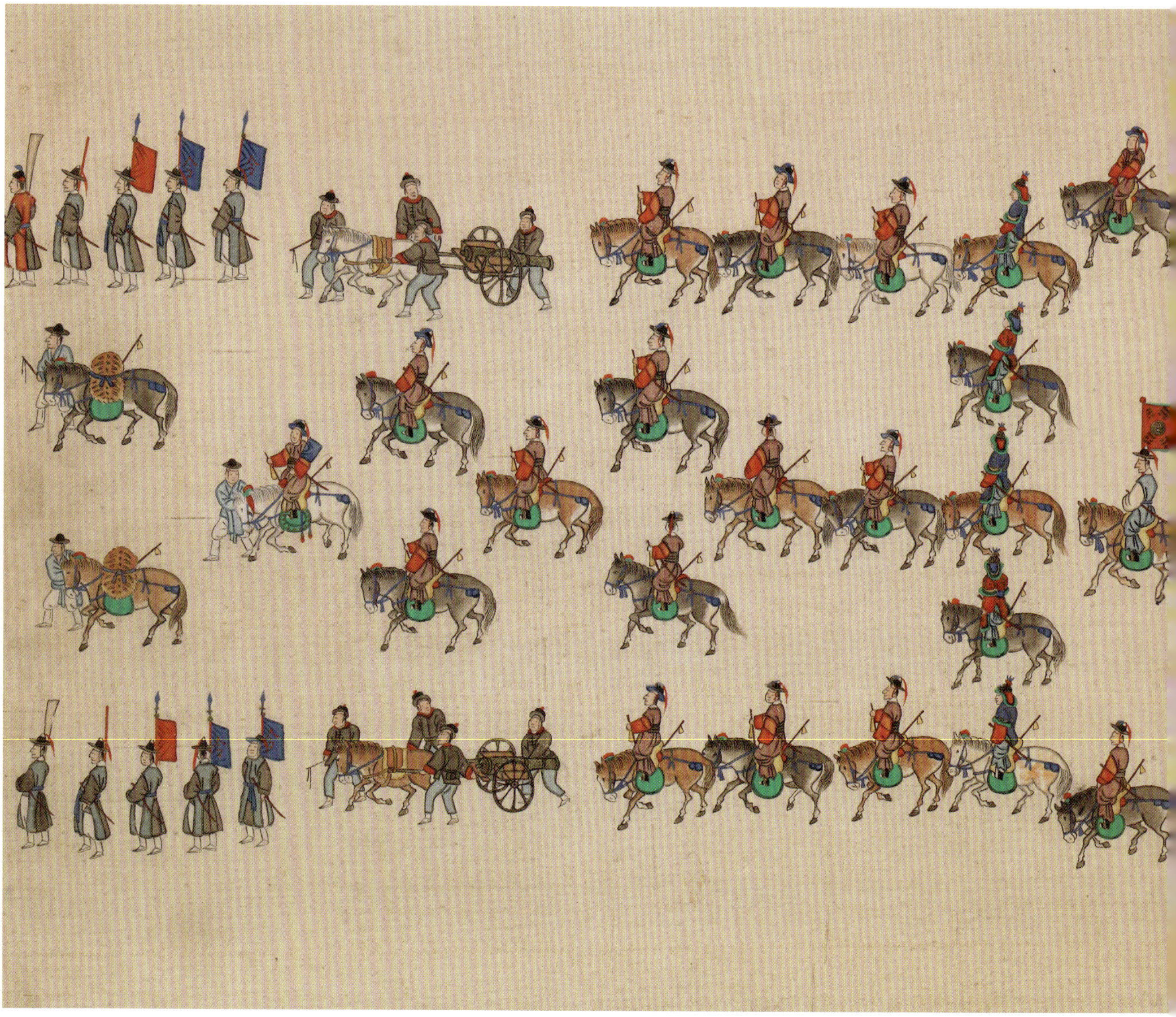

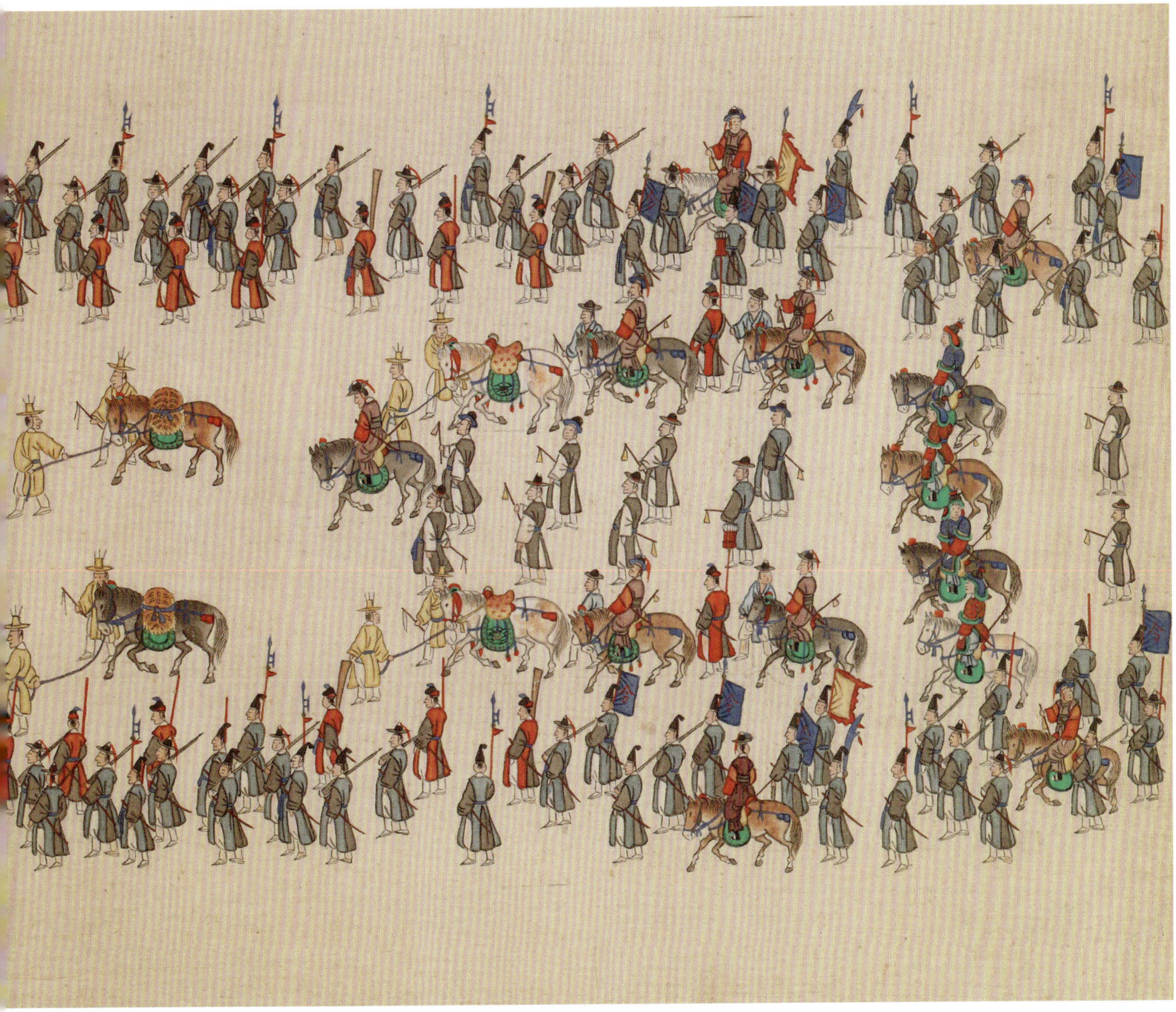

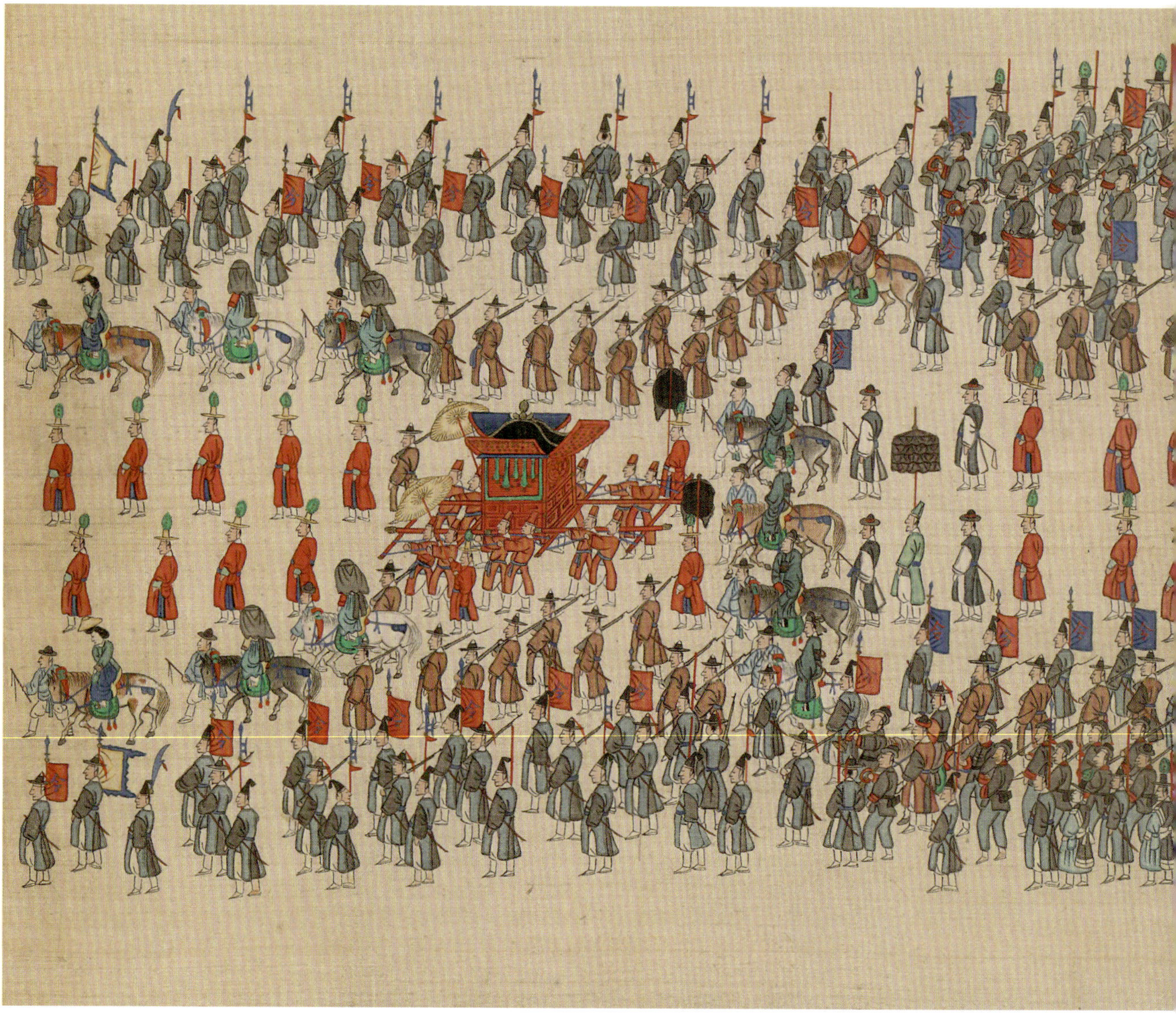

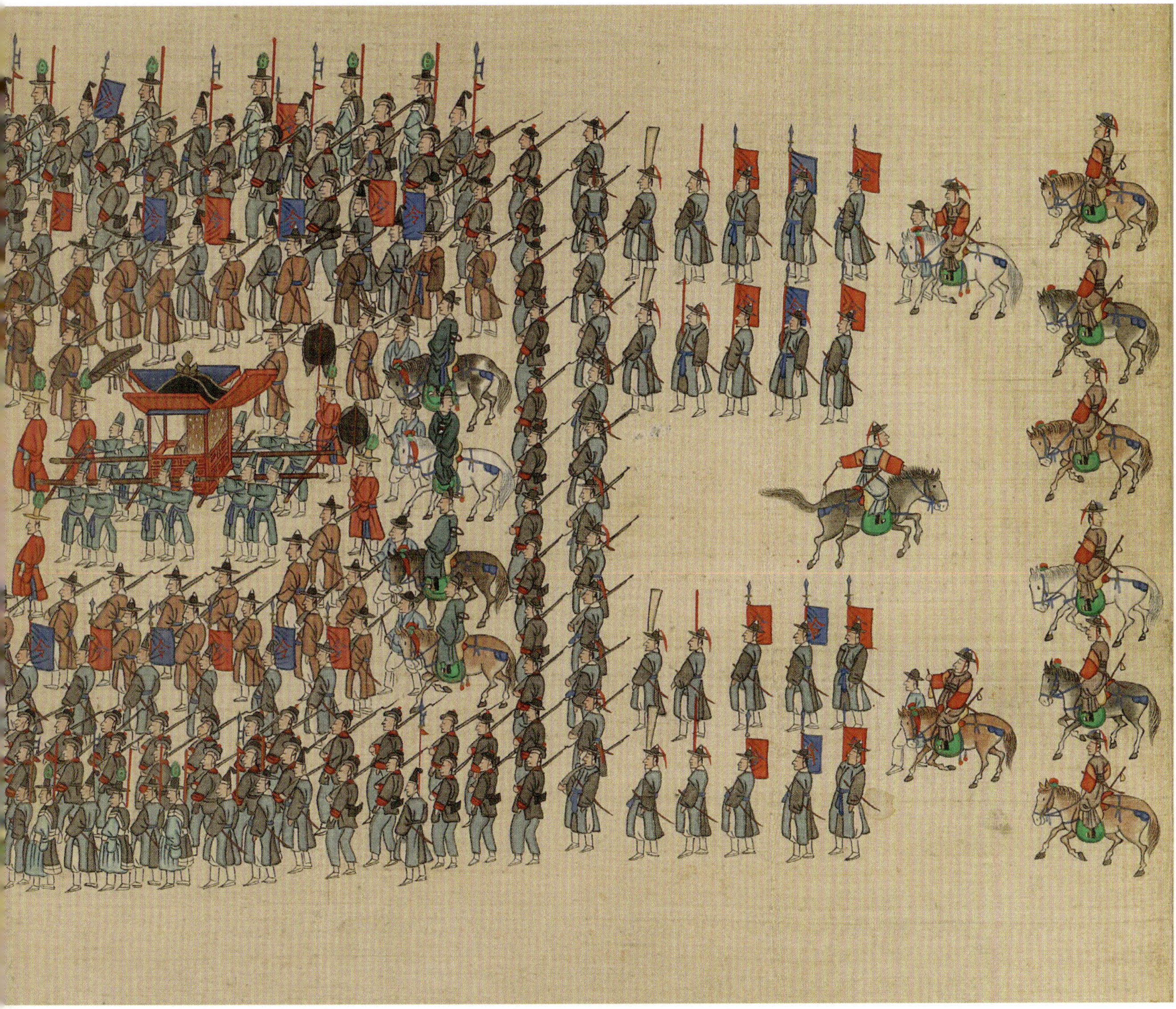

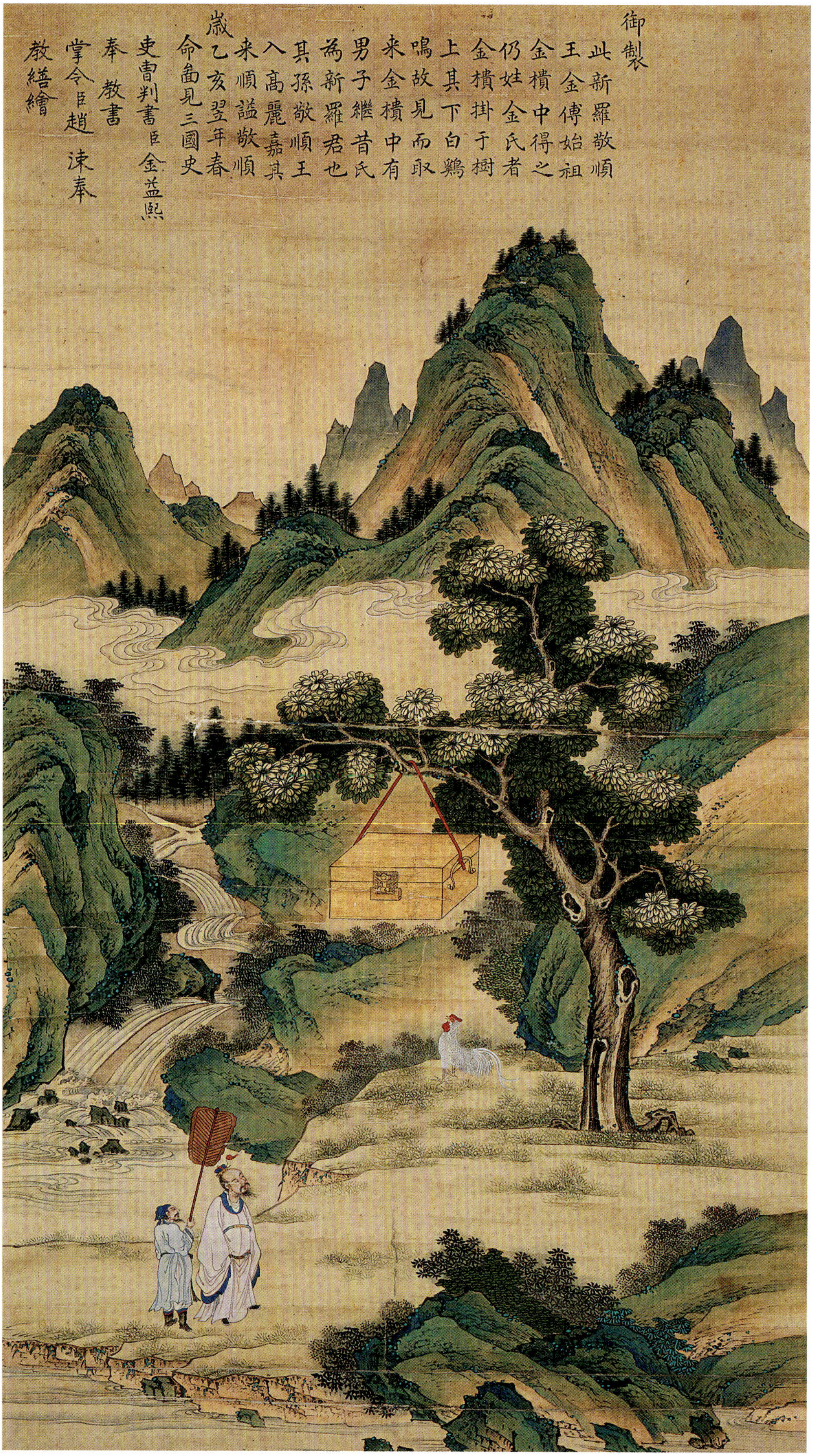
御製
此新羅敬順
王金傳始祖
金櫝中得之
仍姓金氏者
金櫝掛于樹
上其下白鷄
鳴故見而取
来金櫝中有
男子繼昔氏
為新羅君也
其孫敬順王
入高麗嘉其
来順諡敬順
歲乙亥翌年春
命畫見三國史
吏曹判書臣金益熙
奉 教書
掌令臣趙涑奉
教繕繪

Golden Chest *Geumgwedo*

18th century / ink and color on silk / 105.5 × 56 cm / National Museum of Korea

Golden Chest (*Geumgwedo*) depicts the mythical birth of Kim Alji, who is the progenitor of the royal Kim family of the Silla Kingdom (57 BCE–935 CE). According to the legend, a box made of gold was hung on a tree, and underneath a white rooster was crying. Inside the box was a baby boy, Kim Alji, whose last name was said to be bestowed by the king of Silla, Seok Talhae (r. 57–80). The painting's inscription states that King Gyeongsun (Kim Bu, r. 927–935), the last king of Silla, was a descendent of Kim Alji, suggesting that Kim was the forefather of the kingdom's Kim royal family.

The specific creator of this painting remains unclear. The text at the top of the work indicates that the painting was commissioned by King Injo (r. 1623–1649) and painted by literati artist Jo Sok (1595–1668) in the spring of 1636, with calligraphy written by Kim Ik-hee (1610–1656), head of the Board of Personnel. The style of the painting, however, challenges this assertion. The image's blue-green landscape, strict brushstrokes, and thick coloring exhibit the typical painting style of the Office of Paintings. Moreover, contrary to the inscription, Kim Ik-hee did not serve as the head of the board in 1636. For this reason, further research is required to determine the artist and date of production for this work.

Despite such uncertainties, *Geumgwedo* was surely a royal painting commissioned and viewed by the king. Since a good portion of paintings for the royal appreciation were based on Chinese stories or fables, *Geumgwedo* holds a particular significance as it documents the foundation of the Silla Kingdom, an exclusively Korean history.

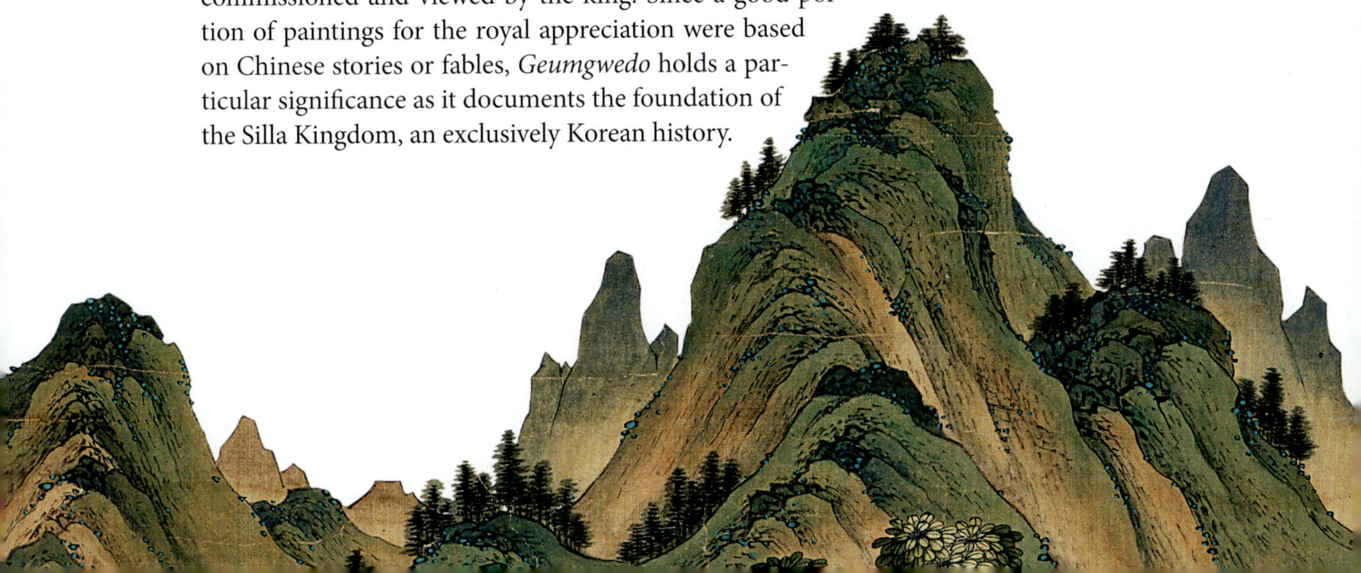

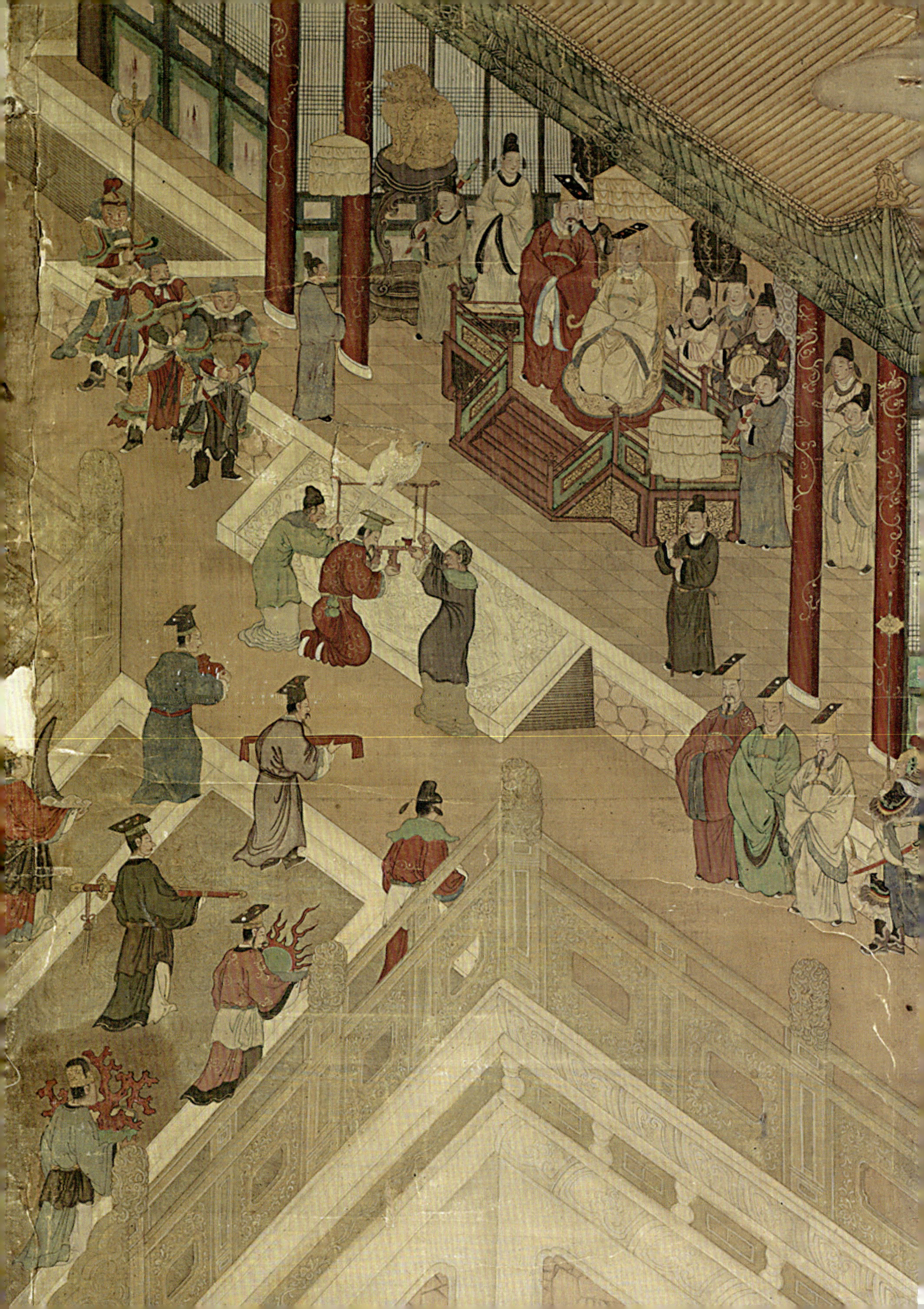

Envoys Paying Tribute to the King

Wanghoedo

Early 19th century / eight-fold screen / ink and color on silk / 140 × 416.5 cm /
Bernadou Collection / Smithsonian National Museum of Natural History

Wanghoe refers to the assembly in which feudal lords and envoys of the neighboring countries gathered during the peaceful era of King Wu (ca.1046–1043 BCE) of the Zhou Dynasty (1046–256 BCE). Understood to be a scene of the king receiving tributes from the envoys of nearby states, the topic was depicted in various ways between the Tang and Qing Dynasties.

In Joseon, *wanghoedo* (paintings of the *wanghoe* gathering) began to emerge during the reign of King Jeongjo in the late eighteenth century as a genre of court painting and continued until the era of King Gojong (r. 1864–1906) in the early twentieth century. The improved attitude toward Qing and the incoming flow of new ideas and experiences fueled by Korean envoys returning from Beijing brought about the more active production of *wanghoedo* in nineteenth-century Joseon.

The first and second panels from the right show a political leader (seated) surrounded by a group of his advisors, while a group of envoys bearing gifts of regional specialties form a line that extends through the full length of the painting. Exotic animals and piles of luxury boxes sitting outside the door reinforce the reach of the leader's influence. The use of perspective adds a sense of depth and dimension to the large palatial complex.

Since the story of *Wanghoedo* is based on an old Chinese anecdote, the picture was never meant to be realistic. The key objective was to depict a time of peace and an ideal political space. In this sense, *Wanghoedo* is comparable with *yojiyeondo* (p. 41, p. 47) for its pursuit of utopia; while the former portrays idealized leadership in the worldly realm, the latter emphasizes respect toward the utmost authority in the ideal world of gods. It seems only natural, then, that the picture, with the clear message of powerful authority and hope for peace, was mostly used as a gift to a king or crown prince to commemorate his entry to the Royal Confucian Academy or recovery from an illness, or to an envoy from a foreign state to be delivered to his king.

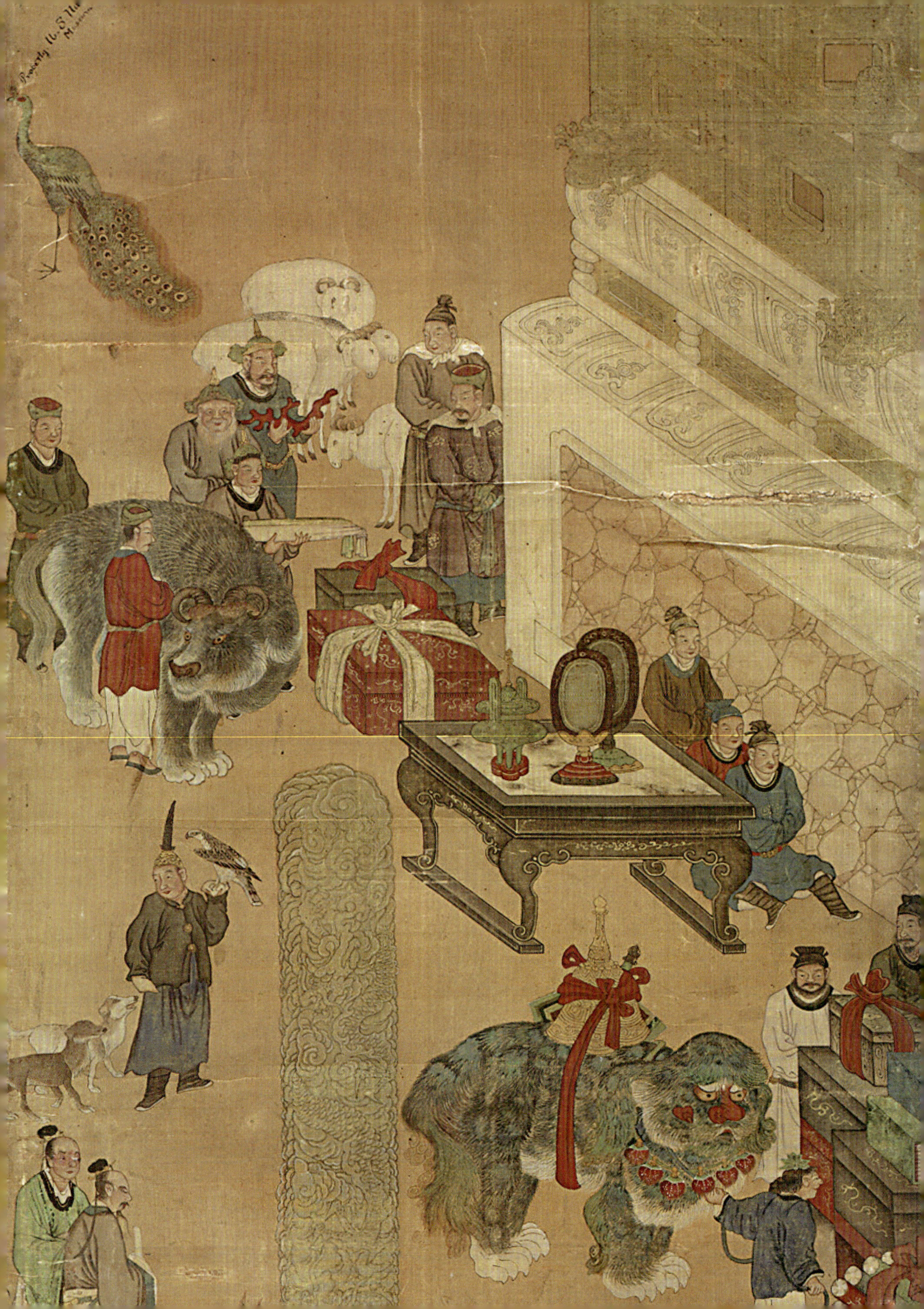

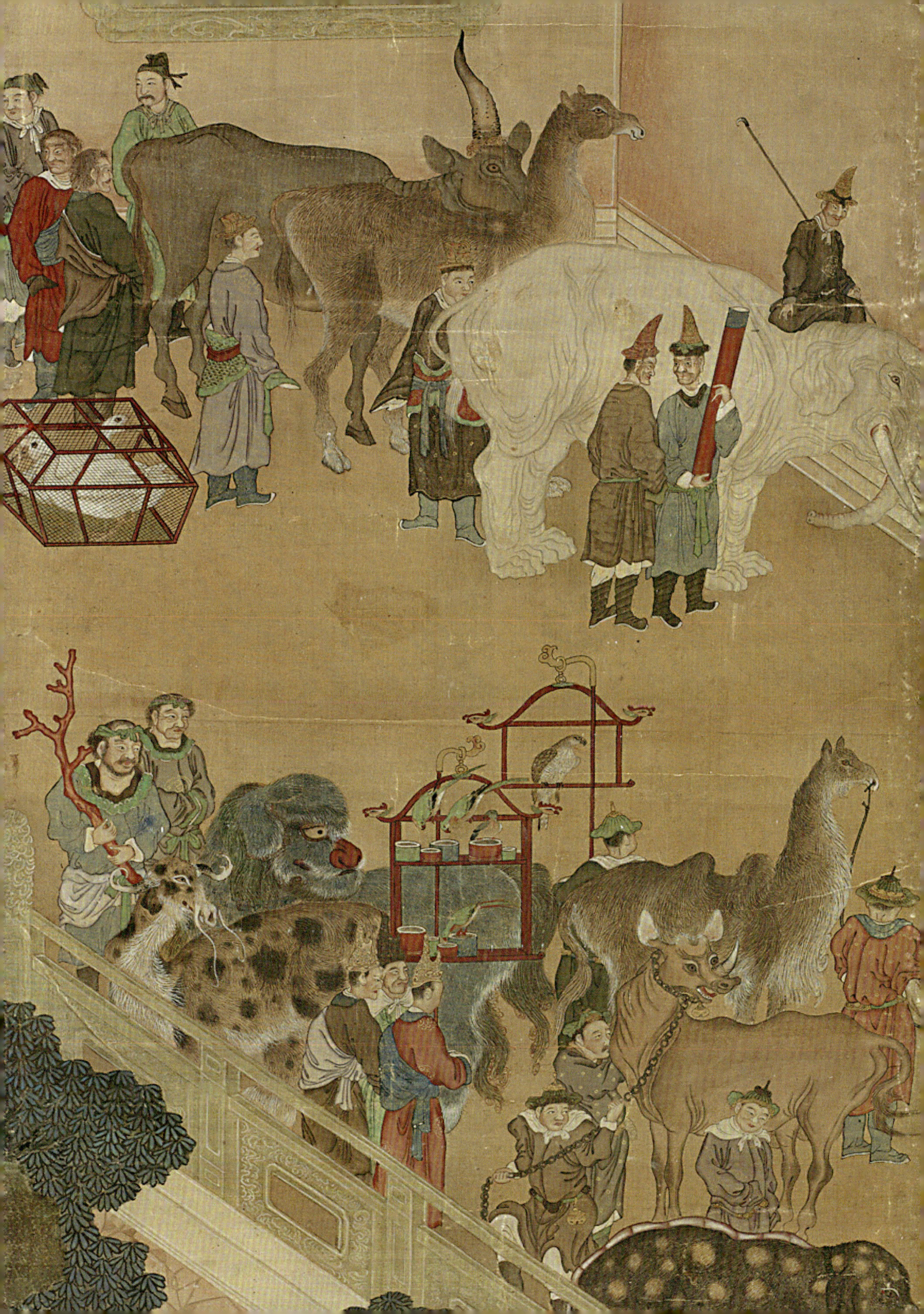

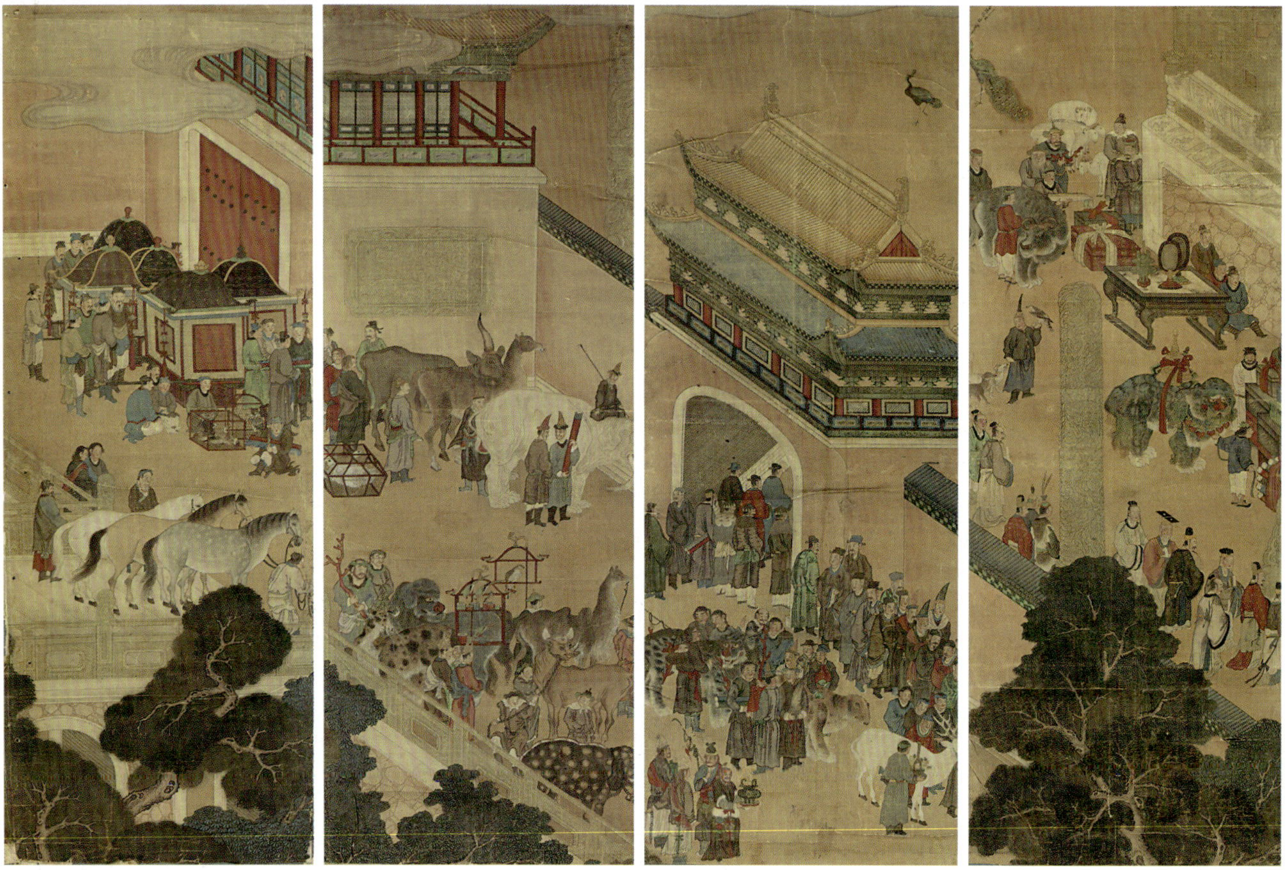

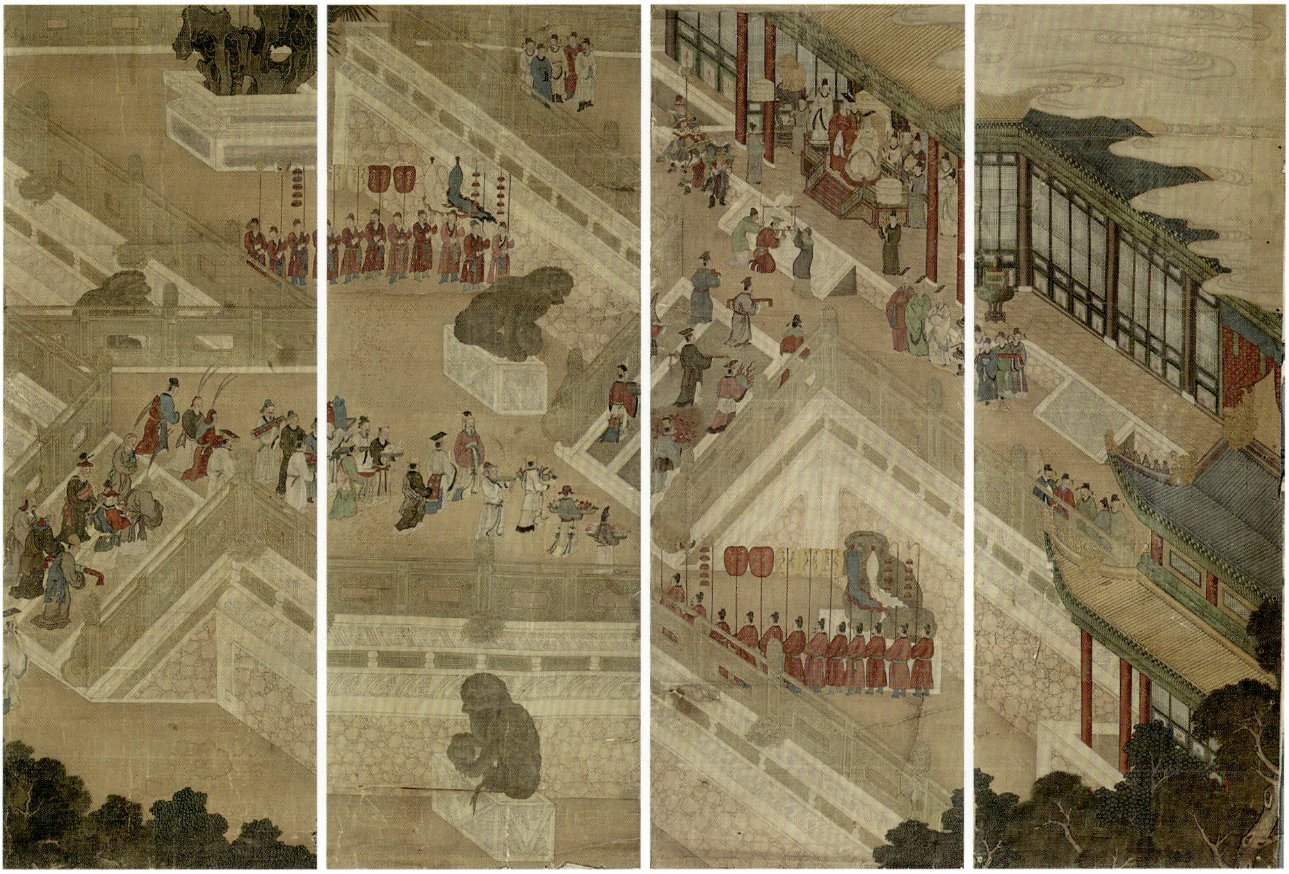

Glossary

abakmu 아박무 牙拍舞
A royal court dance said to have been performed since the Goryeo era. Set to the traditional music genre of *hyangak*, *abakmu* was performed by two dancers who each played a percussion instrument made of ivory known as an *abak*.

baechae 배채 背彩
An artistic technique that involved coloring the rear surface of a piece of paper or silk cloth in such a way that it would show through to the front surface, upon which the artist would paint the final work. This technique would not only enrich a painting's color but would preserve the piece by delaying the processes of peeling or fading.

banchado 반차도 班次圖
A painting or written diagram used in official records that depicted the location and placement of all materials and personnel involved in royal ceremonies and rituals in the Joseon era, including civil and military officials, musicians, instruments, and flags. For practical reasons, *banchado* artists depicted events from a bird's-eye view and utilized deep colors while focusing on minute details. Given that the court recruited the best painters for such records, works of *banchado* constitute some of the most elaborate and exceptional Joseon art remaining today.

Bongsudang 봉수당 奉壽堂
The administrative hall in the court of Hwaseong Palace that was built by King Jeongjo, the twenty-second ruler of Joseon Dynasty. Jeongjo had Bongsudang built to honor the health and long life of his birth mother, Lady Hyegyeong, which is why the name of the building means "pray for longevity."

byeolgung 별궁 別宮
A special palace that was used as a temporary residence for the queen-to-be or crown-princess-to-be during royal marriage ceremonies. It was also where the king met with foreign envoys, or where he stayed before officially ascending to the throne.

gollyongpo 곤룡포 衮龍袍
A royal uniform worn by the king when performing daily duties, with additional fabric embroidered with dragons of gold thread sewn onto the shoulders and chest. When donning a *gollyongpo*, the king would wear a cap known as an *ikseongwan*, a ceremonial belt made of jade, and leather boots that covered the ankles. Joseon royals wore red, which symbolized the king, but King Gojong, who proclaimed the establishment of the Korean Empire in 1907, is noted for having donned a yellow *gollyongpo*, which symbolized the emperor.

Gyeonggijeon Hall 경기전 慶基殿
Located in the city of Jeonju, Jeollabuk-do. One of six special palaces around the country erected specifically to enshrine the portrait of King Taejo, the founding ruler of the Joseon Dynasty. These palaces, known as *jinjeon*, were built in places that were especially relevant to King Taejo's life or in cities that served as the capital from the Three Kingdoms period to the Goryeo era. Gyeonggijeon Hall in Jeonju is the only one of such palaces still standing today.

hyangbalmu 향발무 響鈸舞
A royal court dance said to have been performed since the Goryeo period. Dancers would hold a brass percussion instrument called a *hyangbal* in each hand.

ikseongwan 익선관 翼善冠
A ceremonial cap seen during the Joseon era, worn by the king and crown prince of Joseon alongside a uniform known as the *gollyongpo* when performing daily administrative duties. The top of the cap was adorned with what were supposed to resemble cicada wings, thus the name *ikseongwan*, literally "winged cap."

Kyujanggak 규장각 奎章閣
A palace located in the center of Huwon, the rear garden of Changdeokgung Palace, meant to symbolize the political and cultural prosperity of the reign of King Jeongjo. The building comprises two floors: the first floor constituting Kyujanggak and the second floor being a separate structure called Juhamnu Pavilion. In front of the building is Buyongji Pond, home to an abundant number of lotus flowers. Initially established as a royal library, Kyujanggak developed into an institute for academic and policy research that fostered many political reforms.

pyeonjeon 편전 便殿
The area of the palace where the king normally spent his days while attending to his administrative affairs. The *pyeonjeon* of Gyeongbokgung Palace was known as Sajeongjeon Hall, while its counterpart in Changdeokgung Palace was called Huijeongdang Hall.

seonyurak 선유락 船遊樂
A dance that allegedly originated from the maritime culture of the Silla era, its music and choreography rooted in the surrounding province's *gyobang*, or institutions that taught *gisaeng* (female entertainers) artists how to sing and dance. The dance was first introduced to the Joseon court during the reign of King Jeongjo, an instance of provincial arts becoming popularized in the royal court. Female dancers would surround a beautifully adorned boat, moving in a way that made it appear as if it were sailing foward.

uigwe 의궤 儀軌
A detailed record kept of all major events involving the royal family or state rites, maintained for purposes of careful preparation and future reference. Records were extremely thorough, spanning general function details, the progression of events, financial costs, required materials and personnel, ceremonial procedures, and issues discussed after the event. These meticulous records were also works of art in themselves, as they incorporated exquisite, colored drawings. Korea's *uigwe* collection has been listed as part of the UNESCO Memory of the World registry.

Location of Originals

The British Library
Court Banquet (Jinchando) and *Ceremony of Presenting the Cloth (Jinpyorido)*

Daejojeon Hall in Changdeokgung
Phoenixes (Bonghwangdo)
White Cranes (Baekhakdo)

Dongguk University Museum
The Birthday Banquet for Lady Hyegyeong at Bongsudang (Bongsudang Jinchando)

Ewha Womans University Museum
The Cranes and Peaches of Immortality by the Sea I *(Haehak Bandodo)*

Honolulu Academy of Arts
The Cranes and Peaches of Immortality by the Sea II *(Haehak Bandodo)*

Jordan Schnitzer Museum of Art, University of Oregon
Ten Symbols of Longevity (Sipjangsaengdo)

Korea University Museum
The Eastern Palaces (Donggwoldo)

Leeum, Samsung Museum of Art
Harmony of Auspicious Animals (Seosu Jangsaengdo)
Rank-positioned Procession of a Royal Visit (Dongga Banchado)
Royal Procession Back to Hanyang (Hwaneo Haengnyeoldo)

National Museum of Korea
Golden Chest (Geumgwedo)
Grand Congratulatory Ceremony at Injeongjeon Hall & Day Banquet at Tongmyeongjeon Hall (Injeongjeon Jinhado & Tongmyeongjeon Jinchando)
The Grand Congratulatory Ceremony for the Birth of Crown Prince Yi Cheok (Wangseja Tangang Jinha Dobyeong)
The Feast of Yoji Pond I *(Yojiyeondo)*

The Feast of Yoji Pond II (*Yojiyeondo*)
The Happy Life of Guo Ziyi (*Gwakbunyang Haengrakdo*)
Peonies I (*Morando*)
Scholar's Bookshelf I (*Chaekgado*)
Scholar's Bookshelf II (*Chaekgado*)

National Palace Museum of Korea
Lotus and Water Birds (*Yeonhwa Sugeumdo*)
One Hundred Children (*Baekjado*)
Peonies II (*Morando*)
Sun, Moon, and Five Peaks (*Irwol Obongdo*)
The Sun, Moon, and Peach Trees of Immortality (*Irwol Bandodo*)

National Research Institute of Cultural Heritage
The Crown Prince's Procession Departing from the Palace (*Chulgungdo*)

Royal Portrait Museum
Portrait of King Taejo (*Taejo Eojin*)

Smithsonian National Museum of Natural History
Envoys Paying Tribute to the King (*Wanghoedo*)

Tongdosa Museum
Birds and Flowers (*Hwajodo*)
Books and Scholarly Instruments (*Munbangdo*)

Index

U

W

X

Y

About the Author

Park Jeong-hye is a professor of art history at the Academy of Korean Studies in Korea. She received both her MA and PhD. in art history from Hongik University, Korea. Dr. Park specializes in the court paintings of the Joseon Dynasty, particularly documentary and decorative paintings, *uigwe*, and court painters. She was a member of the Advisory Committee at Bureau of the Cultural Properties in Seoul, Gyeonggi-do and Gyeongsangbuk-do Provinces, and has been an associate member of the Advisory Committee, Cultural Heritage Administration of Korea since 2007.

She is also editor-in-chief of *Korean Journal of Art History*, published by the Art History Association of Korea. Her published works include *Study of the Royal Archival Paintings of the Joseon Dynasty* (Iljisa, 2000), *Royal Painting of the Joseon Dynasty* Vol. 1–3 (co-author, Dolbegae, 2011–2012), and *Banquet Paintings from the Time of King Yeongjo* (The Academy of Korean Studies, 2014).

Credits

Publisher	Kim Hyunggeun
Writer	Park Jeong-hye
Translator	Park Ju-won
Editors	Youn Mi-hyang, Lee Jin-hyuk
Copy Editor	Jaime Stief
Designer	Lee Bok-hyun